THE BEER STEIN BOOK

A 400 YEAR HISTORY

ILLUSTRATED CATALOG
CURRENT PRICES
COLLECTOR'S INFORMATION

BY GARY KIRSNER & JIM GRUHL

EDITOR: BETH KIRSNER

GLENTIQUES, LTD., CORAL SPRINGS, FLORIDA

While every care has been taken in compiling the information contained in this volume, neither the authors, the editor nor the publisher can accept any liablity for loss, financial or otherwise, incurred by reliance placed on the information herein.

Library of Congress Cataloging in Publication Data

Kirsner, Gary, 1945 -

      The beer stein book.

      Revised edition of: The stein book.
      Includes bibliographical references (pp. 357-360)
      1. Steins--Germany--Collectors and collecting--
Catalogs.   I. Gruhl, Jim.   II. Kirsner, Beth, 1967-
III. Title.
NK8647.K49 1990   730'.0943'075   90-2912
ISBN 0-9614130-3-4

Second printing, 1990

Printed in the United States of America
Published by Glentiques, Ltd.
P.O. Box 8807
Coral Springs, FL 33075
Telephone: (305) 344-9856
FAX: (305) 344-4421

CONTENTS

Preface		**5**
1.	**Stein History**	**7**
2.	**Production of Steins**	**15**
3.	**Early Stoneware**	**25**
4.	**Faience**	**43**
5.	**Pewter**	**65**
6.	**Glass**	**73**
7.	**Unusual Materials**	**103**
8.	**Porcelain**	**121**
9.	**Mettlach**	**135**
10.	**Other Etched Ceramics**	**159**
11.	**Pottery and Stoneware**	**185**
12.	**Occupational**	**215**
13.	**Regimental**	**221**
14.	**Military**	**273**
15.	**Character**	**277**
16.	**Brewery**	**337**
17.	**Post-World War II**	**347**
18.	**Bibliography and References**	**357**
Appendix		**361**
Glossary		**367**
Price Changes		**371**
Index		**379**

Front cover photo: Mettlach, 1.0L, 2765, c.1900; Silver, .5L, Russian, late 1800's; Glass, .5L, Bohemian, c.1850.
Rear cover photo: Faience, 1.0L, early 1700's; Stoneware, 1.5L, Altenburg, middle 1700's.

4

One of the earliest drawings of a stein, a flagon type, in the foreground of this 1501 woodcut by Sebastian Brant depicting the feast of Aeneas and Dido.

PREFACE

When *The Stein Book* was being written a number of decisions had to be made to limit the size of the book. Many changes in collecting trends have occurred since then. The inclusion in this book of chapters covering military steins, brewery steins, and post-World War II steins is due to the tremendous increase in collectors' interest in these areas.

Coverage of numerous areas has been vastly strengthened, such as Art Nouveau steins, occupational steins and unusual steins.

The Beer Stein Book still had to be selective. The breadth of the topic has forced the making of some really tough decisions about what to include. Nevertheless, it is hoped that even stein experts will find exciting pictures and new important information about their individual specialties.

During the writing and right after the release of *The Stein Book* and *The Mettlach Book*, the same question was repeatedly asked. "Why would you want to tell everybody about the steins that a few advanced collectors, museums, and dealers know are worth three or four times the price for which they can often be purchased?" It has been suggested that publishing this kind of *inside information* would be bad for the stein dealers' businesses. Again in preparing this book that question has come up, and the answer is the same as before. When a hobby begins to slip under the control of those who have *inside information*, it breeds mistrust, suspicion, and disappointment among the majority of collectors. The publication of "real" prices in previous books has proved that the resulting trust, openness and enthusiasm are great for the hobby as well as for dealers.

This book attempts to answer the most common questions about steins:

- how and why did they originate?
- what do the different types look like?
- which ones are most valuable?
- how old are various types?
- what effect does condition have on what collectors will pay?

Before acknowledging the tremendous assistance that has been graciously contributed by many stein experts, some personal information is reluctantly given. Gary Kirsner studied economics and accounting at New York University and Miami University of Ohio. The business in general antiques which he began in the early 1970's, soon focused almost exclusively on steins. Gary soon grew to be a leader in the purchase and sale of quality steins. With his wife, Karen, and daughters, Beth and Britt, he lives in Coral Springs, Florida.

Jim Gruhl received a doctorate from M.I.T., and currently researches energy and environmental problems. His interest in steins goes back to a boyhood spent in Milwaukee and relatives in the beer industry. Jim has been collecting steins for more than 25 years, and researching steins for about 15 years. He lives next to a canyon near Tucson, Arizona with his wife, Nancy, and children, Amanda and Steven.

Both families have offered important support to tasks involved in assembling this book. There are also a number of other people who deserve specific thanks for their help, information, hospitality, and because they are some of the fine people who make being part of the stein collectors' community such a pleasant experience: Dave Cantwell, Dave Cunningham, Jim DeMars, Dr. Beate Dry-von Zezschwitz, Mark Durban, Bernie Gould, John Harrell, Art Hechler, Harold Hemphill, Bob Lenker, Frank Love, Dick Lovell, John Macyshyn, Irving Miller, Les Paul, Ulrich Schneider, Fredlein Schroeder, John Stuart, Peter Vogt, Jim Widener, and those who wish to remain anonymous. In this group also belong Lotti Lopez and Mike Wald, who deserve *special* thanks for help at several stages in this project.

Because of the success of *The Stein Book*, there are many similar expectations for this book. It expands on that book's ability to:

- show the whole range of steins to collectors, so they will not need to use "trial and error" in order to discover what they like best,

- release steins from collectors who have been holding onto pieces because they didn't know their value,

- build a stronger demand for steins at every level, and

- help collectors build up a lifetime of pricing experience that will improve their confidence and knowledge.

And again with this book, the hope is that people will see stein collecting to be more than just a hobby. It combines beauty, excitement, history, and investment, and it tells us a great deal about past generations and about ourselves.

Gary Kirsner
Jim Gruhl
March, 1990

1. Stein History

Stein is a shortened form of *Steinzeugkrug*, which is the German word for "stoneware jug or tankard." By common usage, however, stein has come to mean any beer container with a hinged lid and a handle, regardless of the material or size. Technically, more appropriate than the word *stein* would be *tankard*, and these two words are used interchangeably in this book. Be warned, however, that some people reserve the word tankard for the all-pewter or all-silver varieties of steins. One final definition: *mug* is universally used as the name for those vessels which have handles but which would never have had a lid. So much for the semantics; those with a deeper interest in definitions should refer to the Glossary.

1.1 Earliest Steins
1525-1700

From about 1340 to 1380, the bubonic plague, or Black Death, killed more than 25 million Europeans! As horrible as this historic event must have been, it prompted tremendous progress for civilization. And of interest here, it is also responsible for the origin of the beer stein.

Recall from above that the distinction between the *mug* and the *stein* is the *hinged lid*. This lid was originally conceived entirely as a sanitary measure. During the summers of the late 1400's, hoards of little flies frequently invaded Central Europe. By the early 1500's, several principalities in what is now Germany had passed laws requiring that all food and beverage containers must be covered to protect consumers against these dirty insects. The common mug also had to be covered, and this was accomplished with the addition of the hinged lid with a thumblift. This ingenious invention soon covered all German beverage containers while still allowing them to be used with one hand.

This *covered container law* and several other public health laws were enthusiastically passed and vigilantly enforced as a result of public fears about a return of the Black Death. In the period from Roman times to the 1300's, sanitation had continually declined. During the years of the Black Death it became obvious to all, with 95% of those in filthy areas dead and only 10% dead in clean surroundings, that the bubonic plague was somehow related to unsanitary conditions.

The lid served to keep flies out of the stein.

The covered container law was only one in a whole series of sanitary regulations that were passed in Germany after the plague: pigpens couldn't be adjacent to streets, old or diseased meat had to be labelled as such, and beer could be brewed only from hops, cereals, yeast, and water.

Strictly enforced regulations concerning the quality and transport of beer in many of the German provinces resulted in a tremendous improvement in the taste of beer, which also had an impact on stein making. Many records show that average beer consumption moved up to about two liters per day in many places. Beerhouses, City Hall cellars, and taverns began to abound in the 1500's. There is an old saying, "the German will place great value on that which brings him his food or drink." Everyone in Germany needed a personal drinking vessel of which to be proud!

Local brews in many other parts of Europe were still being made with rotten bread, cabbages, eggs, and anything else at hand. Soon the Bremen, Hamburg, and other clean, pure Northern German beers became famous and were exported throughout Northern Europe, even as far as the East Indies and Jerusalem. Such beers raised a new need for relatively inexpensive, but durable, large containers; the search for appropriate materials was on.

As for individual beer vessels, up to the 1400's, well-to-do Germans had pewter beakers; a few of the wealthiest had silver vessels. These metal containers and those made of glass, remained too expensive for general use or for large containers. Some wooden beakers were being used, but other than wood, porous earthenware was by far the most common material for beer beakers, mugs, and the larger containers. However, both the wood and the earthenware broke easily, which may have been a blessing because they soaked up beer, giving off a smell that got worse with each subsequent use.

Scientific experimentation was begun to try to improve the earthenware. All such scientific inquiry would previously have been squelched by the all-powerful Roman Catholic Church, long at odds with science. During the Black Death, churches had either claimed prayer would end the plague or they had announced that Revelation had begun — in both cases they lost some of their hold on the public, and more pragmatic scientific views began to prevail. The subsequent rise of science and its marriage with art has been credited with starting the Renaissance.

The obvious experiments to perform with respect to earthenware were to raise the firing temperature of 500°C (900°) past the usual level. Higher temperatures, however, could not be achieved merely by throwing more wood into the furnace; they required new furnace designs. A new design was invented that produced temperatures up to 1200°C (2200°F). It had a furnace on the lower floor, then above it, through some slats, was the ceramic firing chamber entirely enclosed in brick except for small flues. At these extreme temperatures not only was all the moisture driven out of the clay as in earthenware, but the clay *vitrified*, or partially melted, into a solid stone-like material, hence the name *stoneware*.

Stoneware required days of firing and many dozen cords of wood, but the product proved to be far superior to earthenware. It is relatively difficult to chip or crack, and is not porous, making a much more sanitary container.

The expense of stoneware steins, especially after the covered beverage container law required lids, made steins worthy of some fine decorative ceramic art. Renaissance artists supplied many designs for applied and carved stein decorations. Colored glazes complemented these designs nicely. A clear salt glaze had been invented about 1400; a blue glaze from cobalt oxide was also known at that time; a chocolate salt glaze was invented in the 1600's, and a manganese oxide purple glaze was invented around 1650.

Tankards were soon decorated with shields, historical, allegorical, and biblical scenes. Beer drinking had now also become a pleasure for the eyes! And the landless day laborers, the masses who had survived the Black Death, were in a position to command relatively higher wages for their services. They could afford a few modest luxuries, and the personal tankard had become a most important status symbol and display piece for these Germans.

Once again consider the historical situation. The guild system was well in place in the 1500's and the guilds held powerful positions on the city councils. Although no records of it exist, the Pewter Guild was no doubt an important sponsor of the covered container law that prompted creation of the beer stein. The Potters' Guilds are known to have continually pushed up the minimum standards on the quality of both the decorations and the stoneware, thus making steins increasingly more attractive.

The Black Death, by depleting the population, had created a surplus of food, especially grains. Much of this surplus grain made its way into local beers, making a fine pure beverage really worthy of celebration. Eventually surplus grains were able to make their way in large quantity to the breweries in the North (there were only a few cloister brewers in the South at that time). In the 1500's, Hamburg had 600 breweries, producing 25 million liters of beer, and directly or indirectly employing half of the population of that city.

Initially, a few glass bottles were made in Delft, for shipping some of that Northern beer. But soon the fine clay of the Cologne area was being used to make large stoneware jugs. The shipping industry was rejuvenated, and the beer export business and the stein making business were booming and producing some extremely wealthy merchants.

Such wealth did not go uncontested, and the resultant 30 Years' War had changed much by its end in the 1640's. It was a war fought with fire. Virtually all of the Northern breweries were destroyed and most of the Southern vineyards as well. A few Southern breweries in Cloisters survived and more or less by default Bavaria became Central Europe's *beer land*. Beer soon replaced cider and wine as the beverage of choice throughout Germany.

An expanded new market for beer steins developed, and the stoneware industry from the areas of Köln and Koblenz responded. Pewter, silver and glass luxury steins were also available, but the Chinese connection for the luxurious Ming porcelain mugs had been disrupted by rebellions in China in the middle 1600's. No one in Europe knew how to make porcelain, but several German potters were quick to jump in with a porcelain substitute, *faience*.

Faience is earthenware with a porcelain-like white glaze made from tin oxide. German faience was not as durable as the Chinese porcelain, but it was far cheaper and had two aesthetic advantages. First, the motifs on German faience were popular late-Renaissance and early-Baroque designs, not foreign looking Chinese figures. And second, the cobalt oxide of China was contaminated with purple manganese oxide, and the Persian cobalt oxide that the Chinese artists sparingly mixed in, would often diffuse badly. The purer German cobalt oxide supplies were bright blue and allowed for crisp lines. So even when the Chinese porcelain supply was re-established, German faience had gained a firm hold on the stein market.

1.2 Transition Period
1700-1850

Throughout the 1700's, the Pewter Guilds maintained their tight hold on the covered container law. It seems certain that this is responsible for keeping the lidded design of the stein from fading away, for there has always been a tendency to return to beakers and a master stein, or to find some other way of getting around the expense of the individually hinged lids. Yet, by the end of the 1800's, when the covered container law was apparently no longer in force, over 300 years of conditioning had taught Germans to view a stein as incomplete without the lid. Thus, lids, and steins, were here to stay.

Many of those trends that were in place just before 1700 continued to strengthen thereafter. For example, by 1750 there were over 4000 breweries in Bavaria. And the art and production of stoneware and faience steins increased strongly, all the way into the late 1700's.

European porcelain was invented in 1709, but did not begin to have a big impact on stein making until the 1720's. Several porcelain factories were started in the 1700's, but their products were very expensive. Only the wealthiest Germans were drinking their beer from porcelain or glass vessels.

The quality and taste of beer, the *flowing bread*, continued to improve. Besides offering taste and fellowship, beer was considered to be important for the constitution, with qualities inducing strength, health, and relaxation. From the earliest times right up to the 1800's, many considered beer to be the most effective medicine known, the *drink from the gods*.

Although glass beer beakers were used in Roman times, the Church suppressed glassmaking during the Middle Ages as being *heathenish*. The art of making and enameling glass was not re-learned by the Germans until the late 1500's. These early enameled items were mainly beakers and pokals.

A few engraved glass steins began to be used in the 1700's. However, partly because of their fragility, and partly because of their original rarity due to costliness, not many of these early glass steins still exist. The color of this glass was almost always clear, which required some special efforts because the usual *Waldglas* of the time was made partly with wood ashes and had a definite greenish tinge. The use of clear glass would seem to support the theory that an important feature of the early glass stein was to show off the rare clarity and color of the costliest beers, brought from some distance.

Toward the end of the Baroque period, around 1800, pewter and silver tankards were still uncommon in Germany. However, the English, and to some extent the Scandinavians, had by now adopted the "finished" look of a lidded mug. And except for a few ceramic factories, they were exclusively making pewter and silver steins.

The Scandinavians had also perfected a method of making a nice all-wooden tankard complete with a wooden hinge. The few German wooden steins from this period generally have pewter mountings and pewter overlaid designs, and even these were no longer being made by 1800.

Horn drinking vessels, so popular in Roman times, did not adapt well to the covered container law and became rare. Ivory steins were made only for the exceptionally wealthy.

In the 1600's, it was rather easy to determine from where steins had come; every small region had considerable pride in their typical forms. The Bohemian, Austrian, and other Southern tankards were wide and sturdy; the Northerners preferred sleek and tall drinking vessels. The Western steins were gray stoneware with blue decoration; the Eastern steins were brown glazed stoneware.

During the 1700's, however, shape became less important. The faience steins predominantly assumed a pleasing cylindrical shape about twice as high as wide. The stoneware, glass, porcelain, pewter, and other steins soon followed suit. Regional differences of shape and size were replaced by differences in materials and motifs.

Soon after 1800 another transition was begun that was as significant and unpredictable as that which brought on the Renaissance. The Napoleonic and other wars and rebellions of the time so diminished the aristocrats' wealth and power that the newly monied Middle Class became the most important marketplace for steins and other artistic products. This Middle Class cast off the Baroque extravagances, preferring instead a sturdy, functional, *folk art*. In Germany this was known as the *Biedermeier* period.

Baluster Mug
1400-1580

Schnelle
1500-1600

Conical
1530-1700

Flagon
1530-1900

Tapered
1550-1780

Renaissance
1550-1650

Stitze
1570-1750

Double-Handled
1600-1680

Spouted
1600-1700

Globe
1600-1710,
1860-1935

Rorken
1600-1720

Stuart
1600-1710

Stout
1600-1730

Jug 1600-1750

Narrow-Necked
1630-1750

Can
1650-1850

Scandinavian
1650-1850

Frankfurt
1670-1720

Pear
1680-1780

Horn
1700-1870

Cylindrical
1700-1820

Georgian
1710-1930

Pitcher
1730-1820

Melon
1730-1780

Some of the typical shapes of early steins, their most common names and the period when they were most popular.

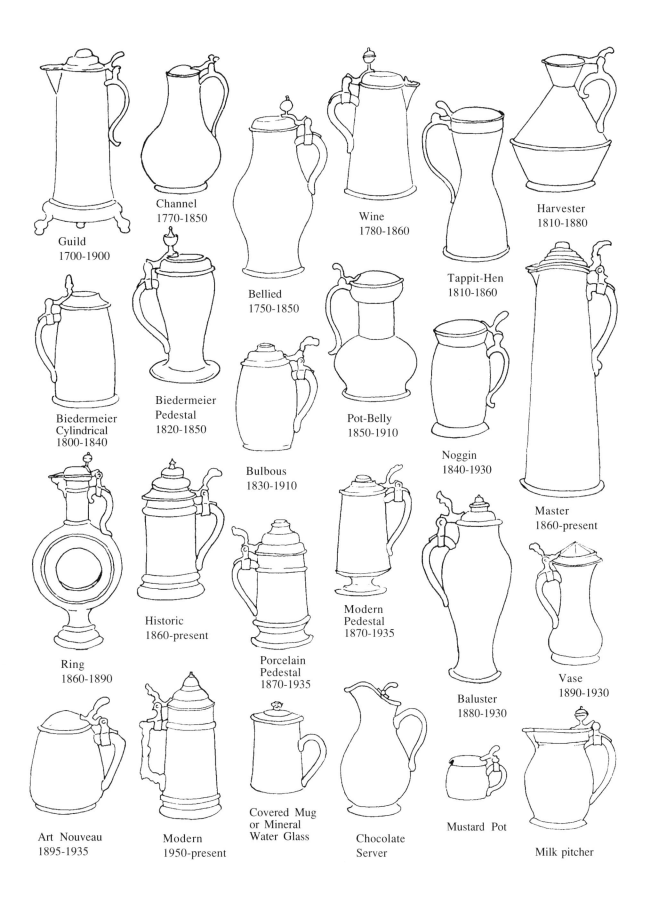

Some typical shapes of later steins, as well as a few of the covered containers that are closest to the stein shape.

Also around 1800 secularization had resulted in many monastery closings, but there were enough private breweries to assure that cloudless beer, without dregs, would still be available to the masses. And perhaps the new pride that developed in the *look* of the clear beer led in part to a major influx of glass steins into the marketplace soon after 1800. These glass steins usually carried enameled folk art designs.

The *straight up,* cylindrical pewter tankards also became very popular at this time. Engraved or stamped designs were common, especially using the same type of *folk art* motifs. Occasionally, pewter steins from this period can be found with remnants of painted decorations. Considering the lack of durability of paint-on-pewter this type of decoration must have been done quite often to have resulted in some surviving examples.

Porcelain and silver steins were still being made in the early 1800's, always with the Renaissance and Baroque designs that still appealed to the wealthy.

In the early 1800's, the preference of the masses was so clearly for glass and pewter that nearly all of the faience workshops were permanently closed. Most stoneware manufacturers stopped making steins and turned to everyday items such as bowls, jars, and wide-mouthed jugs.

The Villeroy and Boch firm of Mettlach has its origin in these times. Although the family was wealthy, the von Bochs had to appeal to the common tastes, with plates and other utilitarian items, in order to stay in business. However, as the Biedermeier period was drawing to a close in 1850, the Mettlach factory, with its aristocratic owners and classically trained artists, was ready to leap ahead with the upcoming change in artistic tastes.

During the early 1800's a great number of archaeological expeditions had uncovered outstanding examples of Greek, Roman, and Renaissance art. By about 1850, the public had been so captivated by the beauty of these finds that they were ready to forsake the mundane, functional styles of the Biedermeier period.

1.3 The Golden Era
1850-1910

By 1850, art students were being instructed entirely by copying the forms and designs of the archaeological finds from the Renaissance and Classical periods. The new style that resulted has been called neo-Renaissance and neo-Classical, or more commonly, *Historicism.* As for beer steins, the white clays of the Köln area were again used to make stoneware steins with Renaissance allegorical motifs. These steins have gray salt-glazed relief decorations, often with porcelain inlaid lids.

Later on, a major resurgence in stoneware steins began when Reinhold Hanke of the Westerwald region started making blue and purple saltglaze Historicism pieces. Molds were used to avoid the expense of the labor-intensive originals. These were no longer unique steins; they were *mass-produced,* as the seams in the

molds clearly attest. But there was an artistic advantage to using molds, and this was exploited to the fullest by Hanke, Dümler, and other stoneware manufacturers. The advantage was that molds could be used to reproduce painstakingly carved, elaborate reliefwork on hundreds of steins quickly.

In the second half of the 1800's, glassmaking techniques had progressed to the point where molds could also be used to mass-produce glass steins. The surprising sturdiness of the thick molded glass steins no doubt helped to increase their popularity. Other glass-maker's tricks were also applied to the production of glass steins. Multicolored glass overlays, acid etchings, staining, and pewter overlaid on glass were used to make some rather spectacular steins.

Advances in the use of moisture-absorbing plaster molds helped the porcelain stein manufacturers. These molds allowed for the use of novel shapes, making the so-called *character* steins much more common. Also, molds could be used to create the lithophane scenes that can be seen in the bottom of many porcelain steins (due to the variation   in the thickness, and thus the translucence, of the porcelain).

The Mettlach factory, with its classically trained artists, was quick to introduce the Renaissance motifs into its new line of relief steins. Experiments with colored glazes and colored clays led to some new, brightly colored Mettlach steins, the *mosaic* and *etched* types. These were popular enough so that many laborers were willing to spend a week's pay on one of these beautiful steins.

By the 1900's, the designs and motifs of Historicism had begun to lose favor. The popular steins now had town scenes, occupational emblems, common social scenes, or remembrances, particularly to military service days. To meet these diverse new demands a great number of potters began to enter the market with stoneware or glazed pottery steins.

A new art style, *Art Nouveau,* was gaining some limited popularity when, around 1910, political and economic turmoil threw the stein industry into a tremendous slowdown. With the subsequent outbreak of World War I, the materials and labor of the pewter industry were converted to munitions products, and stein making virtually ceased.

An early symbol of the brewers.

1.4 The Modern Period
From 1920

Production of stoneware, glass, and porcelain steins, especially character steins, picked up in the 1920's. Except for slowdowns during economic and political disturbances, notably during the early 1930's and the early 1940's, substantial quantities of steins have continued to be manufactured.

The modern period owes a great debt to Historicism, with its reverence for Classical and Renaissance art. It was during the Historicism period, from 1850 to 1900, that most of the great public museums were started. The public, not just the art intellectuals, now wanted to see artistic masterworks, including Renaissance steins. Public appreciation of antique steins led to museum and public collecting of steins.

Antique stein collecting has been a major force shaping stein manufacturing in the modern period. Beginning in about 1900, then reviving in the 1920's, good quality reproductions of antique steins were being made, particularly faience and pewter steins. Many of these early reproductions are clearly marked and are obviously not intended to fool antique stein collectors.

The exceptions to this are some unmarked reproductions of Renaissance stoneware, early pewter, and some rare faience pieces which had reached remarkably high prices in the marketplace, even at the turn of the century. So these are the steins that require the closest scrutiny to determine authenticity. It has really only been since the 1960's or 1970's that most types of antique steins have been valued highly enough so that reproducing steins for the purpose of deception might be considered.

One major new direction in stein production in the Modern period has been the introduction of tremendous numbers of relief pottery steins, especially since World War II.

The last 30 years have seen many changes, with economics playing a key role. The American market has been the primary market for new beer steins of most types, especially the limited editions. Some companies have been very successful with this market, while others have failed to cope with the competition, and have since stopped producing steins.

In the last 20 years, Ceramarte of Brazil has entered the stein producing business and rapidly become one of the dominant producers of new steins. Post-World War II production by this and other companies is discussed in more detail in Section 17.

2. Production of Steins

It would not be practical to make each of the sections of this book self-contained. So to the extent that there are common elements to the production of the various different types of steins, these will be discussed in this section. For example, several of the sections contain steins made from ceramic materials; the description of their production has been brought forward into this section.

2.1 Pewter Mountings

Pewter can contain as much as 90% tin, with the remainder made up of copper, zinc, bismuth, antimony, and occasionally, *small* quantities of lead. Pewter is a very workable metallic alloy that melts at a relatively low temperature. It thus imposes few requirements on the pewter workshop or the pewter craftsman.

In fact, with regard to its undemanding nature, it is rivaled only by lead: lead melts at an even lower temperature than pewter. Nevertheless, ever since the inception of the covered container law, pewter has been the most common choice for the material of a stein's mountings. One reason for this is that lead has a tendency to get very dark, powder, pit, and scale. And an even more important reason why pewter is almost always used for stein mountings is that lead has been known since the Middle Ages to be unacceptable for holding food or drink because of its toxicity to humans.

The various parts of a stein's mounting are shown on page 17, though generally a stein will not contain all the elements shown in the illustration.

Because of the low melting temperature of pewter, pewter mountings can be fastened to most steins with little risk of damaging the already completed body of the stein, whether it is ceramic or glass. Fastening the pewter mounting to the handle of the stein is generally accomplished in one of two ways. The most common method has been to wrap a leather strap around the handle, cover it with clay, then pull the strap out to leave a mold for the melted pewter. Occasionally, wax has been used, covered with clay, then burned out by the molten pewter, hence the so-called *lost-wax* process.

The purpose of the *footring* has always been to protect the bottom of the stein from chipping, cracking, or other damage. Because of their susceptibility to damage, virtually all faience steins, even modern replicas, have had footrings. Footrings will also occasionally be found on stoneware and glass steins, even up to about 1900.

Also of interest is the production of the *hinge*. Before 1860, the outside of the hinge was *closed* over, requiring a good deal of labor; after about 1860, the hinge was drilled and the pin set right in through all the teeth. The hinge pin of these more modern steins thus generally shows on the outside of the hinge.

The most common method for making *lids* and *footrings* has been to cast them, then trim away excess pewter by working these pieces on a lathe. This lathework will leave spinmarks on the inside, and often also the outside, of the lids and footrings. Up until about 1900, pewter had been quite expensive relative to labor. Older types of lids that are cast with a *heavy hand* and not slimmed down on the lathe, are usually reproductions.

The old types of ball *thumblifts*, commonly used in the 1700's, were made by soldering together two cup-shaped pieces of pewter. This saved on both weight and expense. Earlier types of thumblifts, from the 1600's, were generally solid, small figurals, most often shells, and single and double acorns. Thumblifts of the early 1800's ran the whole range from hollow vase-like devices to small solid balls and figurals. Toward the end of the 1800's, the thumblifts were commonly bas-relief decorated tabs or figurals.

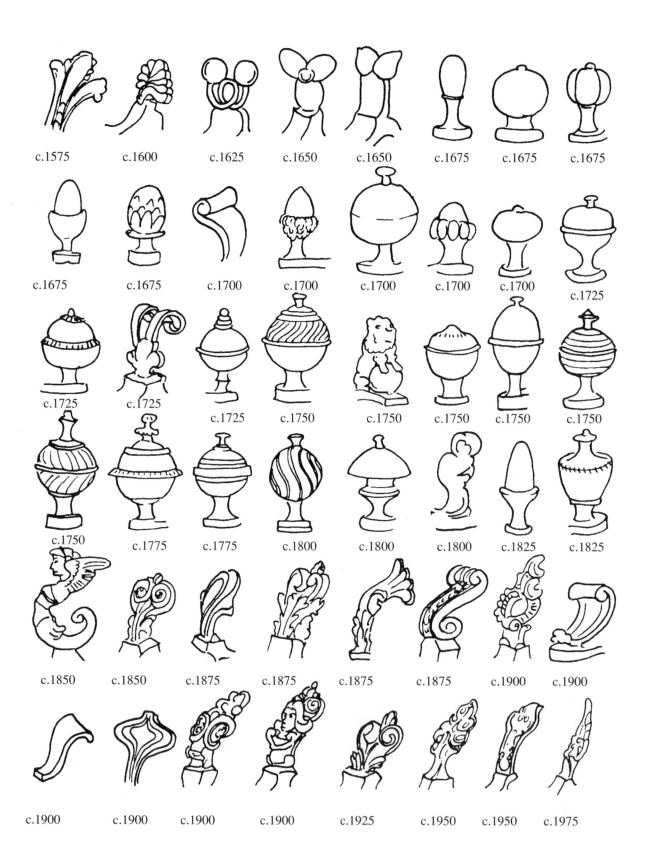

c.1575   c.1600   c.1625   c.1650   c.1650   c.1675   c.1675   c.1675

c.1675   c.1675   c.1700   c.1700   c.1700   c.1700   c.1700
c.1725

c.1725   c.1725
c.1725   c.1750   c.1750   c.1750   c.1750   c.1750

c.1750   c.1775   c.1775   c.1800   c.1800   c.1800   c.1825   c.1825

c.1850   c.1850   c.1875   c.1875   c.1875   c.1875   c.1900   c.1900

c.1900   c.1900   c.1900   c.1900   c.1925   c.1950   c.1950   c.1975

Thumblifts, or thumbpieces, of styles that have been popular in various time periods.

Pewter mountings and patina often convey information about steins. *Patina* can best be described as something that will be lost if pewter is cleaned with an abrasive material. *Patina* encompasses both the evidence of *wear* and the *color* that comes from aging. It gives old pewter a uniformly soft appearance, virtually impossible to reproduce exactly. A check for possible repairs on a stein should thus begin with a careful examination of the strap, the hinge, and the patina, or color, of the pewter.

Being relatively soft, pewter mountings are easily marked with stamps that may give some information about the age and origin of a stein. On early steins these *touchmarks* were the registered symbols of the master pewterers. Reference books that identify touchmarks can be examined at many museums and some libraries.

The results of such touchmark searches, however, are often disappointing, since many of the original pewter guild records have been lost. On average, it seems that the city of the pewterer may be identifiable about one-third of the time, the name of the pewterer perhaps one-tenth of the time.

Dates that occur on touchmarks, and for that matter on lids, can be deceiving. Touchmark dates usually represent the date the pewter guild was founded, often 1708, or the date the master first registered his symbol.

Some of the names and symbols that occasionally occur on pewterwork of the last hundred years are discussed in Section 5.

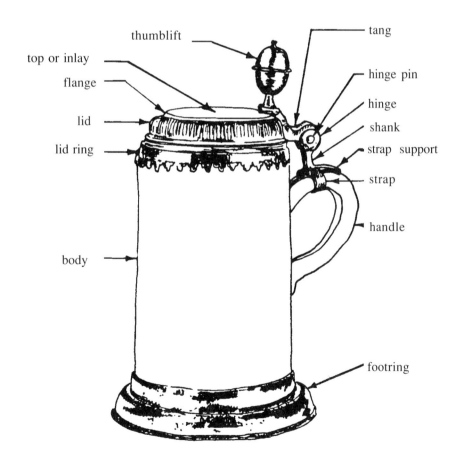

The most common names for the various parts of a stein's mountings.

2.2 Hand-Thrown Ceramics

Earthenware, Hafnerware, pottery, stoneware, *Steingut* or fine stoneware, porcelain, and the other ceramics all differ in only two respects: *firing temperature* and *recipe*, that is to say, the type of clay and other additives. As far as stein production is concerned, ceramic pieces were either *hand-thrown* or *molded*.

In either case, production began by making sure all ingredients were in clay or powder form, which may have required some grinding. The proportions called for in the recipe were then measured out and dumped into a vat with water. The resulting *slurry* was thoroughly mixed and strained to remove impurities.

Two different mechanisms that were used as early potter's wheels.

In the case of the hand-thrown articles, this slurry was dried and kneaded until the *hump* would hold its shape when worked by hand. The hump was then set on a potter's wheel (for early steins these wheels were turned by apprentices) and the cavity was pushed in and the walls pulled up.

Obviously a highlight of the day when "the young, cook's maiden from the castle visits this potter in Grenzau, 1591"

Scrapers were used to bring the outside into a cylindrical shape, as well as to carve excess materials away from the inside, especially the bottom corner. Templates, called *ribs*, were then used to produce the lip and any bands that were desired on the outside.

The hump was then cut away from the wheel by pulling a wire under it, leaving concentric whorls, or by using a knife once the wheel was stopped.

At this point the handle was added, as well as any applied work, incising, or glazing, and the *mug* was ready for firing.

2.3 Slip Molded Ceramics

It is not known exactly when slip molding was invented, but it had become an important stein making technique by the late 1800's.

The slurry was prepared in the same manner as described previously. The drying, however, was not accomplished in a mill or other separate process; instead it took place *right in the mold*.

The molds were made of *plaster* which slowly drew the moisture out of the *slip*, or slurry, that was right against it. The longer the slip was kept in the mold, the thicker the dried portion of the slip became. After a prescribed number of hours the excess slip was poured out and the plaster mold was disassembled.

Because of the time, effort and expense involved in making the plaster mold, slip molded steins are generally made of finer materials, like porcelain. Because slip molding could accommodate almost any kind of shape it helped to make possible the mass production of the oddly shaped *character* steins, shown in Section 15.

2.4 Stein Marks

A large percentage of steins are *not* marked with the name of the manufacturer. There are several theories as to why this is so. It could be that, as with the earliest steins, merchants preferred that their customers not be able to contact the manufacturers directly; thus, they persuaded makers to use only an identifying mold number. It is also known that the Europeans, particularly the Germans, have always been somewhat reluctant to discuss where they purchased items. Whatever the reason, it has made the study of stein producers very difficult. In many cases this study has to begin with locating old catalogs.

Artists' names on steins are even more scarce. Except in the case of some Mettlach steins, a collector would be fortunate to locate the artist's initials somewhere in a stein's design. During the Renaissance revival of the 1800's artists were taught to aspire to the Classics, and as copyists not to sign their names. Perhaps this tradition continued through to the modern era.

Aside from the Mettlach factory, which had an elaborate marking system that is described in *The Mettlach Book*, pp. 15-19, there is little that can be learned from markings on the bottom of steins. The accompanying four pages show symbols that have been identified with particular manufacturers or distributors and dates.

The following are a few other markings that can occasionally be found, and what they mean:

GERMANY, or **Made in Germany**, indicates that the stein was probably meant to be exported to the United States or elsewhere outside Germany; this mark was required after the *1891 Marking Law* and was used until World War II.

WEST GERMANY is a mark used after World War II.

MUSTERSCHUTZ means *protected against copying*.

GESCHÜTZT means *protected* or *patented*.

Gesetzlich Geschützt translated as *legally protected*.

Gegen Nachbildung Geschützt means *protected against copying*.

Reg. U.S. Pat. Off., registered at the U.S. Patent Office, was put on some items intended for sale in the United States.

Incised numbers most often denoted the manufacturer's catalog number of the mold that was used.

Painted numbers usually represent the decoration number.

Steins have occasionally been examined that carried paper labels with prices, export information, or even the manufacturer's or distributor's names. Of course, it is rare that any of these are found to help identify *antique* steins.

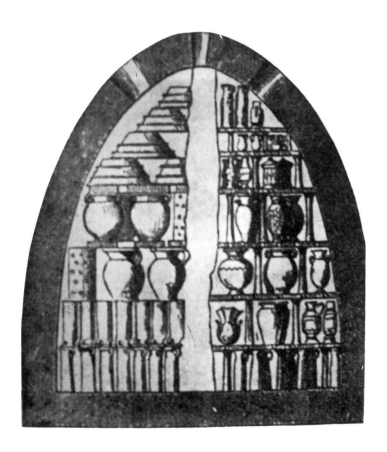

Cross-section of kiln showing a method of stacking the wares; the exhaust vents at the top were used to pour in the approximately 400 pounds of salt at peak temperature.

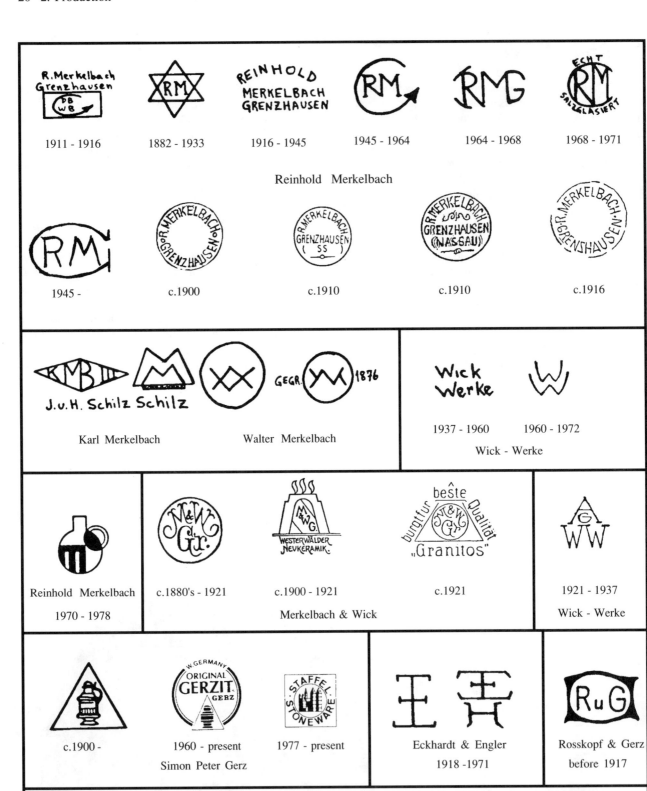

Marks for some of the stein manufacturers.

| 1893 - 1896 | 1897 - 1918 | 1918 - 1930 | 1930 - present |

Albert Jacob Thewalt

D.R.G.M. 154927

Deutsches Reichs Gebrauchsmuster
accompanied with #154927:
Adolf Diesinger, 1901 - 1918

August Corzelius
late 1800's

Werner Corzelius
modern

H. Cremer

Rastal Werk
1959 - present

J. W. Remy   c. 1900 - 1960's

Paulus &
Thewalt
c.1910

P W

Peter Willems
early 1900's

1903 - 1970's   modern

Gilles & Sohn

 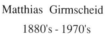

Matthias Girmscheid
1880's - 1970's

GIRMSCHEID

modern

c.1900 - c.1930

Dümler & Breiden

c.1900 -
c.1920's

**FACHSCHULE
·HOEHR·**

Königliche Keramische
Fachschule, early 1900's

Joh. Ferdinand
1920's - 1930's

Hanke **R H** R. H.

Reinhold Hanke   c.1900 - 1930's

Würfel & Müller
modern

**WESTERWALD
ART POTTERY**

Reinhold Hanke
early 1900's

Marks for some of the stein manufacturers.

A. Bauer
c.1900

Bauer Pottery

Gebrüder Benedikt
c.1900

Wachtersbach
Keramik

Hauber & Reuther
1887 - c.1910

Gebrüder Horn
late 1800's

Ferdinand
& Kamp

Ernst Dorfner

Gebrüder Dorfner
1895 - 1914

c.1900   c.1910

Wilhelm Krumeich

Silberdistel

Felsenstein & Mainzer
Nürnberg
(pewter maker &
distributor)

Adolf Schneider
c.1900

Theodor Wieseler (Nürnberg)
(distributor)

L. Ostermayr.

Thoedor
Paetsch
c.1910

W. Goebel
1957 - 1963

Hachiya (Japan)
1950's -

Josef Reinemann   (distributor)

Flix Keramik

Ceramarte (Brazil)
modern

Martin Pauson
(distributor/dealer)

Risler & Cie

Rudolstadt

August Sältzer

Marks for some of the stein manufacturers.

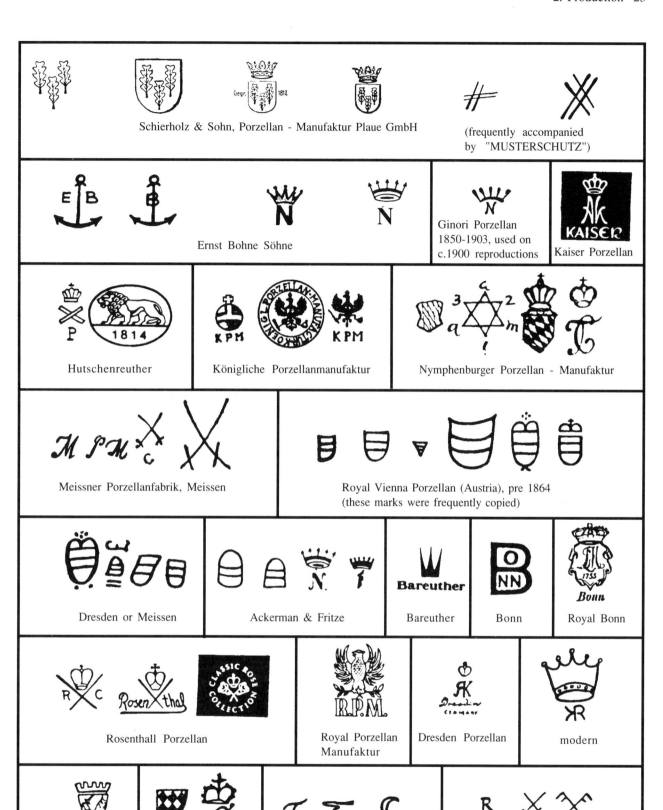

Marks for some of the stein manufacturers.

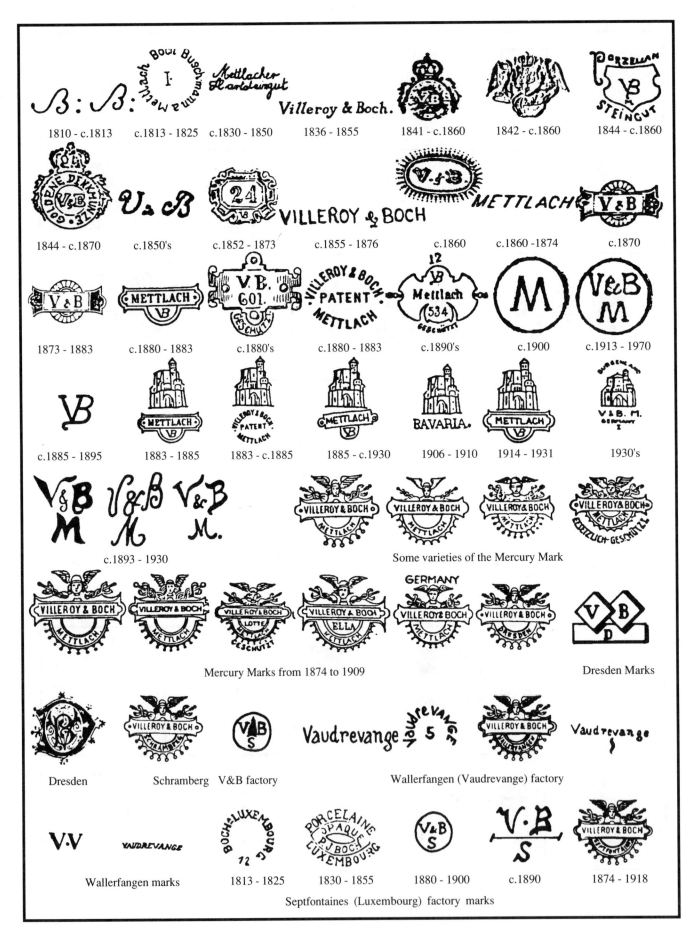

| 1810 - c.1813 | c.1813 - 1825 | c.1830 - 1850 | 1836 - 1855 | 1841 - c.1860 | 1842 - c.1860 | 1844 - c.1860 |

| 1844 - c.1870 | c.1850's | c.1852 - 1873 | c.1855 - 1876 | c.1860 | c.1860 -1874 | c.1870 |

| 1873 - 1883 | c.1880 - 1883 | c.1880's | c.1880 - 1883 | c.1890's | c.1900 | c.1913 - 1970 |

| c.1885 - 1895 | 1883 - 1885 | 1883 - c.1885 | 1885 - c.1930 | 1906 - 1910 | 1914 - 1931 | 1930's |

c.1893 - 1930

Some varieties of the Mercury Mark

Mercury Marks from 1874 to 1909   Dresden Marks

Dresden   Schramberg   V&B factory   Wallerfangen (Vaudrevange) factory

Wallerfangen marks   1813 - 1825   1830 - 1855   1880 - 1900   c.1890   1874 - 1918

Septfontaines (Luxembourg) factory marks

Marks used by the Villeroy and Boch, Mettlach factory and some of its other factories.

3. Early Stoneware

The early history of stoneware steins is virtually the same as the early history of steins, as discussed in Section 1, since stoneware was for some time the only really important material used to make steins. There is a very short chapter in the history of stein making that does precede stoneware and this is related now.

3.1 Earthenware and Hafnerware

Earthenware vessels, especially in a *baluster* shape, were common in the Rhineland area in the 1400's. They were made by firing clay to about 800°C (1500°F) to drive off all the moisture. The resulting pottery was not durable and the surface was quite porous. None of these early pieces have been found with evidence of having had a lid.

Hafnerware, on the other hand, has been found with lids, that is to say, in the true beer stein form. Hafnerware is an earthenware that has been covered by a lead glaze, to make it non-porous and to increase its durability somewhat.

Hafnerware had long been used to make stove tiles and other useful household items. Some decorative glazes have been found on Hafnerware steins, and examples can be found that date from the 1500's to the 1700's. Most of these are from Austria or Southern Germany. They are quite uncommon, however, and do not merit further discussion in this kind of general book.

3.2 Stoneware

The most common of the stoneware steins are those from the Westerwald region. Again, some of the history of these steins was discussed in Section 1. The remainder of this section will thus concentrate on some of the production techniques, factories and their styles, and some information for collectors.

Stoneware is a product of clay that has been heated so intensely, to about 1200°C (2200°F), that the clay has vitrified into stone. It is hard to scratch, even with steel, and is impervious to liquids. Thus, glazes have been added only for aesthetic reasons.

The furnace designs required to obtain such heat took some time to evolve. But it is really the *special clay* that is required that prevented earlier discovery of stoneware. Stoneware clay must be very plastic, free from metallic and alkali impurities, and must fire with little (5% or less) shrinkage, and no warping or cracking. Stoneware clays, sometimes called *white gold*, were originally mined out of potholes, the sides of which were supported by saplings. These clays are still being mined today, but now using extensive shaft and tunneling techniques.

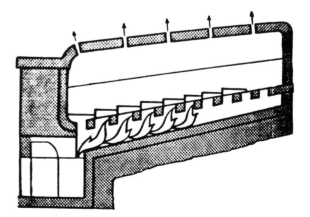

A more modern furnace, or kiln, designed with less vertical transfer of heat than the older upright configurations.

3.3 Stoneware Factories

Although the major deposits of stoneware clays have been in the Westerwald region, these did not become important until the 1600's. Before that time and even after the Westerwald area began production, there were several regional stein producers that had their own distinctive styles and decorative techniques. Examples from most of these factories are shown in the following pictures, so only brief characterizations of the steins produced by these factories are listed here:

Siegburg: early 1500's to late 1500's; white stoneware; clear glaze; slender and tall styles with Renaissance relief decorations; after 1600 the style became much like Westerwald.

Köln-Frechen: early 1500's to 1600; gray stoneware; clear or *leopard* speckled-brown saltglazes; jug shapes, then later cylindrical; bearded man, allegorical, or smooth decor.

Raeren: about 1550 to early 1600's; gray stoneware; clear and blue or brown saltglazes; jug shapes and cylindrical; chip-carving (patterns of vertical creases) with allegorical scenes; then later, bands with coats of arms.

Waldenburg: middle 1500's to late 1600's; gray stoneware; brown glazes with applied decor of allegorical scenes and coats of arms.

Westerwald: 1590 to about 1700; gray stoneware; clear, blue and purple saltglazes; jug shapes with applied decorations; 1670 to about 1800; trend toward cylindrical shapes, first with applied shields and portraits, then in early 1700's with applied diamond-shape decorated bands, later with applied relief, stamped, scratch incised, zig-zag, and chip-carved designs.

Creussen: early 1600's to middle 1700's; brown stoneware; saltglaze and often many colors of enamel; chocolate background color from the combination of the clay, so-called *black salt*, and particular wood used for fuel; squat cylindrical and pear shapes; relief decor; chip-carving; coats of arms, portraits, religious scenes, hunt scenes, and mythological decorations.

Annaberg: middle 1600's to early 1700's; dark brown to grayish brown stoneware; saltglaze and various colors of enamel; squat cylindrical and pear shapes; chip-carving, relief decor, and organic designs.

Freiberg: middle to late 1600's; grayish to olive stoneware; saltglaze and enamels; cylindrical shapes with much chip-carving and stamped designs, often with checkerboard types of decorations.

Duingen: 1600's to about 1800; light brown stoneware; various brown saltglazes; plain bands with an occasional coat of arms.

Muskau: late 1600's to 1700's; gray stoneware; brown, blue and purple saltglazes; pear and cylindrical shapes with crudely scratched or stamped organic decorations.

Altenburg: 1700's to early 1800's; gray stoneware; light brown and creamy white glazes; tall cylindrical shapes with designs often made from many applied *pearls* of glaze, usually depicting folk art designs.

Bunzlau: 1700's; cream stoneware-earthenware; pear and bulbous shapes; brown glazes with occasional cream-colored applied *bisque* decorations, sometimes with smooth *melon* ribs.

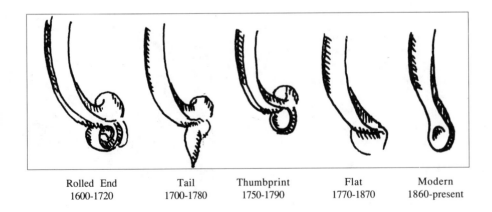

Rolled End	Tail	Thumbprint	Flat	Modern
1600-1720	1700-1780	1750-1790	1770-1870	1860-present

The potter's treatment of the lower end of the handle changed significantly over time, and can sometimes be used to help date Westerwald steins.

3.4 Collecting Early Stoneware

Few of the early stoneware steins were signed by the artist. Some of the famous Raeren and Westerwald steins from around 1590 are signed. Some of the Creussen steins are signed on the bottom with the letters of the artist's name cryptically combined into a clustered stick pattern. Occasionally a Westerwald stein, especially one with a *GR* design (*Georgius Rex*, made for export to England) uses a central applied design that has come from an initialed mold. These are virtually the only identifying marks that will be found on any of these old stoneware steins. The reason, as explained previously, is that stein merchants did not want customers identifying and requesting, or contacting, specific stein makers.

Of interest to some collectors is the area within the broad *Westerwald* region that was responsible for certain steins. It is true that the vast majority of Westerwald steins were produced in the Höhr, Grenzau, and Grenzhausen cluster of neighboring villages. Westerwald-type steins are also known to have been produced in Steinau, other Hessen villages, Siegburg, Raeren, and even possibly around the Frechen area. The pictures in this section identify a couple of the major style variations that are known to have come from specific villages. Examination of leaf designs, deer, ropework, checkerboarding, zig-zag incising, and some floral stamps will help in the identification of similar steins.

There *are* early stoneware steins that come to the marketplace; actually more than one might at first expect. A collector should be aware of several things before considering such a purchase. Reproductions are usually easily identified, but there can be some fakes that are convincing after a cursory examination. So look inside and out at all of the parts of the stein, including the pewterwork.

A second important thing to note is that there are *considerable* differences between the prices of different stoneware steins, as the information later in this section clearly shows. Note also that the value of these steins does not strictly follow age, aesthetic appeal, size, rarity of type, or any other immediately apparent criteria, although each of these will have some bearing on the value. It is important to study the styles and values of the steins pictured.

Finally, it should be noted that the effect of condition on value is difficult to generalize. The value will always be reduced if there is damage or a repair on a stoneware stein. Some collectors, especially those who have previously collected mass-produced steins, are very fastidious about the condition of old stoneware pieces. On the other hand, some long-time collectors and museums tend to place more emphasis on the aesthetic and technical quality of the stein *compared to others* of the *same* type. Each of these old stoneware steins is one-of-a-kind, and damage ought to be considered with this in mind.

There are no particularly dominant strategies for collecting old stoneware steins. Some collectors attempt to acquire examples of all of the various types. Others concentrate on those from one particular region, and this is frequently the Westerwald region because these are the most often encountered. Whatever the strategy it is always better to concentrate on the best quality steins, as these are the most sought after by other collectors and museums, both of which are always looking to *upgrade* their collections.

Evaluation Information

The value range for the steins illustrated in this chapter reflects the normal price that can be expected from a knowledgeable dealer selling to a serious collector in the United States. Prices can vary in other countries; the primary market for these steins is in West Germany. Prices can and will change in the United States to reflect both price changes in West Germany and other countries, as well as changes in currency exchange rates. The values reflect only steins in good to very good condition, and allow for the variations that occur in decorations on hand-produced wares.

a.   Stoneware, 1.0L, Siegburg, relief crests, white saltglaze, dated 1589, $3000-3600.

c.   Stoneware, Frechen, light brown tigerware glaze, English silver mountings, early 1600's, $7000-9000.

b.   Stoneware, Frechen, mottled brown tigerware glaze, silver mountings, stoneware is late 1600's, silver is late 1800's, $1200-1800.

d.   Hafnerware, .75L, relief, originally enameled with brown, red and green, interior has green and tan glaze, c.1680, later pewter mounts, probably used as a model for an ivory stein design, $2000-3000.

e.   Stoneware, 1.0L, Siegburg, relief, three panels with female vices, white saltglaze, signed H.H. (Hans Hilgers), dated 1591, $3000-3600.

f.   Stoneware, 1.0L, Siegburg, relief, three panels, c.1580, $2600-3200.

a. Stoneware, 1.0L, Cologne, light brown, blue enamel on medallion, c.1670, $3000-4000.

b. Stoneware, .75L, Siegburg, orange saltglaze on white body, dated 1598 in medallion, $4000-6000.

c. Earthenware, 2.0L, Wetterau (Hessen), orange/red glaze with yellow etching, middle 1700's, $4500-6000.

d. Hafnerware, .5L, Drinking Bear, dark brown glaze, pewter mounts, c.1700, $5000-8000.

e. Stoneware, 4.0L, Frechen, Bartmann jug, brown glaze, early 1600's $2500-3000.

Courtesy of Peter Vogt Antiquitäten

a.   Stoneware, .5L, Annaberg, relief, brown glaze, enameled, late 1600's, $3500-4500.

b.   Stoneware, 1.0L, Annaberg, relief and cut design, enameled, late 1600's, $3000-3800.

c.   Stoneware, 1.0L, Creussen, cut design, enameled, late 1600's, $3500-4500.

Courtesy of Peter Vogt Antiquitäten

d.   Stoneware, 1.5L, Creussen, relief, enameled, Apostles, late 1600's, $7000-10,000.

e.   Stoneware, 1.5L, Annaberg, relief, dark brown glaze, enameled, bear & dog, late 1600's, $3000-4000.

f.   Stoneware, 1.5L, Annaberg, relief, light blue glaze, enameled, black, white & gold, late 1600's, $5000-7000.

a.   Stoneware, .5L, Creussen, relief, enameled, Christ and Apostles, dated 1703, $5000-7000.

b.   Stoneware, 1.5L, Creussen, relief, enameled, Apostles and lamb, c.1700, $8000-12,000.

c.   Stoneware, .5L, Creussen, relief, enameled, planetary symbols, c.1675, $10,000-14,000.

d.   Stoneware, 1.5L, Annaberg, portrait with cherry borders, brown, enameled, c.1670, $2700-3200.

e.   Stoneware, .5L, Annaberg, couple, brown glaze, enameled, late 1600's, $3000-3600.

f.   Stoneware, .5L, Freiberg, gray, enameled, blue, white & gold, engraved and stamped decor, dated 1667, $7000-10,000.

a. Stoneware, .75L, Muskau, relief, dark brown, green, yellow, white & blue decoration, c.1680, pewter lid, $3000-4000.

b. Stoneware, .5L, Freiburg, brown saltglaze, c.1680, $2000-3000.

c. Stoneware, 1.0L, Muskau, dark brown glaze, c.1690, $3500-4500.

d. Stoneware, .25L, Frechen, brown spotted tiger-ware glaze, c.1650, $4000-5000.

e. Stoneware, .5L, Muskau, cut & relief, black glaze on brown body, c.1700, $1200-1600.

f. Stoneware, 1.0L, Muskau, cut & relief, black glaze on gray body, late 1600's, $1700-2200.

g. Stoneware, 1.0L, Muskau, cut & relief, black glaze on gray body, late 1600's, $4000-5000.

a. Stoneware, 1.5L, Annaberg, relief, dark brown glaze on lighter brown body, lid dated 1700, $3000-3600.

b. Stoneware, 1.0L, Muskau, relief, black glaze on brown body, early 1700's, $1500-2000.

c. Stoneware, .5L, Muskau, relief, black glaze on brown body, late 1700's, $400-600.

Courtesy of Peter Vogt Antiquitäten

d. Stoneware, .75L, Muskau, black glaze, green and white enamel design, late 1600's, $2500-3200.

e. Stoneware, 1.0L, Duingen, relief crest, brown glaze, early 1700's, $1000-1300.

f. Stoneware, .5L, Raeren, relief and engraved, brown/red glaze, dated 1603, $1100-1500.

g. Stoneware, .75L, Raeren, relief and engraved, brown/red glaze, c.1600, $900-1300.

a.   Stoneware, 1.5L, Raeren, swirls, brown glaze, late 1700's, $600-900.

b.   Stoneware, 2.0L, Raeren, relief medallion, brown glaze, early 1700's, $1700-2200.

c.   Stoneware, 2.0L, Raeren, relief medallions, brown glaze, c.1600, $2000-3000.

Courtesy of Peter Vogt Antiquitäten

d.   Stoneware, 1.0L, Altenburg, orange/brown glaze, early 1700's, $500-700.

e.   Stoneware, .75L, Altenburg, light brown glaze, early 1700's, $400-600.

f.   Earthenware, 1.0L, Saxony, tan & red/brown glazes, middle 1700's, $500-700.

g.   Earthenware, .5L, Saxony, tan & red/brown glazes, middle 1700's, $400-600.

a. Stoneware, .5L, Saxony, middle 1700's, silver lid, $400-700.

b. Stoneware, 1.0L, Raeren, relief crest, brown glaze, dated 1719, $1000-1300.

c. Stoneware, 1.0L, Raeren, light brown, early 1700's, $500-700.

d. Stoneware, .5L, Duingen, dark brown, late 1700's, $300-400.

e. Earthenware, .5L, Saxony, swirls, tan and red/brown glazes, middle 1700's, $400-700.

f. Earthenware, .25L, Saxony, glazed redware, c.1700, $800-1100.

g. Earthenware, 1.5L, Saxony, glazed redware, c.1700, $1700-2200.

a. Earthenware, 3.0L, Bunzlau, double-headed eagle, brown glaze with applied cream-colored decor, c.1760, $900-1300.

b. Earthenware, 2.5L, Bunzlau, double-headed eagle, brown glaze with applied cream-colored decor, c.1760, $900-1300.

c. Stoneware, 2.0L, Muskau, brown and black glaze, cut & relief decor, late 1700's, $700-1000.

d. Stoneware, 2.5L, Muskau, brown glaze, middle 1700's, $400-600.

e. Earthenware, 2.5L, Bunzlau, seal of Hamburg, brown glaze with applied cream-colored decor, middle 1700's, $1000-1400.

Courtesy of Peter Vogt Antiquitäten

a. Earthenware, 1.5L, Wetterau (Hessen), orange/red glaze, middle 1700's, $2500-3200.

b. Earthenware, 1.0L, Bunzlau, brown glaze, c.1700, $1000-1500.

c. Stoneware, 1.5L, Muskau, brown glaze, etched design, brown/black glaze on bands & circles, c.1700, $1000-1400.

d. Stoneware, 1.0L, Altenburg, orange/brown glaze, white & blue beading, middle 1700's, $1200-1600.

e. Stoneware, 1.5L, Altenburg, orange/brown glaze, white & blue beading, middle 1700's, $1800-2200.

f. Stoneware, 1.0L, Altenburg, orange/brown glaze, brown rosettes, c.1675, $1000-1500.

Courtesy of Peter Vogt Antiquitäten

a.   Stoneware, 1.0L, Altenburg, swirled pattern, orange/brown glaze, early 1700's, $800-1100.

b.   Stoneware, 1.0L, Altenburg, orange/brown glaze, early 1700's, $700-1000.

c.   Stoneware, .75L, Altenburg, orange/brown glaze, blue and white beaded design, middle 1700's, $1100-1500.

d.   Stoneware, 1.5L, Altenburg, orange/brown glaze, early 1700's, $1200-1600.

e.   Stoneware, 1.0L, Altenburg, orange/brown glaze, relief eagle, white & blue beading, middle 1700's, $2000-2500.

f.   Stoneware, 1.0L, Altenburg, orange/brown glaze, white beading, late 1700's, $1400-1800.

g.   Stoneware, 1.0L, Altenburg, gray glaze, early 1700's, $1200-1600.

Courtesy of Peter Vogt Antiquitäten

a. Stoneware, 1.0L, Altenburg, relief crest, gray glaze, middle 1700's, $1000-1400.

b. Stoneware, 1.0L, Altenburg, gray glaze, white & blue beaded design of man and woman, c.1730, $2400-3000.

c. Stoneware, 1.0L, Altenburg, gray glaze, white beaded design, c.1730, $1200-1600.

d. Stoneware, 1.5L, Altenburg, relief, double-headed eagle, white saltglaze, lid dated 1734, $2200-2700.

e. Stoneware, 1.5L, Altenburg, beaded, Saxon coat of arms, white saltglaze, black enamel, dated 1720, $2500-3000.

Courtesy of Cypress Antiques

a. Stoneware, 2.5L, Altenburg, white glaze, middle 1700's, $3000-3600.

b. Stoneware, 1.0L, Altenburg, orange/brown glaze, white beading, middle 1700's, $2200-2800.

c. Stoneware, .5L, Westerwald, blue and gray saltglaze, cut decor, late 1700's, $1200-1600.

d. Stoneware, .4L, Westerwald, blue, purple, and gray saltglaze, applied decor, c.1710, without lid $400-600, with lid $600-800.

e. Stoneware, .75L, Westerwald, blue, purple, and gray saltglaze, applied decor, c.1700, $700-900.

f. Stoneware, 1.0L, Westerwald, Hausen-style, blue and gray saltglaze, cut, stamped, and applied decor, c.1770, $600-800.

g. Stoneware, .5L, Westerwald, blue, purple, and gray saltglaze, applied decor, c.1680, $700-900.

a. Stoneware, .5L, Westerwald, blue and gray saltglaze, cut, stamped, and zig-zag decor, c.1725, $800-1000.

b. Stoneware, .5L, Westerwald, Steinau-style, blue and gray saltglaze, cut decor, c.1790, $500-750.

c. Stoneware, .75L, Westerwald, Steinau-style, blue and gray saltglaze, cut and stamped decor, 1788, $600-800.

d. Stoneware, .5L, Westerwald, Hausen-style, blue and gray saltglaze, cut decor, c.1790, $350-500.

e. Stoneware, .5L, Westerwald, Steinau-style, blue and gray saltglaze, cut, stamped, and applied decor, c.1770, $500-700.

f. Stoneware, .5L, Westerwald, blue and gray saltglaze, cut, applied, and zig-zag decor, c.1740, note the inlaid lid, $2200-2700.

g. Stoneware, 1.0L, Westerwald, Hausen-style, blue and gray saltglaze, cut and applied decor, c.1770, $600-800.

h. Stoneware, .75L, Westerwald, Hausen-style, blue and gray saltglaze, cut and stamped decor, c.1780, $500-700.

a.   Stoneware, 2.0L, Westerwald, double-headed eagles, cobalt blue & purple glaze on gray body, c.1700, $1000-1500.

b.   Stoneware, 2.0L, Westerwald, coat of arms, cobalt blue & purple glaze on gray body, dated 1687, $1500-2000.

c.   Stoneware, 2.0L, Annaberg, dark brown glaze, late 1600's, $800-1200.

4. Faience

Antique faience pieces can be found with Dutch, French, English, Italian, German and all sorts of other origins, as well as in innumerable shapes: drinking vessels, utensils, and endless numbers of purely decorative items. *Faience* is a tremendously large field of study. However, the focus here is on *steins*, and thus primarily on the *German* faience factories, making this history and discussion much more manageable.

4.1 History of Faience

About the year 800 A.D., Chinese porcelain made its way to the Middle Eastern and European royal courts. Despite major efforts to produce this *white gold* outside China, it was not until 1709 that Johann Böttger and Ehrenfried von Tschirnhaus were able to produce porcelain in Meissen. The 900 or so years of searching produced steadily more attractive substitutes, of which *faience* was perhaps the most convincing.

Faience, as it was originally produced beginning in the Fifteenth Century in Faenza, Italy, was reasonably successful in imitating the white background that gave the Chinese porcelain its contrast and clarity. During the 1400's, faience spread slowly through France to the Northern European countries, and slowly across the Alps into Switzerland and Austria.

Beginning in the 1600's, the then frequent Dutch trade with East Asia brought relatively large quantities of Chinese porcelain to Europe. In the middle of the 1600's, however, revolts in the Ming empire cut off the Chinese supply. The Dutch quickly supplied this disrupted market with wares from its *faience* works. Religious changes in the Netherlands had pushed some of these potters into Germany, and in 1661 at Hanau and 1666 at Frankfurt, German faience production began to supply the waiting German market.

The first of these German, so-called *porcellaine*, steins were unabashed replicas of the authentic Chinese pieces. Their decor included Oriental people in Oriental costume in the midst of Oriental landscapes. The colors were Ming blue on porcelain-like, pure white. Often these steins had finely tooled silver lids, as had been made for the expensive imports.

Predictably, once the stein decor could be controlled by European artists, factories began selling blank white faience bodies to private artists, called *Hausmalers*, who provided decorations. Included were many of the day's finest artists, who painted steins on commission or free-lance, and the results were often magnificent. Every color of glaze was used, as well as the scenes and designs most fashionable in this late-Renaissance and early-Baroque period.

By 1700, with Germany fragmented into hundreds of principalities, many rulers found it profitable to sell licenses or to franchise faience works and exclude imports. Thus, factories were started in almost all the locations where the clay and firewood were available.

The invention of European porcelain in 1709 only slowly began to influence the faience stein market. Initially it was almost as expensive as Chinese porcelain. However, by about 1725, when production began to pick up and a white porcelain background was available, some major shifts began to take place:

(1) the best Hausmalers moved away from faience and began working in porcelain,

(2) the silver lids, often gilded as well, now went only on the porcelain steins,

(3) cheaper factory decorations and pewter mountings opened up the faience stein market to an eager middle class, and

(4) the larger, narrow-necked *Enghalskrug*, and pear *Birnkrug* shapes increasingly gave way to the more masculine, cylindrical *Walzenkrug* shape, in individual sizes of half liter and full liter.

To be sure, even until about 1770, some first-rate artists remained at the faience factories. After 1800, though, faience steins were definitely not up to their former quality. During the Biedermeier period, 1800 to 1850, the middle classes turned to unpretentious, sturdier materials: pewter and thick glass.

Somewhat after the end of the Biedermeier period, an undercurrent of collecting the antique faience items developed. A number of crude reproductions were made around 1900; common types were pear-shaped. In the 1920's some excellent reference books brought collecting out of the selected circles, and something of a faience revival occurred. This revival is easy to understand, since faience and porcelain have always provided the stein artist with a freedom of color and a white, paper-like background unavailable elsewhere.

Another resurgence of good reference books in the 1950's seemed to sharpen the interest of museums, especially in works from their localities. Steins from the 1600's and/or from Hausmalers have largely moved from private collections into museums. Now, the majority of the nice faience steins that come to the marketplace were made in the 1700's and decorated at the factory.

Identifying the workshop and possibly even the artist is of great interest to the collector. The fact that so many pieces are unsigned or, at best, cryptically signed, is an important part of the history of faience (as well as stoneware) steins. All of the guild systems were very strong in the 1600's and into the 1700's. The guild system afforded the few master craftsmen with:

(1) cheap labor in the form of apprentices and journeymen,

(2) absolute control on the numbers of shops, so the master craftsmen could stay well-to-do, and

(3) quality and quantity control.

A worker who provided clay or wood to an unguilded potter could lose supplies from the bakers', butchers', and other guilds. Pewterers' guilds would attach mountings only to steins from guilded potters.

Western German	Upper Plains
Flörsheim 1765-1922	Amberg 1759-1910
Frankfurt am Main 1666-1772	Ansbach 1710-1839
Fulda 1741-1758	Bayreuth 1714-1835
Hanau 1661-1806	Nürnberg 1712-1840
Höchst 1746-1758	Sulzbach 1752-1774
Kassel 1680-1777	**Swaben**
Kelsterbach 1758-1835	Augsburg 1678-1754
Köln 1770-1820	Friedberg 1754-1768
Wiesbaden 1770-1797	Göggingen 1748-1752
Central German	Künersberg 1745-1846
Berlin 1678-1786	Öttingen 1735-1846
Braunschweig 1707-1807	Schrattenhofen 1735-1846
Frankfurt a.d. Oder 1763-1795	**Upper Rhine**
Hannoversch - Münden 1732-1854	Hagenau 1709-1781
Magdeburg 1754-1785	Strassburg 1721-1781
Potsdam 1740-1796	**Baden**
Wrisbergholzen 1735-1834	Durlach 1723-1840
Thüringen	Mosbach 1770-1828
Abtbessingen 1739-1791	**Seas**
Coburg 1739-1786	Hamburg 1625-1655
Dorotheenthal 1707-1806	Kellinghusen 1763-1860
Dresden 1708-1784	Kiel 1763-1787
Erfurt 1717-1792	Lesum 1756-1800
Zerbst 1721-1796	Stockelsdorf 1772-1786
Württemberg	**Austria**
Crailsheim 1720-1827	Gmunden 1582-1820
Göppingen 1741-1812	Salzburg 1590-1790
Ludwigsburg 1757-1824	**Eastern German**
Schrezheim 1752-1852	Glinitz 1767-1800
	Proskau 1763-1793

Faience factories, by region.

And most importantly, merchants' guilds bought steins only from potters' guilds. In return, the merchants required that the steins not be marked. They didn't want buyers to know how to contact the best potters directly, and thus lose their commissions!

Some of the cryptic bottom marks that were used are shown in this section. Also, the pictures in this chapter should help in identifying the styles of different factories and painters. A number of faience books are listed in Section 18 that will provide additional information on glazes, styles, and colors of clays used at the different factories.

It must be noted, however, that there are few *certainties* in faience identification. Some artists are known to have been at *three* different factories in one ten-year period. And, of course, glazes and motifs often moved with the artists. Constant experimentation with clay recipes, slightly different temperatures, even different kinds of wood, could change the color of the fired earthenware. Thus, it is often much easier to identify a stein with a region, than with a specific factory.

Those with further interest in faience factory identification might begin to accumulate a collection of reference texts, such as some of those listed in the bibliography in Section 18.

4.2 Faience Stein Production

Faience manufacturers always located themselves near woods and clay. They experimented with the clay, mixed it with some other earths, sand, lime, and silicic acid, until a recipe was found that would be reasonably resistant, when glazed, to flaking, cracking and crazing.

Once a suitable clay recipe was established, that mixture was combined with water, strained, then dried until workable. The thrower would then fashion a basic shape and let the piece dry further, until *leather hard*. The handle was then attached and a first firing to about 700°C drove off the water and left a hard porous, so-called *bisque* body.

This body was then dipped in a glaze made from tin oxide, powdered glass, and a flux. At this point, factories generally decorated the pieces with pigments that could withstand high temperatures: cobalt blue, manganese violet, antimony yellow, copper green, and sometimes iron red. The second firing, to about 1000°C, melted the tin oxide and pigments into a smooth porcelain-like finish.

Occasionally wares were sent to the second firing with only a white glaze. Afterward, these blanks were then decorated with a far greater variety of low-temperature glazes, even gold leaf, and were fired a third time to about 750°C. Often the pieces for the third firing were set behind protective *muffle bricks* while other wares received the intensely hot second firing. These *muffle-fired* decorations, as were used by the

Hausmalers, can be felt or seen lying on top of the background glaze.

Most factories could not be bothered with the third firing; they usually accomplished all the decorations with pigments that could withstand the second firing, or occasionally (such as with some Ansbach or Schrezheim steins) just *cold-painted* the decorations. After much handling such cold-painted decorations became very worn, and are often totally removed to make a plain faience stein (usually leaving a plain turquoise, white or yellow background).

4.3 Collecting Faience

At best, with its porous earthenware body, faience is not particularly durable. Even with the original protective lid and footring, old faience steins generally have nicks, hairline cracks, or worse damages. Of course, collectors generally have an aversion to buying glued together pieces. Such steins aside, the age and aesthetic quality of a stein are more important than absolutely perfect condition.

Most reproductions can be spotted easily, as the decorations are usually crudely painted. However, recently some better quality reproductions have been made. Reproductions also generally have *cast* lids and thumblifts, rather than carefully handspun and soldered pewterwork. Old lids occasionally can be found fastened to reproduction bodies, but the patina and file marks around the strap or shaft will almost inevitably show what has been done. See Section 17 for more information on new faience steins.

There are not many faience collecting strategies of note. However, shape is often of concern in developing a collection. Collectors who collect steins from many different types of materials seem to prefer cylindrically shaped faience steins, which appear more in place with the other types of steins. On the other hand, collectors who concentrate totally on faience, more often relish the *earlier* narrow-necked and pear-shaped forms. Very few American faience stein collectors try to concentrate on a particular motif or factory; it is much more popular to seek diversity.

The faience steins shown on the following pages have been identified by several experts and their descriptions are reasonably accurate. Still, a substantial amount of uncertainty exists regarding the factories. For this reason, the words *possibly* and *probably* have been included in some of the following descriptions.

Unless otherwise noted, the prices have been set presuming these steins are in reasonably good shape, which would allow for a couple of faint, very short hairlines and/or some minor chipping on the handle or rim. For a stein that has large pieces missing, the value will drop closer to that of the pewter mountings, perhaps as little as $100 or $200.

Factory and artist marks used on the bottom of some faience steins.

Lesum	Ludwigsburg	Magdeburg
Mainz	Marburg	Mosbach
Münden	Niederweiler	Nürnberg
Offenbach	Öttingen	Poppelsdorf
Potsdam	Proskau	Reval
Rheinsberg	Rudolstadt	Schleswig
Schrattenhofen	Schrezheim	Stockelsdorf
Stralsund	Strassburg	Sulzbach
Wiesbaden	Wrisbergholzen	Zerbst

Factory and artist marks used on the bottom of some faience steins.

Evaluation Information

The value range for the steins illustrated in this chapter reflects the normal price that can be expected from a knowledgeable dealer selling to a serious collector in the United States. Prices can vary in other countries; the primary market for these steins is in West Germany. Prices can and will change in the United States to reflect both price changes in West Germany and other countries, as well as changes in currency exchange rates. The values reflect only steins in good to very good condition, and allow for the variations that occur in decorations on hand-produced wares.

Courtesy of Cypress Antiques

a.   Faience, 1.5L, Frankfurt, early 1700's, $2500-3500.

b.   Faience, .5L, possibly Ansbach, middle 1700's, $600-800.

c.   Faience, 1.0L, Delft, early 1700's, $700-1000.

d.   Faience, .5L, Hanau, middle 1700's, $700-1000.

e.   Faience, .25L, Hanau, middle 1700's, $600-800.

a.   Faience, .75L, Crailsheim, middle 1700's, $4000-5000.

b.   Faience, .75L, Crailsheim, middle 1700's, $4000-5000.

c.   Faience, .75L, Crailsheim, middle 1700's, $4000-5000.

d.   Faience, .75L, Crailsheim, c.1760, $3500-4500.

e.   Faience, .75L, Crailsheim, late 1700's, $3000-4000.

f.   Faience, .75L, Crailsheim, middle 1700's, $4000-5000.

g.   Faience, .75L, Crailsheim, c.1800, $1800-2400.

h.   Faience, .75L, Crailsheim, late 1700's, $3500-4500.

a. Faience, .75L, Öttingen-Schrattenhofen, middle
    1700's, $5000-6000.

b. Faience, .75L, Salzburg, late 1700's, $1200-1600.

c. Faience, .75L, Salzburg, late 1700's, $1100-1500.

d. Faience, .75L, possibly Durlach, early 1700's,
    $2400-3000.

Courtesy of Peter Vogt Antiquitäten

e. Faience, 1.0L, Nürnberg, c.1750, $3000-4000.

f. Faience, .5L, Nürnberg, middle 1700's,
    $2400-3000.

g. Faience, 1.0L, Nürnberg, middle 1700's,
    $2800-3600.

h. Faience, 1.0L, Nürnberg, c.1750, $2200-2800.

a.   Faience, 1.0L, Bayreuth, c.1770, $2000-2600.

b.   Faience, 2.0L, Thüringen region, middle 1700's, $2800-3600.

c.   Faience, .75L, Nürnberg, oasis scene, middle 1700's, $3400-4200.

d.   Faience, .4L, creamware, c.1800, $600-900.

e.   Faience, 1.0L, creamware, c.1800, $700-1100.

f.   Faience, .4L, creamware, c.1800, $600-900.

g.   Faience, .75L, creamware, c.1800, $700-1100.

a. Faience, .75L, Nürnberg, marked *I...*, crescent moon Madonna, by G.F. Kordenbusch, 1765, $3000-3600.

b. Faience, .75L, Potsdam, marked *P/R*, nobleman, c.1780, $2000-2600.

c. Faience, 1.0L, Thüringen region, middle 1700's, $2000-2600.

d. Faience, .75L, Thüringen region, princess, c.1770, $2200-2800.

e. Faience, .75L, Erfurt, c.1740, $1400-1800.

f. Faience, .75L, Ansbach, middle 1700's, $1400-1800.

g. Faience, .75L, Erfurt, c.1800, $1800-2400.

h. Faience, .75L, Thüringen region, middle 1700's, $1400-1800.

a. Faience, .75L, Erfurt, c.1780, $1400-1800.

b. Faience, .5L, Thüringen region, late 1700's, $1800-2200.

c. Faience, .75L, Thüringen region, c.1780, $2600-3200.

d. Faience, .75L, Erfurt, c.1790, $2600-3200.

e. Faience, .75L, probably Frankfurt Oder, late 1700's, $1200-1600.

f. Faience, .5L, Thüringen region, c.1760, $2000-2600.

g. Faience, .5L, probably Crailsheim, c.1800, $1000-1400.

h. Faience, .75L, Thüringen region, c.1780, $1100-1500.

a.   Faience, .75L, Thüringen region, c.1770,
       $2200-2800.

b.   Faience, 1.0L, Thüringen region, c.1770,
       $2500-3200.

c.   Faience, .75L, Bayreuth, late 1700's, $1800-2400.

d.   Faience, 1.0L, Crailsheim, c.1800, $1000-1400.

e.   Faience, 1.0L, Berlin, c.1770, $1800-2400.

f.   Faience, .75L, Thüringen region, late 1700's,
       $1600-2200.

g.   Faience, .75L, probably Erfurt, c.1770,
       $1600-2200.

h.   Faience, .75L, Thüringen region, late 1700's,
       $1600-2200.

Courtesy of Peter Vogt Antiquitäten

a. Faience, 1.0L, Erfurt, late 1700's, $1000-1400.

b. Faience, 1.0L, Bayreuth, c.1770, $1100-1500.

c. Faience, 1.0L, Dorotheenthal, late 1700's, $1300-1800.

d. Faience, .75L, Magdeburg, late 1700's, $1000-1400.

e. Faience, 1.0L, Thüringen region, c.1770, $2000-2600.

f. Faience, 1.0L, possibly Dorotheenthal, middle 1700's, $2600-3400.

g. Faience, .75L, Proskau, c.1790, $2600-3400.

h. Faience, 1.0L, probably Thüringen region, c.1770, $1800-2400.

a.   Faience, .75L, Thüringen region, late 1700's, $2000-2600.

b.   Faience, 1.0L, Thüringen region, c.1780, $1500-1900.

c.   Faience, .75L, Bayreuth, c.1790, $1400-1800.

d.   Faience, 1.0L, Bayreuth, c.1790, $1100-1500.

e.   Faience, 1.0L, Magdeburg, late 1700's, $1000-1400.

f.   Faience, 1.0L, Bayreuth, middle 1700's, $1100-1500.

g.   Faience, .75L, Schrezheim, early 1800's, $500-800.

h.   Faience, 1.0L, Dorotheenthal, late 1700's, $1100-1500.

a.   Faience, .75L, Schrezheim, late 1700's, $700-1000.

b.   Faience, 1.0L, Thüringen region, c.1780, $1200-1600.

c.   Faience, .5L, Thüringen region, c.1780, $1000-1400.

d.   Faience, .5L, Thüringen region, late 1700's, $2200-2700.

e.   Faience, .75L, Hannoversch-Münden, late 1700's, $600-900.

f.   Faience, .75L, Hannoversch-Münden, early 1800's, $500-700.

g.   Faience, .5L, Thüringen region, late 1700's, $1500-1900.

a.   Faience, .5L, Öttingen-Schrattenhofen, middle
     1700's, $2600-3400.

b.   Faience, .75L, Berlin-Funcke factory, middle 1700's,
     $2000-2600.

c.   Faience, .5L, probably Bayreuth, c.1780,
     $900-1300.

d.   Faience, .75L, Erfurt, late 1700's, $1000-1400.

e.   Faience, .75L, Salzburg, late 1700's, $700-1000.

f.   Faience, .75L, possibly Thüringen region, c.1770,
     $2000-2500.

g.   Faience, .75L, Thüringen region, late 1700's,
     $1200-1600.

h.   Faience, .75L, Ansbach, late 1700's, $2200-2700.

Courtesy of Peter Vogt Antiquitäten

a.   Faience, 1.0L, Hanau, middle 1700's, $900-1300.

b.   Faience, .75L, Nürnberg, middle 1700's, $2400-3000.

c.   Faience, .75L, Schrezheim, c.1800, $900-1300.

d.   Faience, 1.0L, Ansbach, c.1780, $1200-1600.

e.   Faience, .75L, Crailsheim, c.1800, $2800-3400.

f.   Faience, .75L, Ansbach, middle 1700's, $2400-3000.

g.   Faience, .75L, Dorotheenthal, late 1700's, $1200-1600.

h.   Faience, .75L, Frankfurt Oder, middle 1700's, $1200-1600.

a. Faience, 1.0L, Thüringen region, middle 1700's, $1400-1800.

b. Faience, .5L, Thüringen region, late 1700's, $900-1300.

c. Faience, .75L, Braunschweig, c.1800, $500-700.

d. Faience, .5L, Berlin, c.1780, $1000-1400.

e. Faience, .5L, Ansbach, c.1760, $900-1300.

f. Faience, .5L, Ansbach, middle 1700's, $1000-1400.

g. Faience, .5L, possibly Magdeburg, tailor's emblem, late 1700's, $2400-3000.

a. Faience, 1.0L, Thüringen region, middle 1700's,
    $1100-1500.

b. Faience, 1.0L, Thüringen region, middle 1700's,
    $1100-1500.

c. Faience, 1.0L, Thüringen region, late 1700's,
    $1000-1400.

d. Faience, 1.0L, Bayreuth, c.1770, $1400-1800.

e. Faience, .75L, Nürnberg, late 1700's, $800-1100.

f. Faience, .75L, Thüringen region, late 1700's,
    $900-1200.

g. Faience, 1.0L, Thüringen region, late 1700's,
    $900-1200.

h. Faience, .75L, Thüringen region, late 1700's,
    $1000-1400.

a. Faience, 1.0L, Bayreuth, late 1700's, $1000-1400.

b. Faience, .75L, Bayreuth, late 1700's, $800-1100.

c. Faience, .75L, Bayreuth, late 1700's, $700-1000.

d. Faience, 1.0L, Thüringen region, late 1700's, $900-1300.

e. Faience, .5L, probably Berlin, middle 1700's, $700-1000.

f. Faience, .5L, Bayreuth, late 1700's, $900-1200.

g. Faience, .75L, probably Schrezheim, c.1800, $500-700.

h. Faience, 1.0L, Ansbach, middle 1700's, $1000-1400.

Courtesy of Peter Vogt Antiquitäten

a.   Faience, .75L, Öttingen-Schrattenhofen, c.1780, $800-1200.

b.   Faience, .75L, Öttingen-Schrattenhofen, c.1780, $800-1200.

c.   Faience, .75L, Schrezheim, middle 1700's, $800-1200.

d.   Faience, .75L, Magdeburg, c.1780, $700-1000.

e.   Faience, 1.0L, Bayreuth, c.1770, $700-1000.

f.   Faience, 1.0L, Bayreuth, c.1770, $900-1300.

g.   Faience, 1.0L, Thüringen region, middle 1700's, $1000-1400.

h.   Faience, 1.0L, Ansbach, late 1700's, $800-1100.

Courtesy of Peter Vogt Antiquitäten

a. Faience, 1.0L, Hannoversch-Münden, late 1700's, $400-600.

b. Faience, 1.0L, Hannoversch-Münden, late 1700's, $300-500.

c. Faience, 1.0L, Hannoversch-Münden, late 1700's, $300-500.

d. Faience, 1.0L, Austrian, late 1700's, $600-900.

e. Faience, .75L, Gmunden, c.1800, $500-700.

f. Faience, 1.0L, Gmunden, late 1700's, $500-700

a.   Faience, .5L, Schrezheim, by J.A. Bechdolff, c.1775,
     $9000-13,000.

b.   Faience, 1.0L, Künersberg, by J.C. Rupprecht,
     c.1760, $20,000-30,000.

c.   Faience, 1.0L, Nürnberg, Hausmaler, by Johann
     Schaper, dated 1670, copper gilt lid,
     $20,000-30,000.

d.   Faience, 1.0L, Bayreuth, c.1730, rare dark
     brown/red glaze, $10,000-15,000.

a. Faience, 1.0L, Crailsheim, c.1780, $4500-6000.

b. Faience, 1.0L, Crailsheim, c.1780, St. George slaying the dragon, $4500-6000.

c. Faience, 1.0L, Crailsheim, c.1760, $5000-6500.

d. Faience, .75L, Nürnberg, c.1760, $3500-4500.

e. Faience, 2.0L, Nürnberg, c.1730, Adam & Eve, $5000-7000.

f. Faience, 1.0L, Nürnberg, c.1730, Rebecca at the Well, $3500-4500.

a. Faience, 1.0L, Bayreuth, c.1750, $1500-2000.

b. Faience, 1.0L, Künersberg, c.1750, $4000-6000.

c. Faience, 1.0L, Crailsheim, c.1780, $5000-6500.

d. Faience, 1.0L, Gmunden, Austrian, early 1800's, $500-750.

e. Faience, .75L, Ansbach, Miller occupation, c.1780, $3000-4000.

f. Faience, .75L, Ansbach, Shoemaker occupation, dated 1750, $3000-4000.

g. Faience, 1.0L, Schrezheim, Baker occupation, c.1790, $2000-3000.

h. Faience, 1.0L, Erfurt, Blacksmith occupation, dated 1777, $2000-3000.

Above, top row, left to right:

a. Stoneware, 1.0L, Westerwald, cut and stamped decor, unusual stoneware lid, c.1760, $2000-2600.

b. Stoneware, 1.0L, Siegburg, relief, three panels, c.1600, $3000-3600.

c. Stoneware, 1.5L, Creussen, relief, Apostles, c.1680, $1500-2500.

d. Stoneware, 1.5L, Annaberg, relief, enameled, c.1700, $3000-4000.

Above, bottom row, left to right:

e. Stoneware, .75L, Westerwald, applied relief, saltglaze, c.1700, $1200-1800.

f. Stoneware, 1.0L, Annaberg, relief, enameled, c.1660, $8000-12,000.

g. Stoneware, 1.0L, Annaberg, relief, enameled, late 1600's, $3000-3800.

h. Stoneware, .5L, Freiberg, enameled, engraved and stamped decor, c.1670, $6000-8000.

Left:

i. Stoneware, 1.0L, Annaberg, four sided, enameled, late 1600's, $4500-6000.

a. Stoneware, 1.0L, Frechen, light brown tigerware glaze, English silver mountings, early 1600's, $7000-9000.

b. Stone, 1.0L, a soft stone, polished, c.1760, pewter mountings, $2500-3500.

c. Earthenware, 1.5L, probably northern Germany, faience glaze, c.1770, pewter mountings, $8000-11,000.

d. Earthenware, 1.0L, Wetterau (Hessen), etching, middle 1700's, $3500-4500.

e. Ivory, 10.5" ht., middle 1800's, silver mountings, $2200-2800.

f. Ivory, 10.5" ht., 1700's, silver lid & base, $3000-4000.

g. Ivory, 9" ht., signed R. Rusolpk, Stuttgart, late 1800's, $2800-3400.

a. Cobalt blue glass, .5L, engraved, St. Ann, dated 1818, pewter lid, $1500-2000.

b. Cut overlaid glass, .5L, Bohemian, c.1850, glass inlaid lid, $7000-9000.

Opposite, top row, left to right:

a. Enameled glass, .5L, Art Nouveau, c.1900, pewter lid, $350-500.

b. Opaline glass, .2L, enameled, late 1800's, glass inlaid lid, $400-600.

c. Cut overlaid glass, .3L, enameled, middle 1800's, porcelain inlaid lid, $500-700.

d. Swirl glass, .5L, three layers of glass, middle 1800's, glass inlaid lid, $1600-2200.

e. Cut overlaid glass, .5L, middle 1800's, porcelain inlaid lid, $700-900.

f. Cut overlaid glass, .5L, enameled, late 1800's, porcelain inlaid lid, $600-800.

Opposite, bottom row, left to right:

g. Enameled glass, .5L, Art Nouveau, c.1900, pewter lid, $500-700.

h. Amber glass, .5L, late 1800's, pewter lid, footring & overlay, $475-550.

i. Cut overlaid glass, .5L, middle 1800's, porcelain inlaid lid, $2000-2600.

j. Cobalt blue glass, .5L, engraved, early 1800's, pewter lid & footring, $800-1100.

k. Enameled glass, .5L, c.1800, pewter lid & footring, $1100-1500.

c. Engraved glass, .75L, late 1800's, pewter lid, $900-1200.

d. Engraved & cut glass, .75L, deep engraving, handle also engraved, late 1800's, $4000-5000.

e. Enameled glass, 1.25L, Austrian double-headed eagle, c.1800, $2500-3500.

f. Biedermeier glass, 1.0L, Saxony, enameled flowers, middle 1800's, $500-650.

l.   Engraved glass, .75L, dated 1763, Apostles, pewter
     lid, $1500-2000.

m.   Engraved glass, .5L, dated 1779, $500-700.

n.   Engraved glass, .75L, c.1750, $1000-1500.

o.   Engraved glass, 1.0L, c.1800, $500-700.

Above, top row, left to right:

a. Silver gilt, .5L, Austrian, silver coins, early 1900's, $700-1000.

b. Enamel on silver, .75L, Austrian, c.1880, $4000-5000.

c. Silver, 1.0L, character Bartmankrug, c.1890, $1600-2400.

Above, bottom row, left to right:

d. Silver, 1.5L, relief, middle 1800's, $2000-2600.

e. Silver, 2.0L, Norwegian, relief, King Olaf's death in 1387, dated 1905, $3000-4000.

f. Enamel on silver, 1.0L, Austrian, c.1880, $4000-5000.

5. Pewter

Some information on pewter is presented in Subsection 2.1, Pewter Mountings. History and production information can be found there. This section provides additional detail and pictures of steins that have been made entirely of pewter. Unfortunately, it is not possible to cover the popular areas of American and English pewter tankards. There are, however, many fine references in that field, often combined with discussions of other pewter utensils, and these are usually available at libraries and museums.

5.1 History of Pewter Steins

For centuries pewter was the most popular material for eating and drinking utensils. Pewter does not tarnish, rust or break, and of great importance in the stein business, it does not give a taste to beer, as do copper, silver, and iron. It was not until the 1700's that stoneware replaced pewter as the material of choice for most steins.

The shaping and decoration of pewter is so easy that there have been many very different techniques used in making pewter steins. In the 1500's, pewter steins were either decorated in cast or hammered *relief* or by *engraving* or incising. The handles were relatively thin, S-shaped straps of pewter. Motifs commonly contained allegorical scenes within arcades or bands. At that time, the most outstanding relief pewter steins were being produced in Saxony and Nürnberg. The quality of the engraved decorations on pewter steins made during the 1500's and 1600's usually depended on whether the pewterer did it himself, or sent it to a specialist, such as a copper-plate engraver.

The next innovation in pewter stein design came in the late 1600's with the so-called *Lichtenhainer* steins. They are not really made using *anchored-grooves* as their name suggests, but are simply pewter strips laid into carved oak staves. Since these steins, mainly from Kulmbach or Scandinavian areas, are primarily *wood*, they are pictured and described further in Section 7.

Occasionally pewter steins from the 1600's and 1700's are found gilded, but this is not common. Enameling of pewter steins, however, may have been somewhat more popular, especially in the 1700's and early 1800's when pewter steins were having trouble competing with the more colorful faience, stoneware, and glass steins.

Around 1800, and especially in the ensuing Biedermeier period, many pewter steins were produced in the Walzenkrug shape, cylindrical and about twice as high as wide. Tiny zigzag, or *wrigglework*, engraving was quite popular in Germany and Switzerland then, and the designs were typically *folk art*, as was the fashion in that period.

After 1850, during the *Historicism* period, neo-Renaissance designs abounded on pewter steins: cartouches, masks, fruit bundles, garlands, and other classical devices arranged in panels or covering the stein bodies.

At the beginning of this century, pewter steins underwent their last important stylistic change, often being used to capture the sinuous lines of the *Art Nouveau* period.

It is probably true that the outstanding metalworking artists have always worked with silver or gold, rather than pewter. However, pewter steins from the 1600's by Günther, Wiegold, Wildt, and other top artists are as eagerly sought as any metal tankards.

Regional differences in shape can help in the identification of pewter steins. *Rorken*, or footed vase shapes, are more commonly from northern Germany. Pear-shaped pewter steins are often from Schlesien, Bohemia, Hungary, or southern Germany. Also from southern Germany, as well as Austria and Switzerland, come the tall, tapered pewter steins.

5.2 Production and Marks

Due to the scarcity and great expense of pewter in early times, designs were often hammered into molds, to save material that would be lost in casting. Lids, handles, and thumblifts were also often made in separate pieces and soldered together. Early molds were usually made from mixtures of calves' hair and clay, except for complicated molds which were often made of stoneware. Metal molds began to be used in the late 1500's for complicated relief pieces. They slowly gained popularity among craftsmen until, by the 1800's, iron molds had become very popular for the making of pewter steins.

Touchmarks can frequently be used to identify the origin of pewter steins made between 1600 and 1800. Not only are the master pewterer's touchmarks often visible, but the town's touchmark is commonly seen on steins, especially on those from the middle 1700's. Although touchmarks are known to have been used even in the 1500's, few very early steins are marked.

During the 1800's, pewterers began using their full name when they stamped steins, often with their city's name as well, thus removing much of the mystery of touchmark identification.

Pewter comes in three basic types, or recipes. The best *genuine* (*Lautere*) pewter has a light color, is lead-free tin with small additions of copper, brass, or bismuth. *Probezinn*, or *proved* pewter, occasionally called *Reichsprobe*, *Probe*, or similar names, contains about a ten to one ratio of tin to lead. *Low* (*geringen*) pewter has a six to one ratio. Beginning in the 1700's a fourth type of pewter was developed when *antimony* was added to pewter alloys to make a very different material, *Britannia metal*, some examples of which are shown in Section 7.

The *quality* of the pewter is often found stamped on steins. Sometimes *KL* is used for *genuine* (*klar und lauter* = *clear and pure*); X is for *Probezinn*. Sometimes just the ratio appears, like *10:1*. In the 1800's it was common to see *Feinzinn*, or *Englishzinn* for lead-free pewter; in the 1700's this was often represented by a touchmark that had an *angel* with a sword and balance or a palm frond and trumpet.

One final mark of importance is *KAYSERZINN*, or *KZ*. This is an antimony-pewter alloy used by the *Kayser* factory from the late 1800's to the early 1900's.

5.3 Collecting Pewter

A great deal of reproduction of early styles was undertaken during the Historicism period. These were not originally intended as *fakes*, but removal of   the manufacturer's name at a later time has sometimes been done to mislead buyers. Most of these reproductions make extensive and unfaithful use of casting, often in sand or gypsum/plaster molds which are not as sharp as originals. Knowledge of marks, purities, and the study of originals will greatly help the beginning collector in identifying these reproductions.

Pewter can get *sick*, either with a black flaking disease or a powdering disease. In either case the pewter may slowly be eaten away until there are actually holes in it. Leaving steins wrapped in accidently dampened newspapers (which contain sulfur) will greatly accelerate the damage done by these diseases. *Polishing* (and darkening, if desired) is virtually the only way to arrest these diseases, which can, incidentally, spread to neighboring pieces.

Courtesy of Cypress Antiques

a.   Engraved pewter, 1.5L, marriage stein, dated 1787, $1200-1800.

Courtesy of Peter Vogt Antiquitäten

a. Pewter, 1.0L, Saxony, c.1820, $250-350.

b. Pewter, 1.0L, Wasserburg, c.1750, $300-400.

c. Pewter, 1.5L, Salzburg, c.1780, $350-450.

d. Pewter, .75L, Saxony, c.1800, $250-350.

e. Stamped, engraved pewter, 1.0L, Normandy, early 1700's, $600-800.

f. Engraved pewter, 1.0L, Saxony, dated 1829, $300-500.

g. Relief pewter, .5L, Germania, late 1800's, $150-250.

a.   Relief pewter, 1.5L, c.1870, $300-450.

c.   Relief pewter, 1.5L, tailor, c.1870, $450-600.

b.   Relief pewter, 1.5L, knight, c.1870, $400-550.

a. Relief pewter, 1.5L, blacksmith, c.1870, $450-600.

c. Relief pewter, 1.5L, carpenter, c.1870, $450-600.

b. Relief pewter, 1.5L, baker, c.1870, $450-600.

Opposite:

d. Relief pewter, 1.5L, Ferdinand and his dog, c.1870, $450-600.

e. Relief pewter, 1.5L, knight, c.1870, $400-550.

f. Relief pewter, 1.5L, knight, c.1870, $400-550.

d. Relief pewter, .5L, marked F. Barth, München, dated 1872, Pillow Fight, $700-900.

a.   Relief pewter, .5L, hunter, c.1900, $100-175.

b.   Relief pewter, .5L, woman sharpshooter, c.1900,
     $100-175.

c.   Relief pewter, 1.5L, courting and dancing, c.1900,
     $150-250.

d.   Relief pewter, 1.0L, forest scenes, c.1900,
     $150-250.

e.   Relief pewter, 1.5L, Imperial eagle, c.1900,
     $250-350.

f.   Relief pewter, 2.0L, marked Osiris, c.1900,
     $100-200.

g.   Relief pewter, 1.0L, Falstaff scene, c.1900,
     $150-250.

h.   Engraved pewter, .5L, c.1900, $150-250.

a. Relief pewter, .25L, *St. Louis* souvenir, dated 1904, $50-100.

b. Relief pewter, .25L, *Anaconda, Montana* souvenir, c.1900, $50-100.

c. Relief pewter, .25L, *Santa Barbara* souvenir, c.1900, $50-100.

d. Relief pewter, .25L, c.1900, $40-70.

e. Relief pewter, .2L, *Winnepeg, Canada* souvenir, c.1900, $40-70.

f. Relief pewter, .1L, *Chicago* souvenir, c.1900, $50-100.

g. Relief pewter, 1.0L, Bacchus and revellers, late 1800's, $200-300

h. Relief pewter, 1.0L, mascaroons and cartouches, dated 1898, $200-300.

i. Relief pewter, .5L, mascaroons and eagles, late 1800's, $150-250.

j. Relief pewter, .5L, eagle, late 1800's, $125-200.

a. Relief pewter, .5L, marked Riceszinn, devil, late 1800's, $125-200.

b. Relief pewter, .5L, tavern scene, late 1800's, $100-175.

c. Relief pewter, .5L, marked F.&M.N., tavern scene, late 1800's, $125-200.

d. Relief pewter, .5L, marked Orivit, king, knight, maiden, late 1800's, $300-400.

e. Relief pewter, 1.0L, double-headed eagle, late 1800's, $250-350.

f. Relief pewter, 1.0L, shooting festival, late 1800's, $250-350.

g. Relief pewter, 1.0L, marked F.& M.N., four seasons in panels, $200-300.

6. Glass

The tremendous variety of ways glass has been used to produce beer steins makes it very difficult to select generalized comments and representative pictures. Some references listed in Section 18 can supply more specifics; unfortunately, these concentrate on the earliest glass steins, with little available on glass steins made after 1850.

6.1 History of Glass Steins

The variety of ways glass has been used is certainly due to the fact that it is a material that has been known and loved for thousands of years, and thus it has received the attention of many innovative craftsmen.

Glass steins are known to have been made in the 1530's and 1540's. A couple of examples that exist have large *finials,* but no thumblifts. It seems possible that thumblifts, which became popular shortly thereafter, may have been finials displaced to make it easier to open the lid.

So few glass steins exist from the 1500's and 1600's that it is difficult to generalize about their materials, shapes, or decorations. The glass was sometimes greenish to brownish in color; sometimes it was milk glass. Some had applied glass *prunts*, others were enameled with portraits or heraldic symbols. The enameled steins show the influence of French and Italian Renaissance designs, readily explained by the fact that the French had re-introduced the lost art of enameling to the Germans in the 1400's, with the Italian influence coming in the middle 1500's.

Enameling glass just involves the painting of powdered, colored glass, flux, and a vehicle onto glass, then heating at a sufficient temperature to fuse the design to the glass. So-called *cold-painting*, with lacquers or oil paints, is known to have been used on early glass steins. It is not durable, however, and may account for some glass bodies now being plain, yet having rather elaborate old mountings.

From the late 1600's to about 1800, milk glass was a commonly used *porcelain substitute*. Milk glass was made by mixing tin oxide, the same white coloring agent used in faience, into the raw materials for glass. The early decorations on milk glass steins, as on many enameled glass items of this period, were similar to those appearing on the faience steins of those times: first Chinese motifs, then the so-called Indian and German flowers, and finally genre scenes. Like the faience steins, these motifs turned from Baroque to folk art by about 1800.

Also in the 1700's, some spectacular engravings were being cut into clear and colored glass steins, steins that were almost always cylindrically shaped. Common themes were floral, heraldic, hunting, portraits, celebrations and cities; some of the earlier themes were mythological or religious.

Silver and pewter mountings were about equally popular on glass steins around 1700. Somewhat later, *pewter* mountings became far more common. By then, silver mountings were apparently reserved only for spectacular glass steins, such as those that were ornately engraved (often diamond-cut) or those of ruby or cranberry glass (made using *gold* as the coloring agent in the glass).

During the Biedermeier period, 1800 to 1850, glass steins began moving from the cylindrical *Walzenkrug* shape into a shape tapered slightly toward the top and often also pulled into a partial pedestal near the base. Folk art enameled designs were used, often with wedding scenes or small panels with inscriptions about weddings or remembrances. These were probably the most popular steins of any kind during this period.

The following period, Historicism, brought a strong interest in Renaissance enameled decorations, occasionally found on cut colored glass. Glass that was cut or engraved through one or more different colored layers, gained in popularity through the middle 1800's. Subsection 6.2 relates the techniques used to make these steins, often depicting deer, forests, buildings, geometric patterns, or other folk themes. Geometric patterns created by deep cutting or mold blown techniques were also popular in the middle 1800's.

Around 1870, elaborate pewter piercework or lattice overlays began to be constructed right over colored glass steins. Toward 1900, the pewterwork became more elaborate and comprehensive, often including the handle, so that the colored glass *cup* could be separately manufactured and dropped into the pewter *shell*.

Enameled decoration of steins continued to be popular in the late 1800's and early 1900's, but the themes changed from neo-Renaissance to those of more social significance. Also during this period there developed a strong interest in *clear* glass steins of every reasonable shape: cylindrical, pedestal, pear, vase, conical, spherical, and all combinations. These may have included adding prunts, cutting, engraving, etching, enameling, or adding *rigaree* ribbons.

Such steins have continued to be popular until today, although the hand work has generally disappeared. Occasionally these modern glass steins will carry an enameled design, which has been printed or silk-screened onto a decal that was then fired onto the stein. As with stoneware, there are still a few craftsmen who are making steins using some of the old glass-making techniques.

6.2 Production

Glass is the product of a silicic acid (often from sand) and an alkali (often from soda and ash). It must be brought to a temperature of about 1100°C (2000°F) in order to form a *melt*. Great amounts of wood are required if wood is to be used as fuel, which led to most *glasshouses* being located in forests. Some coal-fired glass furnaces were used, but these only became common in the 1800's. Some time after 1900, electricity became the most popular energy source for glass furnaces.

For the earliest glass steins, a long pipe, called a *punty* or *pontil*, was used to take a blob of glass from the furnace, which was then pressed, spun, drawn, and/or blown into cylindrical shape. The end was trimmed off, and the handle was formed and pressed into place. When somewhat cooled, the *mug* was broken away from the pipe, leaving a *pontil mark* on the bottom. This mark often has its rough edges ground smooth, but is clearly visible on glass steins made preceding about 1870, and on the fewer and fewer hand-made steins produced since then.

A new *mold blown* technique was developed around 1840. Glass steins of this type were made by putting a partially blown and shaped blob of glass *into a mold*, then further blowing it until it touched the sides and picked up the pattern of the mold. Steins from three-part molds or dip molds have soft contours, unlike sharper pressed or cut glass, and they will still have pontil marks. These mold blown glass steins can also be identified by hollows and patterns on the *outside*, that to some extent correspond to patterns *inside* the steins. Sand spots, bubbles or *seeds*, swirls, or streaks may often be seen in these steins, as in all earlier handmade glass. The sizes are usually regular, such as quarter, half, and whole liters. The lids are the same as those that are characteristic of most steins made from about 1840 to 1880: porcelain inlaid, cut glass inlaid, and heavy steepled pewter, occasionally with faceted colored glass *jewels*.

In the middle of the 1800's the demand for glass bottles and jars generated tremendous economic incentive for the invention of bottle-making machines. The widespread use of coal as an abundant furnace fuel made such mass production possible. By the 1870's, automatic machinery had replaced the mold blown processes, creating the so-called pressed glass steins. Nearly always using clear glass, these steins are usually seen with the same types of lids as the mold blown steins. Into the 1900's, the pewter lids became markedly less heavy and less ornate.

Colors are imparted to glass intentionally or unintentionally by *metal oxides*. As mentioned previously, the iron oxide in sand and other raw materials imparts a greenish blue tinge. Metallic impurities in wood ash tend to produce a grayish green tint. Colors which may be used intentionally include:

cobalt oxide for royal blue;
manganese oxide for violet;
chromium oxides and nickel oxides for greens;
tin oxides for milk or white;
gold for cranberry;
silver for gray;
copper sulfate for turquoise;
cadmium oxides for red; and so on.

Most of these colors were available in the 1200's, long before stein making started, and were subsequently refined during the Medici's synthetic gem experiments and by others later experimenting with colored glass for stained glass windows.

Some other techniques are often used to add color to glass. If a blob of molten clear glass is touched to a blob of another color, usually red, blue, violet, green, or yellow, it will pick up a thin outer layer of that color. This layer can then be engraved, cut, or etched (with hydrofluoric acid) through to the clear glass. Some beautiful steins have been produced using multiple layers of this *overlaid* glass.

Clear or colored glass can also be *stained* with silver nitrate or some other stains that are fired into the surface layers of the glass. These stains are always in the range from light yellow to orange-yellow, and they can be engraved, cut, or etched through to clear, similar to the techniques used on overlaid glass.

6.3 Collecting Glass Steins

Flashed glass has a thin layer of colored, translucent enamel fired onto its surface; most often the enamel is a ruby color with a slight bluish surface sheen. Flashed glass is easily cut through to clear to provide decorative effects, such as scenes of spas, buildings, or deer.

Of these three types of surface colors, the *overlay* is the richest, most even, and most difficult to produce. Compared to the other two techniques, it can easily be identified by its noticeable *thickness* at all places where it has been cut through.

As beautiful as colored glass can be, the quest for a formula for any specific color pales in comparison to the fanatical search for a perfectly clear glass. The raw materials required to make a glass of so-called *superior brilliance* have to be surprisingly pure. Even stirring the raw materials for glass with an *iron* tool will be enough to impart to the glass that common greenish blue tinge of iron oxide.

In the middle 1800's it became common to mask this iron oxide tint with small quantities of manganese oxide, but this *decolorizer* becomes unstable in sunlight and changes to light purple. During World War I manganese became a strategic mineral, and since it was unavailable for glass manufacture, it was replaced by the straw-coloring selenium. Since the late 1920's, whenever a reasonably clear glass was desired without the expense of using a *crystal* recipe, traces of selenium (straw-colored) and cobalt (bluish) have been mixed to yield a glass with a very light gray color. Clear glass steins can often be identified with these periods by looking into the edge of the base, or the lip, for a *concentrated* view of the color of the glass.

The Historicism of the 1800's brought about the reproduction of many Renaissance enameled glass pieces; however, few were steins (most were beakers and pokals, often with the Imperial Eagle motif). Streaks and seeds in the glass, and great attention to detail in the originals, are the best ways of identifying age. Enameled names of manufacturers who reproduced the steins can be expected to have been polished off.

The most difficult copies to detect are those that use authentic old glass bodies, originally decorated very sparsely or polished clean, and then enameled using old designs. To properly bake such enamel designs onto a stein, however, requires the removal and reattachment of the mountings, which can usually be easily detected.

The same types of problems are encountered in the identification of reproduced engraved glass steins. And the same solutions exist: examining the detail of the engraving, replaced lids, and so on.

Care of glass steins is simple, but important. To protect against damage from heat, they should be kept out of direct sunlight and away from fireplaces, stoves, and furnace vents when these are in use. Especially vulnerable are the very old and very thin-walled steins.

Since there is such a great variety of glass steins, most glass stein collectors tend to specialize in a particular type or types. Many of these types can be recognized by those that are grouped together in the following pictures. Again, with such a great variety there are some types of steins that don't come up for sale very often. This makes it difficult for many collectors to accumulate a good *feel* for prices; therefore, this section offers a fairly comprehensive selection of pictures.

a.　Engraved glass, 1.0L, eagles with butcher emblem, inlaid glass medallion, late 1700's, pewter lid & footring, $3000-4000.

a. Engraved glass, 1.0L, dated 1771, pewter lid & footring, $1000-1400.

b. Engraved glass, 1.0L, late 1700's, pewter lid, $700-1000.

c. Engraved glass, 1.0L, middle 1700's, pewter lid & footring, $900-1200.

Courtesy of Cypress Antiques

d. Engraved glass, 1.0L, middle 1700's, occupational brewer, pewter lid & footring, $2400-3200.

e. Engraved glass, 1.0L, early 1700's, pewter lid & footring, $3500-4500.

f. Engraved glass, 1.0L, Christ on cross, dated 1728 on glass, pewter lid, $3000-4000.

a. Enameled glass, 1.0L, horse, c.1800, pewter lid & footring, $2000-2600.

b. Enameled glass, 1.0L, birds, c.1800, pewter lid & footring, $1700-2200.

c. Enameled glass, .75L, heart & cross, early 1800's, pewter lid & footring, $1500-2000.

d. Biedermeier glass, 1.0L, enameled flowers, early 1800's, pewter lid & footring, $600-800.

e. Biedermeier glass, 1.0L, Saxony, enameled flowers, middle 1800's, pewter lid & footring, $500-650.

f. Biedermeier glass, 1.0L, Saxony, enameled flowers, middle 1800's, pewter lid, $500-650.

g. Biedermeier glass, .5L, enameled flowers, middle 1800's, pewter lid, $300-500.

a.   Milk glass, .5L, enameled horse, c.1800, pewter lid & footring, $1500-2000.

b.   Milk glass, .5L, enameled Holy Child, c.1800, pewter lid & footring, $2000-2600.

c.   Milk glass, .5L, engraved and enameled design, early 1800's, pewter lid & footring, $700-1000.

d.   Milk glass, .5L, enameled flower, dated 1795, pewter lid & footring, $800-1100.

Courtesy of Thirsty Knight Antiques

e.   Milk glass, .5L, engraved and enameled design, early 1800's, pewter lid, $650-900.

f.   Milk glass, .5L, engraved and enameled design, early 1800's, pewter lid & footring, $800-1100.

g.   Milk glass, .5L, enameled children, early 1800's, pewter lid & footring, $1200-1500.

h.   Milk glass, .5L, enameled flowers, early 1800's, pewter lid & footring, $900-1200.

Courtesy of Thirsty Knight Antiques

a. Milk glass, 1.0L, enameled flowers, late 1700's, pewter lid & footring, $1100-1400.

b. Milk glass, 1.0L, enameled flowers, late 1700's, pewter lid & footring, $1100-1400.

c. Milk glass, 1.0L, enameled heart and birds, early 1800's, pewter lid & footring, $1500-2000.

d. Milk glass, .5L, enameled flowers, early 1800's, pewter lid, $600-900.

e. Milk glass, .5L, enameled flowers, early 1800's, pewter lid, $700-1000.

f. Milk glass, .5L, enameled flowers, c.1830, pewter lid, $500-700.

a. Milk glass, 1.0L, enameled, late 1700's, pewter lid
    & footring, $900-1200.

b. Milk glass, .5L, enameled, early 1800's, pewter lid
    & footring, $500-700.

c. Milk glass, 1.0L, enameled, early 1800's, pewter
    lid, $1300-1700.

d. Biedermeier glass, .5L, cobalt blue glass, gold and
    white enamel, early 1800's, pewter lid & footring,
    $650-850.

e. Biedermeier glass, 1.0L, cobalt blue glass, gold
    and white enamel, early 1800's, pewter lid &
    footring, $700-1000.

f. Biedermeier glass, 1.0L, orange glass, gold and
    white enamel, middle 1800's, pewter lid &
    footring, $700-1000.

Courtesy of Cypress Antiques

a. Ruby glass, .5L, cut, deep red color, c.1890, silver-plated lid, $500-650.

b. Ruby glass, .5L, cut, deep red color, c.1870, silver lid with inlaid glass, $700-900.

c. Opaline glass, .5L, blue, c.1890, glass inlaid lid, $350-500.

d. Cut overlaid glass, .5L, blue on clear, gold enamel, silver-plated lid, $600-800.

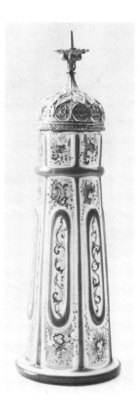

Courtesy of Cypress Antiques

e. Glass boot, 1.0L, etched, dated 1876, silver mounts, $1500-2000.

f. Biedermeier glass, 1.0L, Saxony, enameled, c.1840, pewter lid, $700-900.

g. Cut overlaid glass, 1.0L, blue and white on clear, gold and red enamel, middle 1800's, silver gilt lid, $2200-2800.

a. Opaline glass, .5L, white, enameled, c.1870, silver lid, $800-1100.

b. Opaline glass, .5L, white, gold enamel, c.1870, silver lid with inlaid glass, $1100-1500.

c. Cut overlaid glass, .5L, white on clear, enameled, middle 1800's, glass inlaid lid, $600-800.

d. Cut overlaid glass, .5L, white on clear, enameled spa scenes, middle 1800's, silver lid, $600-800.

Courtesy of Cypress Antiques

e. Swirl glass, 1.0L, clear and white glass, early 1800's, pewter lid, $1800-2300.

f. Opaline glass, .5L, white, c.1890, inlaid glass lid with figural satyr, $500-700.

g. Opaline glass, .5L, blue/white, c.1870, silver lid, $600-800.

a. Cut glass, 2.0L, late 1800's, pewter lid, $300-450.

b. Cut glass, 3.0L, dated 1878, pewter lid, $450-600.

c. Glass, 2.0L, green prunts, late 1800's, pewter lid, $500-700.

d. Amber glass, 2.0L, c.1900, pewter lid, handle, base & overlay, $550-700.

e. Amber glass, 1.5L, c.1900, pewter lid, handle, base & overlay, $350-500.

a. Engraved and overlaid glass, .5L, red on clear, late 1800's, glass inlaid lid, $1400-1800.

b. Cut overlaid glass, .5L, red on clear, middle 1800's, silver gilt lid, $1400-1800.

c. Bohemian glass, .5L, red, middle 1800's, silver gilt mountings & overlay, $1000-1400.

d. Cut overlaid glass, .5L, white on pink, middle 1800's, glass inlaid lid, $500-700.

e. Cut overlaid glass, .25L, pink and white on clear, middle 1800's, porcelain inlaid lid, $550-750.

f. Opaline glass, .5L, pink, gold enamel, c.1870, glass inlaid lid, $1000-1300.

a. Cut overlaid glass, .5L, blue and white on clear, middle 1800's, glass inlaid lid, $700-900.

b. Cut overlaid glass, .5L, blue and white on clear, middle 1800's, glass inlaid lid, $700-900.

c. Swirl glass, .5L, blue and white, Venetian style, early 1800's, glass inlaid lid, $1400-1800.

d. Cut overlaid glass, .5L, white on blue, red and gold enamel, middle 1800's, porcelain inlaid lid, $2000-2600.

e. Cut overlaid glass, .5L, black and white on clear, late 1800's, pewter lid, $600-800.

f. Cut overlaid glass, .5L, blue and white on clear, middle 1800's, silver-plated lid, $600-800.

g. Cut overlaid glass, .5L, blue and white on clear, middle 1800's, glass inlaid lid, $600-800.

h. Cut overlaid glass, .5L, blue and white on clear, middle 1800's, silver lid, $500-700.

Courtesy of Cypress Antiques

Courtesy of Cypress Antiques

a.   Engraved glass, 1.0L, Bohemian, deer and mountain scene, very deep engraving, c.1757, silver lid & footring with malachite stones, $6000-8000.

b.   Engraved and cut glass, .5L, red flashed over clear, deer, late 1800's, glass inlaid lid, $800-1100.

c.   Engraved and cut glass, .5L, blue flashed over clear, horses, deep engraving, late 1800's, glass inlaid lid, $2000-2500.

d.   Cut glass, .5L, red flashed over clear, buildings on side panels, late 1800's, glass inlaid lid, $300-450.

e.   Cut overlaid glass, .5L, red over clear, middle 1800's, glass inlaid lid, $650-850.

f.   Engraved and cut glass, .5L, red flashed over clear, deer, late 1800's, glass inlaid lid, $800-1100.

g.   Engraved and cut glass, .5L, blue flashed over clear, horses, deep engraving, late 1800's, glass inlaid lid, $2000-2500.

a.   Engraved glass, .5L, building, late 1800's, silver-plated lid, $175-250.

b.   Engraved glass, .75L, deer, late 1800's, pewter lid, $900-1200.

c.   Engraved glass .5L, deer, late 1800's, glass inlaid lid, $225-325.

d.   Engraved glass, .5L, deer, late 1800's, glass inlaid lid, $225-325.

e.   Engraved glass, .5L, red flashed over clear, hunter in field, late 1800's, glass inlaid lid, $400-600.

f.   Engraved glass, .5L, red flashed over clear, spas, including *Brand*, glass inlaid lid, late 1800's, $200-300.

g.   Engraved glass, .5L, red flashed over clear, spas, including *Schlossburg*, glass inlaid lid, late 1800's, $200-300.

h.   Engraved glass, .5L, red flashed over clear, *Kursaal zu Hamburg*, glass inlaid lid, late 1800's, $225-325.

i.   Engraved glass, .2L, red flashed over clear, *Theaterterasse i. Teplitz*, glass inlaid lid, late 1800's, $150-250.

a.   Cranberry glass, .5L, threaded design, late 1800's, pewter lid and base, $350-450.

b.   Cranberry glass, .5L, inverted thumbprint pattern, late 1800's, pewter lid, $300-400.

c.   Cranberry glass, .5L, threaded design, cranberry to clear, late 1800's, pewter lid & footring, $350-450.

d.   Cut glass, .5L, cranberry flashed over clear, swirled design, late 1800's, pewter lid, $350-450.

e.   Amber glass, .5L, c.1900, pewter lid and overlaid pewter medallion of farmer with wagon, $350-450.

f.   Glass, .5L, amber, green prunts, late 1800's, green glass lid overlaid with pewter, pewter footring, $350-450.

g.   Cranberry glass, .25L, late 1800's, pewter lid, handle, base & overlay, $200-300.

h.   Biedermeier glass, .5L, cobalt blue, c.1840, pewter lid & footring, $300-450.

a. Cut glass, .5L, late 1800's, pewter lid & base, $200-300.

b. Glass, .5L, green prunts, late 1800's, green glass lid overlaid with pewter, pewter base, $275-375.

c. Cut glass, .5L, late 1800's, pewter lid & base, $225-325.

d. Glass, .5L, swirl, etched, rigaree bands, dated 1912, pewter lid, $175-275.

e. Cut glass, .5L, late 1800's, pewter lid, $175-275.

f. Cut glass, .5L, dated 1848, pewter lid, $200-300.

g. Cut glass, .5L, late 1800's, pewter lid with small porcelain inlay, $225-325.

h. Cut glass, .5L, late 1800's, pewter lid, $175-275.

a. Cranberry glass, .5L, late 1800's, pewter lid, footring & overlay, $475-550.

b. Cranberry glass, .5L, late 1800's, pewter lid, footring & overlay, $400-550.

c. Cranberry glass, .5L, late 1800's, copper gilt lid, footring & overlay, $600-800.

d. Green glass, .5L, late 1800's, green glass insert in pewter lid, pewter base & overlay, $400-550.

e. Amber glass, .5L, late 1800's, pewter lid, footring & overlay, $350-450.

f. Green glass, 1.0L, dated 1894, pewter lid, footring & overlay, $500-700.

g. Green glass, .5L, late 1800's, pewter lid, footring & overlay, $325-425.

a. Glass, .5L, blue prunts, late 1800's, pewter lid, $275-375.

b. Amber glass, .3L, prunts, late 1800's, pewter lid & base, $250-350.

c. Amber glass, .5L, late 1800's, pewter lid & base, $275-375.

d. Amber glass, .5L, inverted thumbprint pattern, late 1800's, pewter lid, base & overlay, $350-450.

e. Cranberry cut glass, .5L, late 1800's, pewter lid & footring, $400-550.

f. Cranberry glass, .5L, late 1800's, cranberry glass insert in pewter lid, pewter base & overlay, $450-550.

g. Cranberry glass, .5L, dated 1893, pewter lid, base & overlay, $350-450.

h. Turquoise glass, .5L, c.1900, pewter lid & base, $300-400.

a.   Etched glass, .5L, late 1800's, pewter lid, $350-550.

b.   Cut glass, .5L, late 1800's, pewter lid, $400-600.

c.   Cut glass, .5L, late 1800's, pewter lid, $400-600.

d.   Cut glass, .5L, late 1800's, pewter lid, $500-700.

e.   Cut glass, .5L, c.1850, pewter lid, $200-300.

f.   Cut glass, .5L, c.1840, pewter lid, $200-300.

g.   Etched glass, .5L, c.1840, pewter lid, $200-300.

h.   Mold blown glass, .3L, c.1860, glass inlaid lid, $150-250.

a. Cut glass, .5L, late 1800's, pewter lid, dwarf thumblift, $150-250.

b. Cut and engraved glass, .5L, flowers, dated 1898, silver-plated lid, $150-250.

c. Glass, .5L, faceted, c.1910, silver-plated lid, Eisenbahn (railroad) thumblift, $300-400.

d. Cut glass, .5L, late 1800's, pewter lid, dwarf thumblift & finial, $200-300.

e. Enameled glass, .5L, dated 1915, pewter lid, $200-300.

f. Pressed glass, .5L, late 1800's, black glass inlaid lid, fireman's helmet, $300-400.

g. Cut glass, .5L, late 1800's, pewter lid, dwarf thumblift, $150-250.

h. Cut glass, .5L, scalloped base, late 1800's, pewter lid, $200-300.

a. Glass, .5L, faceted, dated 1870, silver-plated lid, Germania finial, $350-500.

b. Pressed glass, .3L, c.1900, silver-plated lid, brass Jäger tschako finial, $250-350.

c. Glass, .5L, faceted, dated 1893, silver-plated lid, engraved: *Stoss an Kamerun Lebel* (give a toast to life in Cameröun), $150-250.

d. Pressed glass, .5L, enameled, Geneva fraternity, dated 1915, pewter lid, $100-150.

e. Glass, .5L, faceted, c.1900, pewter lid, helmet finial, $250-350.

f. Glass, .5L, faceted, dated 1879, silver-plated lid with helmet finial, $350-450.

g. Glass, .5L, c.1900, pewter lid, brass fireman's helmet, $250-350.

h. Glass, .5L, faceted, silver lid, dated 1861-1911, Berlin, Husaren helmet finial, $350-450.

a. Enameled glass, .4L, c.1900, pewter lid, $200-300.

b. Enameled glass, .5L, white enamel, late 1800's, prism glass inlaid lid, $350-450.

c. Enameled glass, .3L, late 1800's, pewter lid, $300-400.

d. Enameled glass, .3L, white enamel, beer delivery wagon, early 1900's, pewter lid, $400-600.

Courtesy of Cypress Antiques

e. Enameled glass, .5L, blue, c.1900, glass inlaid lid, $150-250.

f. Enameled glass, .5L, green, blue prunts, c.1900, porcelain inlaid lid, *Garde Ulan Potsdam*, $350-500.

g. Glass, 1.0L, English, green, blue rigaree bands, faceted, c.1870, silver lid & footring, $900-1200.

h. Glass, .5L, blue prunts, c.1880, pewter lid, dwarf thumblift, $350-500.

a.   Amber glass, .5L, blue applied rigaree bands and
     prunts, late 1800's, pewter lid, $250-350.

b.   Enameled glass, .5L, amber, flowers, late 1800's,
     silver lid, $300-400.

c.   Enameled glass, .5L, amber, flowers, late 1800's,
     glass inlaid lid, $300-400.

d.   Enameled glass, .5L, white enamel, late 1800's,
     glass inlaid lid, $300-400.

e.   Enameled glass, .5L, amber, enameled rifles and
     target, dated 1890, pewter lid, $275-375.

f.   Enameled glass, .5L, amber, c.1900, pewter lid,
     $225-325.

g.   Enameled glass, .5L, amber, Berlin crest, c.1900,
     pewter lid, $300-400.

h.   Enameled glass, .5L, amber, c.1900, silver lid,
     $300-400.

a.   Enameled glass, .5L, c.1900, pewter lid, $140-200.

b.   Enameled glass, .3L, blue, late 1800's, glass inlaid lid, $100-160.

c.   Enameled glass, .25L, green, c.1900, glass inlaid lid, $150-220.

d.   Enameled glass, .5L, green, late 1800's, glass inlaid lid, $450-650.

e.   Enameled glass, .5L, designed by Franz Ringer, early 1900's, pewter lid, $350-550.

f.   Enameled glass, .5L, designed by Franz Ringer, early 1900's, pewter lid, $350-550.

g.   Enameled glass, .5L, c.1900, pewter lid, $200-300.

h.   Enameled glass, .5L, c.1900, pewter lid, $100-160.

Courtesy of Cypress Antiques

a. Cut glass, .5L, green cut to form leaves, Art Nouveau, late 1800's, pewter lid, $250-350.

b. Enameled glass, .5L, hops decor, Art Nouveau, late 1800's, pewter lid, $300-400.

c. Enameled glass, 1.0L, Art Nouveau, late 1800's, pewter lid, $350-450.

d. Glass & silver, .5L, Art Nouveau, dated 1900, silver lid, $400-600.

e. Enameled glass, .3L, amber, c.1900, glass inlaid lid, $200-300.

f. Enameled glass, .5L, amber, c.1900, glass inlaid lid, $250-350.

g. Enameled glass, .3L, tan, c.1900, glass inlaid lid, $300-400.

h. Enameled glass, .25L, blue, Mary Gregory type, c.1900, glass inlaid lid, $150-220.

i. Enameled glass, .25L, blue, c.1900, glass inlaid lid, $100-160.

a. Enameled glass, .5L, amber, Munich Child, late 1800's, pewter lid & footring, $200-300.

b. Enameled glass, .125L, amber, Munich Child, late 1800's, pewter lid, $100-160.

c. Enameled glass, .125L, amber, Munich Child, late 1800's, pewter lid, $100-160.

d. Enameled glass, .5L, amber, Munich Child, late 1800's, pewter lid & footring, $225-325.

e. Enameled glass, 2.0L, amber, cavalier, late 1800's, pewter lid, $300-400.

f. Enameled glass, 2.5L, green, *Trumpeter from Sackingen*, late 1800's, pewter lid, $350-450.

g. Enameled glass, 2.5L, amber, flowers, late 1800's, pewter lid, $250-350.

a. Cut glass, .5L, frosted, enameled, c.1860, porcelain inlaid lid, $200-300.

b. Cut glass, .5L, frosted, enameled, c.1860, porcelain inlaid lid, $200-300.

c. Cut glass, .5L, enameled, c.1860, pewter lid, $175-275.

d. Cut glass, .5L, frosted, c.1860, porcelain inlaid lid, $200-300.

e. Cut glass, .5L, middle 1800's, porcelain inlaid lid, $175-250.

f. Pressed glass, .5L, c.1900, porcelain inlaid lid, $60-100.

g. Pressed glass, .5L, c.1900, pewter lid, $60-100.

h. Pressed glass, .5L, c.1900, copper and pewter lid, $100-160.

Above and below:

a.   Etched glass, .5L, late 1800's, porcelain inlaid lid, farmer occupation, hand-painted, $150-250.

b.   Cut glass, .5L, etched, late 1800's, porcelain inlaid lid, girl, hand-painted, $140-200.

c.   Pressed glass, .5L, c.1900, porcelain inlaid lid, clown, hand-painted, $80-120.

d.   Pressed glass, .5L, c.1900, porcelain inlaid lid, hunter, transfer, $80-120.

a.   Enameled glass, 2.0L, enameled knight,
     late 1800's, pewter lid, $600-800.

b.   Enameled glass, 3.0L, amber, knights,
     prunts, c.1900, pewter lid, $500-700.

c.   Enameled glass, 1.5L stein, and matching amber
     glasses, c.1870, pewter lid, bases & overlays,
     $800-1200.

d.   Enameled glass, 2.0L, crest, prunts, late 1800's,
     glass inlaid lid, $600-800.

7. Unusual Materials

Included in this section are steins made from silver, wood, ivory, and other miscellaneous materials. Either because of expense or because of their form, none of these materials lent themselves to mass production processes. They were hand-worked, often with great detail, and mostly fell into their period of decline at the beginning of the 1800's. Each has an interesting history, but they are now encountered by collectors so infrequently that they do not warrant extensive discussions.

7.1 Silver Steins

Silver is often considered the most valuable material to be used regularly in stein making. Gold was very rarely used because it was expensive and so soft that it would be too easily dented.

Early silver steins or silver mountings usually show traces of having been *gilded*. This was apparently *not* intended as a *deception*, rather it was just a means of avoiding the polishing that was made necessary by the oxidation of exposed silver. Beginning in the 1700's, gilding was no longer commonly used, with silver being appreciated for its own qualities, regardless of the polishing required.

Silver is often *alloyed*, usually with copper, to reduce its cost and increase its strength. The purity of the silver in the earliest days of stein making was stamped according to the number of *sixteenths* representing the fraction of silver, for example 11 or 12. In more recent times this fraction has been changed to *thousandths*, such as 825.

Silver steins of the 1500's and early 1600's were decorated with hand-hammered relief and/or engravings. They were often tall, slim, and tapered toward the top. They were used for beer, cider, and wine, which were most often drunk *warm*, sometimes *hot*. With silver's high conductivity of heat, it was important that thumblifts

be made thin and handles hollow (also reducing the cost and weight of silver steins).

Silver tankards were the first, in the middle 1600's, to consistently use the *Walzenkrug*, or cylindrical shape, about twice as high as wide. These steins were most often just engraved.

Toward the end of the 1600's, casting techniques provided deep and elaborate relief. However this type of stein faded quickly, in favor of simpler engraved designs again, which carried right through to the 1800's.

The 1800's began a period of *revivals*, especially of earlier cast pieces. In 1884, a marking rule was passed requiring that a crescent moon, crown, and purity be stamped on all German silver steins. This can be very helpful in identifying some of the later reproductions.

Identifying authentic early silver steins requires some understanding of styles, techniques, and marks, especially goldsmiths' marks, which should be sharp, not smooth as on many reproductions. It also should be noted that reproductions made during the late 1800's, the Historicism era, were *not* intended as *fakes* and often carried marks clearly identifying their manufacturer and period. When it appears that marks have been polished out, extra scrutiny should be used.

7.2 Wooden Steins

Wood was one of the most popular materials for making beer *beakers* in the Middle Ages. Wood's downfall began in the 1500's, due to the difficulties involved in making a durable hinge for the lid. Occasionally, good examples are seen of all-wooden steins, and when they are from the 1600's, the carving is generally very detailed and in high relief.

As mentioned in Section 5, the pewter mounted and pewter inlaid wooden steins were first popular from the late 1600's to the middle 1700's. The *Lichtenhainer* name given to these steins is actually derived from the popular beer brewed in this region around Kulmbach. Natural motifs, such as plants and animals, dominate the inlaid designs on these steins.

Beginning in the early 1800's some very nice all-wooden steins were being produced in Norway and other Scandinavian countries. These are usually found made from birch burl, with feet and thumblifts often in the shape of lions. Earlier examples have bodies carved with plant forms; later examples generally have smooth sides.

Around 1900, the St. Louis Silver Co. produced several types of steins made from oak staves and held together with silver-plated overlays and mountings. Also at the time, a number of lathe-produced steins were made, often put together from separate pieces, with bodies carrying woodburnt decorations.

7.3 Other Materials

Horn, amber, stone, coconuts, various metals such as hammered brass, and many other materials have been used to make steins. Of particular note among these are the *ivory* steins, which received the attention of some great craftsmen.

Ivory steins were not really possible until the Dutch East Indies Trade Co. began to bring African ivory to Europe in the 1600's. Steins were carved in Nürnberg and the vicinity, usually in high relief. When the drilling, carving, and filling were finished, the scenes were polished with wood ashes and oil.

Cracks and discolorations have hurt the appearance of most ivory steins, but the workmanship is still evident. Toward the 1700's, the scenes changed, for the most part, from cherubs and mythological scenes to hunts, battles, and city scenes.

Checks in the ivory are not good indicators of age, as they can be produced by soaking in hot water then quickly drying. A yellowish to orange color may be a sign that a piece was *torched* or buried (in dung) to simulate patina. Authentic old ivory steins, however, are often as *white* as originals, due to the bleaching action of light. Very fine workmanship on carvings and on mountings can be another good way to recognize old steins of almost any type.

Some of the tools and equipment that were in a metalwork shop of the late 1500's.

Courtesy of Cypress Antiques

Courtesy of Cypress Antiques

a.   Serpentine, 1.0L, German, gray/green, faceted, pewter mounts, c.1730, $3500-4500.

b.   Serpentine, .4L, German, dark green, silver lid & base, c.1640, $7000-9000.

c.   Horn, .5L, English, silver lid & base, late 1800's, $1000-1300.

d.   Horn, .5L, silver plated lid & base, late 1800's, $600-900.

e.   Silver, .3L, silver gilt, Egyptian turquoise and rubies, probably 1 7 0 0 ' s , $3000-5000.

Courtesy of Cypress Antiques

a. Wood, 1.5L, Norwegian, carved, c.1690,
    $8000-12,000.

b. Wood, 1.5L, Norwegian, carved by Samuel
    Fanden, c.1660, $14,000-18,000.

Courtesy of Cypress Antiques

c. Wood, 1.0L, German, pearwood, intricately
    carved, four seasons, c.1760, $5000-8000.

d. Wood, 2.0L, walnut, carved relief, silver lid,
    handle & base, c.1740, $15,000-20,000.

e. Wood, .5L, North German or Swedish, carved
    relief, Roman scene, carved handle of Viking,
    inlaid lid of carved flower, pewter bands &
    liner, probably c.1620, $6000-8000.

a. Wood, 1.0L, Norwegian, burl, middle 1800's, $600-800.

b. Wood, .75L, Norwegian, burl, c.1800, $600-900.

c. Wood, 1.0L, Norwegian, painted leaves, early 1800's, $700-1000.

d. Wood, 1.5L, Norwegian, carved, c.1900, $700-1000.

e. Wood, 1.5L, Norwegian, carved, c.1900, copy of earlier style, $600-800.

Courtesy of Cypress Antiques

a.   Lichtenhainer, .5L, wood &
      pewter, 1600's, $2000-2800.

b.   Wood, 1.5L, Norwegian, burl, c.1770, $1200-1600.

Courtesy of Cypress Antiques

c.   Wood, .3L, Norwegian, burl, c.1770, $800-1200.

d.   Wood, 2.5L, Norwegian, burl, c.1770, $2500-3000.

a. Wood, 1.0L, Norwegian, burl, middle 1700's, $1800-2300.

b. Wood & pewter, 1.0L, German, late 1800's, $500-700.

c. Wood & pewter, 1.5L, probably northern German, late 1800's, $600-900.

d. Wood & pewter, .5L, German, late 1800's, $400-600.

e. Wood, 1.0L, *Daubenkrug* (slats), glass bottom, c.1780, pewter lid & footrim, $500-700.

f. Wood, .75L, *Daubenkrug* (slats), engraved horse in glass bottom, c.1800, pewter lid, $600-900.

Courtesy of Peter Vogt Antiquitäten

a. Wood, 2.0L, slats, dated 1714, $1000-1400.

b. Wooden drinking horn, .5L, carved, c.1900, $400-600.

c. Wood, 1.5L, St. Louis Silver Co., c.1900, silver-plated mountings, $250-350.

d. Wood, 1.0L, St. Louis Silver Co., c.1900, silver-plated mountings, $200-300.

e. Wood, .5L, St. Louis Silver Co., c.1900, silver-plated mountings, $150-250.

f. Wood, 2.0L, St. Louis Silver Co., c.1900, silver-plated mountings, $250-350.

a.   Wood & pewter, 1.5L, Norwegian, late 1800's, $500-700.

b.   Wood, 1.5L, etched eagle, c.1900, $200-300.

c.   Wood, 1.0L, etched, man drinking, c.1900, $100-200.

d.   Wood, .5L, carved, deer running, c.1900, $250-350.

e.   Ivory, 15" ht., Italian, 1800's, $2000-3000.

f.   Ivory, 11" ht., carved relief, silver gilt lid & base, 1700's, $5000-7000.

a.   Ivory, 11" ht., 1700's, silver lid & base, $3000-4000.

b.   Ivory, 9.5" ht., 1800's, brass lid & base, $1800-2600.

c.   Ivory, 9" ht., 1700's, silver lid & base, $1000-1800.

d.   Ivory, 14" ht., 1800's, $3000-4000.

e.   Ivory, 14" ht., 1700's, silver lid & base, $4000-5000.

a.   Ivory, 9.5" ht., 1800's, $1400-2000.

c.   Ivory, 9" ht., late 1700's, $2500-3500.

b.   Ivory, 8.5" ht., 1800's, brass lid & base, $1500-2200.

d.   Ivory, 16.5" ht., 1800's, $3000-4000.

e.   Ivory, 16.5" ht., 1800's, silver lid & base, $2500-3500.

Courtesy of Cypress Antiques

a. Ostrich Egg, 1.0L, Augsburg, character, soldier with chain-mail helmet, silver mounts, carved wood handle, c.1775, $7500-10,000.

Courtesy of Thirsty Knight Antiques

b. Ostrich egg, 1.0L, c.1870, pewter mounts, $1500-2000.

Courtesy of Thirsty Knight Antiques

c. Meerschaum, 14" ht., marked Elkington & Co., brass plated mounts, c.1885, $3000-4000.

Courtesy of Thirsty Knight Antiques

d. Enamel on copper, .5L, Austrian, middle 1800's, $2400-3000.

Courtesy of Cypress Antiques

e. Enamel on silver, .5L, blue & white, enamel interior, gold & silver threading & mounts, early 1800's, $4000-6000.

f. Marble, .3L, German, silver base, inlaid lid with silver rim, late 1800's, $2500-3000.

Courtesy of Cypress Antiques

Courtesy of Thirsty Knight Antiques

Courtesy of Cypress Antiques

a.   Enamel on silver, 1.0L, Austrian, silver mounts by Hermann Bohn, c.1885, $8000-11,000.

b.   Leather, 1.0L, enameled, birds, pewter lid dated 1769, $3000-4000.

c.   Leather, 2.0L, relief silver lid, base & crest, Oliver Cromwell granted the right to protect England and the crown, dated 1655, $10,000-15,000.

d.   Bronze, 1.0L, relief, marked Elkington, Department of Science & Art, c.1885, $1200-2000.

e.   Bronze, 1.5L, cast relief, dark patina & polished, middle 1800's, $2000-3000.

a.   Silver, .5L, English, late 1800's, $600-800.

b.   Silver, 1.0L, Norwegian, dated 1815, $1300-1700.

c.   Silver, 1.0, silver gilt interior, late 1800's, $800-1100.

d.   Silver, .5L, Nürnberg, late 1700's, $2000-2800.

e.   Silver, 1.0L, German, Augsburg, repoussé, cherubs, late 1600's, $4000-6000.

f.   Silver, 1.0L, marked Whiting, New York, inscribed Larchmont Yacht Club Regatta, July 4, 1895, $600-800.

g.   Silver, 1.5L, German, Augsburg, coins, late 1700's, $3000-4000.

Courtesy of Cypress Antiques

a. Silver, .5L, German, c.1660, $6000-8000.

b. Silver, .5L, Russian, engraved, dated 1861, $2800-3800.

c. Silver, 1.0L, Scottish, George IV, commemorates retirement of sheriff in 1623, $10,000-12,000.

d. Silver, .5L, Russian, silver gilt interior, shape of Estonian wood tankard, dated 1841, $2000-2500.

e. Silver, 18" ht., Continental, relief, late 1800's, $3000-4000.

f. Silver, 15" ht., English, relief, late 1800's, $2000-2500.

a. Silver, .5L, Russian, St. Petersburg, repoussé & chased, silver gilt inside and on highlights, late 1800's, $1800-2500.

b. Silver, .5L, Russian, by Wilhelm Fredrich Sengbush, St. Petersburg, 1856, repoussé & chased, $1200-1600.

c. Silver, .4L, Russian, by Carl Adolf Seipel, St. Petersburg, 1857, repoussé & chased, $800-1200.

d. Silver, .75L, Norwegian, coin on lid, late 1800's, $1200-1800.

e. Silver, 18" ht., relief, Cain & Abel and other Biblical scenes, late 1800's, $2500-3500.

f. Silver, 15" ht., German, relief, silver gilt lid and interior, late 1800's, $2500-3500.

a.   Silver, 1.0L, English, presented to the Lord of the
     Manor, Hamptons, 1862, $1000-1500.

b.   Silver, 1.5L, 1700's, $3000-4500.

c.   Silver, 1.0L, English, repoussé, cherubs, 1800's,
     $1200-1800.

d.   Silver plated, 17" ht., coin design, late 1800's,
     $500-800.

e.   Silver, 15.5" ht., German, repoussé, battle scene,
     late 1800's, $2200-3000.

f.   Silver plated, 17" ht. relief, hunting scene, late
     1800's, $500-800.

a.   Glass horn, 17.5" ht., amber, pewter mounts, c.1900, $1200-1800.

b.   Brass and blown glass, 1.5L, bronze patina, amber glass, Bock finial, late 1800's, $1000-1500.

c.   Metal, 1.5L, brass-plated, relief, c.1900, $75-125.

d.   Metal, .75L, brass-plated, relief, c.1900, $50-100.

e.   Metal, 1.0L, brass-plated, relief, c.1900, $75-125.

f.   Metal, 1.5L, brass-plated, relief, c.1900, $75-125.

8. Porcelain

In Subsection 1.2 of the Stein History chapter, and in Subsection 4.1, History of Faience, there are some important discussions about the origins of European porcelain steins. This Section will provide additional information on porcelain steins.

There were three basic reasons why Oriental porcelain steins were not imported after the discovery of porcelain making in Europe, and price (originally about the same) was not a factor. First, the *kaolin*, or white clay, available in Europe produced a harder porcelain than the so-called *softer* Oriental varieties. Second, the cobalt oxide available in Europe was naturally purer, and resulted in sharper, less diffused, blue decorations. And most importantly, the European artists and decorators knew best how to appeal to European tastes. Thus, the Oriental chapter in the history of steins virtually closed soon after the successful experiments of Johann Böttger and Walter von Tschirnhaus in Meissen, in 1708 and 1709 .

8.1 History of Porcelain Steins

Walzenkrug is the shape of most porcelain steins, a shape which probably originated with the silver steins of the 1600's, and which was popularized by the faience and stoneware steins of the 1700's. Unlike those faience and stoneware steins, however, *pewter* mountings are rarely found on early porcelain steins. The expense of the porcelain made *silver*, often gilded, the material of choice of lids, thumblifts, and footrings. Porcelain lids, or inlays, became increasingly common until they were used exclusively in the 1800's. In turn, these lids were finally replaced altogether by steepled pewter lids in the late 1800's.

At first, Böttger was unable to make a white porcelain and a few steins were produced in the early *brown color*. These were mostly very plain steins, with occasional examples engraved or decorated with gold. In the earliest days after *white* porcelain had been developed, a few *relief* steins were made , but these gave way when they could not be made to match the intricate details of the glaze decorations.

Artists who decorated porcelain in the early 1700's were often quite famous in their time. Until about 1730, though, they seem to have followed the customary Oriental motifs, as if they were making reproductions. Soon after 1730, however, these Oriental designs quickly lost favor and gave way to the more fashionable Renaissance and Baroque scenes and decorative devices, including exotic floral motifs.

Toward the end of the 1700's, the *German flowers*, painted in a very naturalistic style, became popular. Copies of famous paintings, often executed by *Hausmalers* (independent, individual decorators) were common themes around 1800.

Around the same time, *transfer-printing* techniques, also known as *print-under-glaze*, were brought to Germany from England. Decorations could thus be cheaply mass-produced, and these were often used on porcelain mugs of this period. Apparently, the expensive silver mountings of the true porcelain *steins* were rarely mixed with the cheap, new, transfer decoration techniques; at least not until the late 1800's.

By the late 1800's, transfer-printing and pewter lids were commonplace on porcelain steins. Numerous examples are pictured in this section and in the Occupational and Regimental sections.

8.2 Production and Collecting

Porcelain recipes are composed of kaolin, feldspar, some quartz, and traces of various other materials, such as whiting. Once prepared, the materials could either be worked on a potter's wheel or, for relief sections or unusual shapes, thinned to a slip and poured into a gypsum or plaster mold. Section 2 describes these processes in more detail. Handles, relief areas, or separately constructed portions of the stein were then *glued* together with additional slip.

Once air-dried to a leather-hard consistency, the stein bodies received a bisque firing to about 900°C (or about 1600°F). The glazes used to decorate porcelain steins are merely coloring agents or dyes mixed into the porcelain slips. These glazes soaked into the porous surfaces, and good decorations required a sure hand. This decoration was completed before the second firing to about 1400°C (about 2500°F). In a process similar to that described in Subsection 4.2, porcelain bodies could receive a third, lower-temperature firing, which allowed for the use of a myriad of low-temperature colors of glaze, as well as gold. This process was called *muffle-painting* or *muffle-firing*.

Porcelain collectors would be advised to become familiar with the porcelain marks shown at the end of Section 2. Comparing the consistency of the ages of the mark, the design, and the lid, will provide good protection against the mistaken purchase of reproductions. *Signed* pieces, especially those signed by famous artists, should be suspect, and subject to extra scrutiny. Reproductions are also often crudely executed, and a visit to a museum, or a fine collection, will show the quality that should be expected of various eras. The most common reproductions of porcelain steins have been the porcelain character steins produced after World War II. Examinations of the marks and the decorations, often full color, should remove any doubts about authenticity. More information about post-World War II character steins can be found in Sections 15 and 17.

Courtesy of Cypress Antiques

a.   Porcelain, 1.0L, by Johann Böttger, chocolate brown color, first European porcelain, c.1710, silver rim, mount and thumblift, porcelain lid with strawberry silver finial, $40,000-50,000.

Courtesy of Cypress Antiques

a. Porcelain, 1.0L, *Meissen* mark, hand-painted, c. 1750, porcelain inlaid lid, $10,000-13,000.

b. Porcelain, 1.0L, *Nymphenburg* mark, Hausmaler tankard by Johann Huber, dated 1778, silver gilt lid & footring, $12,000-15,000.

c. Porcelain, .5L, *Meissen* mark, hand-painted, late 1800's, porcelain lid, $1800-2300.

d. Porcelain, 1.0L, *Meissen* mark, hand-painted, late 1800's, porcelain lid, $2000-2500.

e. Porcelain, 1.0L, *Meissen* mark, hand-painted, dated 1738 on lid, made in late 1800's, porcelain lid, $1500-2000.

f.. Porcelain, 1.0L, *Meissen* mark, hand-painted, late 1800's, porcelain lid, $2000-2500.

g. Porcelain, 1.0L, *Meissen* mark, hand-painted, late 1800's, porcelain lid, $1700-2200.

a.   Porcelain, 1.0L, *Meissen* mark, hand-painted, late 1800's, porcelain lid, $1700-2200.

b.   Porcelain, 1.0L, *Meissen* mark, hand-painted, late 1800's, porcelain lid, $1300-1700.

c.   Porcelain, .75L, *Meissen* mark, hand-painted, late 1800's, porcelain lid, $1800-2300.

d.   Porcelain, 4.0L, unmarked, probably Dresden, hand-painted, relief flowers, late 1800's, porcelain lid, $3000-4000.

a. Porcelain, 1.0L, marked with crown over N, Capo di Monte style, relief, late 1800's, porcelain inlaid lid, $350-550.

b. Porcelain, .5L, marked with crown over N, Capo di Monte style, relief, late 1800's, porcelain inlaid lid, $300-500.

c. Porcelain, .5L, marked with crown over N, Capo di Monte style, relief, middle 1800's, gold on copper lid with porcelain finial, $400-600.

d. Porcelain, .5L, marked with crown over N, Capo di Monte style, relief, late 1800's, porcelain lid, $400-600.

Courtesy of Cypress Antiques

e. Porcelain, .5L, marked with beehive, hand-painted, c.1900, porcelain inlaid lid, silver mounts, $1700-2100.

f. Porcelain, .5L, marked with beehive, hand-painted, c.1900, porcelain inlaid lid, $1700-2100.

g. Porcelain, .5L, marked with beehive, hand-painted, Admiral Dewey, c.1900, porcelain inlaid lid, $1800-2400.

h. Porcelain, .5L, Chinese Export, hand-painted, c.1675, silver gilt lid and footring (Austrian), $4000-6000.

a. Porcelain, .5L, marked with beehive and *Germany*, hand-painted, c.1900, porcelain inlaid lid, $1600-2000.

b. Porcelain, .5L, marked with beehive, hand-painted, c.1900, porcelain inlaid lid, $1600-2000.

c. Porcelain, .5L, marked with beehive, hand-painted, c.1900, porcelain inlaid lid, $1600-2000.

d. Porcelain, .5L, marked with beehive, hand-painted, c.1900, porcelain inlaid lid, $1600-2000.

e. Porcelain, .5L, marked with beehive, hand-painted, c.1900, porcelain inlaid lid, $1700-2100.

f. Porcelain, .5L, marked with beehive, hand-painted, *Meine et Amor*, c.1900, porcelain inlaid lid, $1700-2100.

g. Porcelain, .25L, marked with beehive, hand-painted, *Reflexion*, c.1900, porcelain inlaid lid, $1000-1300.

h. Porcelain, .25L, marked with beehive, hand-painted, *Erbluth*, c.1900, porcelain inlaid lid, $1000-1300.

a. Porcelain, .5L, marked with beehive, hand-painted, c.1900, brass mountings, $1200-1600.

b. Porcelain, .5L, marked with beehive, hand-painted, c.1900, porcelain inlaid lid, $1600-2000.

c. Porcelain, .25L, marked with beehive, hand-painted, c.1900, porcelain lid, $900-1200.

Courtesy of Thirsty Knight Antiques

d. Porcelain, .1L, marked with beehive, hand-painted, c.1900, porcelain inlaid lid, $600-800.

e. Porcelain, .25L, marked with beehive, hand-painted, c.1900, porcelain inlaid lid, $1100-1400.

f. Porcelain, .5L, marked with beehive, hand-painted, c.1900, porcelain inlaid lid, $1600-2000.

g. Porcelain, .5L, marked Dresden and with Meissen crossed swords, c.1900, porcelain inlaid lid, $700-1000.

a.   Porcelain, 1.0L, marked with beehive, hand-painted, c.1900, porcelain lid, $2600-3200.

b.   Porcelain, .05L, marked *Dresden*, hand-painted, c.1900, porcelain inlaid lid, $600-800.

c.   Porcelain, .05L, marked with beehive, hand-painted, c.1900, porcelain inlaid lid, $600-800.

d.   Porcelain, .5L, marked Royal Worcester, hand-painted, c.1880, porcelain lid, $1000-1300.

e.   Porcelain, .3L, unmarked, made in Dresden, hand-painted, late 1800's, porcelain inlaid lid, $1500-2000.

f.   Porcelain, .25L, marked Dresden and with beehive, hand-painted, c.1900, porcelain inlaid lid, $1100-1400.

g.   Porcelain, .25L, marked Dresden and with beehive, hand-painted, c.1900, porcelain inlaid lid, $1100-1400.

a. Porcelain, .5L, marked Musterschutz (Schierholz), relief and hand-painted, dancing girls, c.1900, porcelain lid, $350-500.

b. Porcelain, .75L, Meissen mark, relief dancing figures, hand-painted, middle 1800's, porcelain lid, $1700-2200.

c. Porcelain, 1.0L, unmarked, made by Royal Copenhagen, blue on white, c.1830, silver lid, $650-850.

d. Porcelain, 1.5L, unmarked, made by Rauenstein, hand-painted, blue, red and gold, late 1800's, inlaid lid, $200-300.

e. Porcelain, 2.0L, unmarked, made by Rauenstein, hand-painted, blue, red and gold, birds and flowers, late 1800's, porcelain inlaid lid, $200-300.

f. Porcelain, 1.0L, unmarked, made by Royal Copenhagen, blue on white, late 1800's, silver lid, $500-700.

a.   Porcelain, 1.5L, marked KPM, Berlin, hand-painted, hunter, late 1800's, pewter lid, $300-400.

b.   Porcelain, 2.5L, marked KPM, Berlin, hand-painted, eagle, late 1800's, pewter lid, $300-400.

c.   Porcelain, 2.0L, marked KPM, Berlin, hand-painted, late 1800's, pewter lid, $200-300.

d.   Porcelain, .5L, unmarked, relief and hand-painted, *3. Deutsches Turnfest, Leipzig, 1863*, pewter lid, $200-300.

e.   Porcelain, .5L, unmarked, relief, white on gray marbleized background, late 1800's, set on porcelain lid, $250-350.

f.   Porcelain, .5L, unmarked, relief, white on brown background, deer and hunter, late 1800's, porcelain inlaid lid, $300-500.

g.   Porcelain, .5L, unmarked, relief and hand-painted, targets on side, late 1800's, pewter lid, $125-200.

a. Porcelain, 1.0L, unmarked, hand-painted, deer, late 1800's, porcelain inlaid lid, $600-800.

b. Porcelain, .5L, unmarked, hand-painted, hunters, lithophane, c.1900, pewter lid with relief scene of barkeeper, $125-200.

c. Porcelain, .5L, unmarked, hand-painted, knight on horse, lithophane, c.1900, pewter lid and footring, $250-400.

d. Porcelain, .5L, unmarked, hand-painted, crest, *George von Groote, S/L., Hans Graf Blumenthal, z.fr.Erg.,Coblenz,17-VI,1889,* lithophane, pewter lid. $150-250.

Courtesy of Thirsty Knight Antiques

e. Porcelain, 1.0L, relief, white on green marbleized background, maiden, bird and dog, c.1900, porcelain lid, $500-700.

f. Porcelain, .5L, unmarked, bisque glaze, Wagner, c.1900, porcelain inlaid lid, $400-600.

g. Porcelain, .5L, unmarked, bisque glaze, Beethoven, c.1900, porcelain inlaid lid, $400-600.

a.   Porcelain, .5L, unmarked, *Sangerrunde, d. B.B. München*, lithophane, c.1900, pewter lid, $150-250.

b.   Porcelain, .5L, unmarked, folk dancing club, *1896*, lithophane, pewter lid, $125-200.

c.   Porcelain, .5L, unmarked, bicycle rider, lithophane, c.1900, pewter lid, $300-450.

d.   Porcelain, .5L, unmarked, *Radfahrer Club Huglfing* (bicycle club), two side scenes with bicycles, lithophane, dated 1920, pewter lid, $250-350.

e.   Porcelain, .5L, unmarked, flowers, lithophane, c.1900, pewter lid, $75-125.

f.   Porcelain, .5L, unmarked, flowers, lithophane, c.1900, pewter lid, $75-125.

g.   Porcelain, 1.0L, unmarked, military recruits, *1879-89, Rothenburg*, lithophane, pewter lid, $200-300.

h.   Porcelain, 1.0L, unmarked, zither, lithophane, c.1900, pewter lid, $150-250.

a. Porcelain, .5L, unmarked, verse, lithophane, c.1900, pewter lid, $75-125.

b. Porcelain, .5L, unmarked, *Lindau im Bodensee*, lithophane, c.1900, pewter lid, $75-125.

c. Porcelain, .5L, unmarked, hand-painted, Ludwig II, lithophane, c.1900, pewter lid, $125-200.

d. Porcelain, .5L, marked HR 188/20, hand-painted, c.1900, pewter lid, $125-200.

e. Porcelain, .5L, unmarked, bowling, lithophane, c.1900, pewter lid, $150-250.

f. Porcelain, .5L, unmarked, Lohengrin, lithophane, c.1900, pewter lid, $150-250.

g. Porcelain, 1.0L, unmarked, Lohengrin, lithophane, c.1900, pewter lid, $200-300.

h. Porcelain, 1.0L, unmarked, people talking, lithophane, c.1900, pewter lid, $200-300.

a.   Porcelain, .3L, unmarked, man and woman, lithophane, c.1900, pewter lid, $100-175.

b.   Porcelain, .5L, unmarked, blue and white, *straw flowers*, lithophane, c.1900, inlaid lid, $150-250.

c.   Porcelain, .5L, marked Gebr. Schönau, Swaine & Co., blue and white, windmill, lithophane, c.1900, inlaid lid, $150-250.

d.   Porcelain, 1.5L, marked Gebr. Schönau, Swaine & Co., blue & white, windmill, lithophane, c.1900, inlaid lid, $150-250.

NOTE: Steins b, c and d (and others of this type) are frequently marked Delft.

e.   Porcelain, .5L, unmarked, *Gruss aus Landshut*, lithophane, c.1900, pewter lid, $75-125.

f.   Porcelain, .5L, unmarked, photo, lithophane, c.1900, pewter lid, $100-175.

g.   Porcelain, .5L, unmarked, deer, lithophane, c.1900, pewter lid, $75-125.

h.   Porcelain, .5L, unmarked, hunters and game warden, lithophane, c.1900, pewter lid, $200-300.

9. Mettlach

Ever since they were first produced in about 1850, Mettlach steins have been cherished as very high quality art objects. *The Mettlach Book*, with information, pictures, and prices similar to this book's, has been devoted entirely to Mettlach wares. Most of that book is relevant to the interests of stein collectors. Some of that information is repeated here; those with further interest should consult that reference.

9.1 Mettlach History

Mettlach, from the Latin word for *mid-lakes*, is a small village on the Saar River in what is now the far western part of West Germany, near both Luxembourg and France. Although the ceramic products made there were produced by the Villeroy and Boch Company, they have commonly been called *Mettlach* wares. Apparently this has been done partly to avoid confusion with the very different products made at the eight Villeroy and Boch factories in other cities, and partly because the name Mettlach dominates the important incised *old tower* or *castle* trademark used by the Mettlach factory.

Pierre-Joseph Boch, the founder of the family pottery business, had a son Jean Francis Boch, who studied chemistry and mineralogy at the École des Sciences in Paris. After Jean Francis completed his studies, he began searching for a place to begin a pottery so he could make use of his education. In 1809, utilizing the fortunes of his family and of his wife, Rosalie Buschmann, he purchased the old Benedictine Abbey of Mettlach, including its expansive central buildings and its famous old tower, as the site for their firm, Boch-Buschmann.

The government had imposed a condition on the sale of the buildings that the abundant hard coal, and not the scarce wood, be used to fire the kilns. This presented a tremendous obstacle because it required the invention of a coal-burning kiln, which was only accomplished in 1816, but it did result in a far superior and more uniform firing.

Mettlach innovations did not come solely through necessity. Water power was harnessed for turning the potters' wheels and for the clay preparation machinery. These novel labor-saving advances helped the company cope with the skyrocketing wage demands of the new middle class following the French Revolution. Other advances came when the copper-plate engraving and transfer-printing techniques from Staffordshire, England were brought to Mettlach in 1820, and excellent common wares were produced that appealed to the newly monied middle class. Art studios, archives, museums, art schools, and famous artists were all brought to Mettlach in an effort to further promote the artistic accomplishments of the factory.

In 1836, with the business in the hands of Jean Francis' son Eugene, a merger with Nicholas Villeroy's factory was undertaken in order to eliminate the only significant competition that had arisen in the region. This created the Villeroy and Boch Company. Soon afterward, the influence of the Empire and Biedermeier styles, which demanded only mundane wares, diminished. Mettlach found a market for the decorative relief beakers and steins, in the style of Historicism, which they then produced in great numbers.

The golden age of Mettlach lasted from approximately 1880 to 1910, during which, using guarded secret techniques, the etched, glazed, and cameo wares were at the pinnacle of their production. New designs and an explosion of color went into the production of the Mettlach items. An extensive display at the 1885 Antwerp World's Fair propelled Mettlach into the forefront of the ceramics field, with reviewers using descriptions such as *Vollkommenes* (perfection) and *geradezu unerreicht* (frankly unrivalled). Production quantities continued to grow until at its height the Mettlach plant employed about 1250 people.

About 1909, and certainly by the start of the First World War, business seems to have slacked off considerably. Researchers of this subject tend to blame unfavorable economic conditions and a lack of skilled labor. In 1921, a great fire destroyed molds, production records, and formulas for the production processes and materials, including the 30 colored clay slips, 150 underglaze colors, and 176 colored hard glazes. From 1925 until the early 1930's, a few etched and PUG articles were again being produced at the Mettlach plant. Although the Mettlach factory continued to produce tiles, dishes, plumbing fixtures, and other wares, there was almost a fifty year lapse before Mettlach revived stein and plaque manufacturing. Although some of the most desirable steins and plaques have been reproduced, the processes and materials are mostly different. The quality of these reproduced pieces is very admirable, but they are not the same as the original chromolith items. More information about currently produced Mettlach steins can be found in Section 17.

9.2 Production Techniques

The Villeroy and Boch Company produced steins and other wares that were, almost without exception, both original in design and in production technique. The majority of V&B steins have certain common characteristics. They were made from a very hard, impervious stoneware material which was homogeneous and vitrified. A pure white, porcelain-like glaze was applied to all insides, except those marked BAVARIA, which are a gray color inside and out. The same general type of stoneware that formed the bodies of the wares was also used in the decorations on the etched, relief, and mosaic items. Mold marks are generally not visible, indicating a very careful cleaning of the seams after the body was formed, or the use of potters' wheels to form or clean the bodies.

The earliest steins produced at Mettlach were bas-relief in style, commonly called *relief*. The earliest decorations usually consisted of green or brown leaves and vines, eventually evolving into figures and other more decorative relief scenes. These earliest relief steins were produced from the 1840's through the early 1880's, when diversification into a variety of other production methods took place.

The designs on the relief wares seem to have been produced in two ways. In rare instances, it appears that the relief has been applied by hand; apparently, the common method was to form the design in a full-bodied mold. After an opaque tan relief material was set into the mold, a colored background stoneware-slip was painted into the mold, usually of a light blue, green, brown, grey, or coral red color.

Cameo and relief wares are often confused with each other. Their production processes seem to be quite similar, except that: (1) the cameos do not protrude as far from the body as the reliefs, thus calling for closer tolerances, and (2) the material used in the cameo reliefwork is a more translucent, porcelain-like material that allows for shadings of background colors to show through the thinnest portions of the relief. The resultant product is similar to the gemstone and shell cameos, from which they get their name.

The simplest steins to produce were the *print under glaze*, or PUG steins. After the blank body was formed, fired, and glazed, a decal-type or transfer-printed scene was applied, and the body was covered with an additional coat of transparent glaze, and then refired. Actually, the process could best be described as print between glazes. After the final firing, the transfer scene had become an integral part of the product.

The decorations on the Mettlach *faience*, *Delft*, and *Rookwood* steins were primarily accomplished, with a few possible exceptions, via hand-painting.

When the name *Mettlach* is recognized, it is most commonly associated with the *etched*, or *chromolith*, steins. With no tangible evidence other than *autopsies* of broken pieces, there have been a number of theories advanced to explain the process for making chromolith products.

There are some elements that are common to many of the chromolith theories. The design is generally recognized to be a separate section which was applied and fused to the body with pressure and great heat. The hard white glaze on the interior was applied separately and vitrified during one of the firings. While it would appear that the design materials were wrapped around the body, there are some knowledgeable researchers who feel that the body could have been poured into the design.

A *reverse painting* theory seems to be picking up more support lately, and it claims the following. A flat or curved tray was developed which had the etched lines in reverse, that is protruding, from its surface. Colored clay slips were hand painted onto this perhaps plaster or metal tray. Colors for which atomizer sprayed shadings were required, were sprayed after all other colors had been painted, and then painted over with the solid background color. An eighth inch, or so, layer of slip or moist stoneware was then placed on the tray and the decoration was lifted from the design tray and set into the appropriate portion of a body or a body mold. The rest of the body had already been, or was then, poured or hand worked into its mold, which was then cleaned on a potter's wheel.

In virtually all theories it is believed that the handle was applied separately on most of the steins. Bases were sometimes also applied, but the frieze bands are generally felt to be integral to the body of the steins. After the decoration had been fired it is usually believed that the black lines that form the distinctive outlining in the decoration, were produced by rubbing a black glaze into the incised lines.

The so-called *Art Nouveau* wares are *etched* with the bold sinuous designs that became so popular at the beginning of the 20th Century. The designs are often dominated by either a blue and tan or a rust and green color scheme. The *mosaic* wares generally followed the relief era and preceded the etched era. Although some mosaic pieces contain etched sections, for the most part they were totally decorated with colored glazes on surfaces that are actually quite complex compared to the usual etched pieces. The glazed wares are similar to mosaics but have no protrusions from the surface. The relative undesirability of many of the mosaic and glazed pieces is due more to their simple, repetitive, floral and geometric design than to a disenchantment with the results of the techniques themselves.

Estimations of the number of steins originally produced are fraught with uncertainties. A *tremendous* number of steins were destroyed over the years, particularly during the wars. There are any number of soldiers who have recalled machine-gunning hundreds of shelves full of steins throughout Germany — apparently this had become an important form of cultural vandalism for the invading forces. This destruction has rendered the U.S. inventory a significant part of the current world supply. Based partly upon extrapolation back from recent observations, and partly from the use of cost and wage figures, it seems improbable that the *average* production of a particular Mettlach item could have exceeded 2000 pieces. The *most common* items, however, definitely had more than 2000 produced, perhaps 10,000 or more. In the case of the *extremely rare* steins, it seems unlikely that more than 100 were ever produced.

9.3 Marks

Many of the trademarks used by Villeroy & Boch, Mettlach are shown below and at the end of Section 2. Fortunately, throughout the important Mettlach period from about 1880 to 1910 the factory marked their products consistently and profusely. Of course, some of these marks are of little importance to collectors because they were intended for the identification of individual craftsmen and for quality control purposes. However, some of the marks are interesting to collectors and these are the ones described here.

A most important mark is the one that shows the *form* number, sometimes called the *mold* or *stock* number; it is the large Arabic number impressed into the base or back of Mettlach wares. This is generally a three- or four-digit number and is usually located below the trademark. Even when the trademark is not present, the distinctive crisp style of the form number can be used, together with an examination of quality, to identify Mettlach items.

A *decoration* number was used for identifying the design of PUG, Rookwood, and some faience products. This number was stamped on PUGs and Rookwoods, and painted on faiences, usually in black or blue, and generally occurred with Geschützt (patented) or DEC. (abbreviation for *Dekoration*?).

The exact year of production can often be discerned from the marks on an item. All of the known dating systems are described in *The Mettlach Book*. The most important date code is the two-digit incised number that often is located to the right of and below the trademark, as can be seen in the figure below. Items made from 1882 to 1887 have an 82 to 87 incised inside a small rectangle. For 1888 and after, the rectangle was not used, so for example 88 is 1888, 95 is 1895, 00 is 1900, and 05 is 1905, and so on.

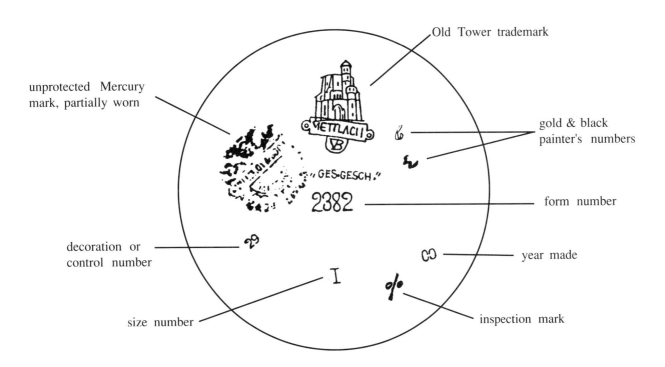

Bottom of a well-marked Mettlach stein: a 1.0L 2382 made in 1900; the MADE IN GERMANY barely visible around the bottom of the Mercury mark indicated that this stein was probably exported.

a. Mettlach 1745, .25L, relief, inlaid lid, $120-170.

b. Mettlach 2077, .3L, relief, inlaid lid, $110-160.

c. Mettlach 2211, .3L, relief, inlaid lid, $130-170.

d. Mettlach 2232, .3L, relief, inlaid lid, $160-210.

e. Mettlach 171, .5L, relief, inlaid lid, $130-170; .25L, $100-150.

f. Mettlach 228, .5L, relief, inlaid lid, $225-325.

g. Mettlach 2182, .5L, relief, inlaid lid, $200-300.

h. Mettlach 2358, .5L, relief, inlaid lid, $200-300.

a.	Mettlach 1155, .5L, mosaic, inlaid lid, $325-425.

b.	Mettlach 1192, .5L, mosaic, inlaid lid, $375-475.

c.	Mettlach 1288, .5L, mosaic, inlaid lid, $300-400.

d.	Mettlach 1803, .25L, mosaic, inlaid lid, $225-325.

e.	Mettlach 2800, .5L, etched, Art Nouveau, inlaid lid, $300-400.

f.	Mettlach 2811, .5L, etched, Art Nouveau, inlaid lid, $350-450.

g.	Mettlach 2892, .5L, etched, Art Nouveau, inlaid lid, $300-400.

h.	Mettlach 2935, .5L, etched, Art Nouveau, inlaid lid, $350-450.

a. Mettlach 626(280), .5L, PUG, pewter lid,
    $150-225.

b. Mettlach 1212(1909), .5L, PUG, pewter lid,
    $225-300.

c. Mettlach 1055(2271), .5L, PUG, pewter lid,
    $225-300.

d. Mettlach 1110(1526), 1.0L, PUG, pewter lid,
    $275-375.

e. Mettlach 726(1909), .5L, PUG, pewter lid,
    $250-325.

f. Mettlach 732(1909), .5L, PUG, pewter lid,
    $225-300.

g. Mettlach 983(1909), .5L, PUG, pewter lid,
    $225-300.

h. Mettlach 1143(1909), .5L, PUG, pewter lid,
    $250-350.

a. Mettlach 1073(1909), .5L, PUG, pewter lid, $225-300.

b. Mettlach 1102(1909), .5L, PUG, pewter lid, $250-350.

c. Mettlach 1109(1909), .5L, PUG, pewter lid, $250-350.

d. Mettlach 1181(1909), .5L, PUG, pewter lid, $250-350.

e. Mettlach 1010(1909), .5L, PUG, pewter lid, $200-250.

f. Mettlach 1077(1526), .5L, PUG, pewter lid, $150-200.

g. Mettlach 1098(1526), .5L, PUG, pewter lid, $200-275.

h. Mettlach 961(2179), .25L, PUG, pewter lid, $150-200.

a. Mettlach 284, .5L, hand-painted, *Corpus Juris*, pewter lid, $250-350.

b. Mettlach 406, .5L, hand-painted, Albrecht Dürer, pewter lid, $300-400.

c. Mettlach 2140, .5L, PUG, Signature stein, inlaid lid, $350-450.

d. Mettlach 2222, .5L, PUG, Signature stein, inlaid lid, $375-475.

e. Mettlach 1533, .5L, tapestry, pewter lid, $225-275; 1.0L, $250-325.

f. Mettlach 1641, .5L, tapestry, pewter lid, $225-275; 1.0L, $250-325.

g. Mettlach 1642, .5L, tapestry, pewter lid, $225-275; 1.0L, $250-325.

h. Mettlach 1662, .5L, tapestry, pewter lid, $250-300; 1.0L, $275-350.

a. Mettlach 2018, .5L, character, Pug Dog, stoneware lid, $900-1100.

b. Mettlach 2036, .5L, character, Owl, stoneware lid, $850-1050.

c. Mettlach 2069, .5L, character, Monkey, stoneware lid, $2000-2400.

d. Mettlach 2106, .5L, etched & relief, inlaid lid, $2000-2500.

e. Mettlach 2130, .5L, cameo, Gambrinus, inlaid lid, $550-750; also a relief version, $225-325.

f. Mettlach 2479, .5L, cameo, Hildebrand stein, inlaid lid, $550-750; .25L, $350-450.

g. Mettlach 2652, .25L, cameo, Rodenstein stein, inlaid lid, $350-450; .5L, $500-700.

h. Mettlach 2627, .5L, cameo, inlaid lid, $700-900; .3L, $450-550.

a.   Mettlach 1675, .5L, etched, Heidelberg, inlaid lid, $450-550.

b.   Mettlach 1742, .5L, etched, Göttingen, inlaid lid, $500-600.

c.   Mettlach 1863, .5L, etched, Stuttgart, inlaid lid, $500-600.

d.   Mettlach 3200, .5L, etched, Heidelberg, inlaid lid, $575-675.

e.   Mettlach 2277, .5L, etched, Nürnberg, inlaid lid, $500-600.

f.   Mettlach 2829, 1.0L, etched & relief, Rodenstein, inlaid lid, $2300-2900.; .5L, $1700-2100.

g.   Mettlach 2828, .5L, etched & relief, Wartburg, inlaid lid, $1800-2200; 1.0L, $2600-3000.

h.   Mettlach 2024, .5L, etched & glazed, Berlin, inlaid lid, $550-700.

a.   Mettlach 2002, .5L, etched, Munich, inlaid lid, $375-450; 1.0L, $525-625.

b.   Mettlach 2917, .5L, etched & relief, Munich, inlaid lid, $2400-3000; 1.0L, $3500-4200.

c.   Mettlach 2585, .5L, etched & relief, Munich, inlaid lid, $550-675; 1.0L, $900-1100.

d.   Mettlach 3043, .5L, etched & glazed, Munich, inlaid lid, $1400-1800.

e.   Mettlach 2391, 1.0L, etched, Lohengrin stein, inlaid lid, $1500-1800; .5L, $700-850.

f.   Mettlach 2394, .5L, etched, Siegfried's youth, inlaid lid, $700-850.

g.   Mettlach 2401, .5L, etched, Tannhauser in the Venusberg, inlaid lid, $700-850; 1.0L, $1000-1400.

h.   Mettlach 2402, .5L, etched, The Courting of Siegfried, inlaid lid, $700-850.

a.   Mettlach 2382, .5L, etched, Thirsty Knight stein, inlaid lid, $600-700; 1.0L, $800-1000.

b.   Mettlach 2580, .5L, etched, *Die Kannenburg* stein, inlaid lid, $650-775; 1.0L, $800-1000.

c.   Mettlach 2765, .5L, etched, Knight on White Horse stein, inlaid lid, $2200-2600; 1.0L, $3400-3900.

d.   Mettlach 2776, .5L, etched, Keeper of the wine cellar, inlaid lid, $650-800.

e.   Mettlach 1997, .5L, etched & PUG, *George Ehert* brewer, inlaid lid, $250-325.

f.   Mettlach 2900, .5L, etched, *Argentina Quilmes* brewery, inlaid lid, $350-450.

g.   Mettlach 1403, .5L, etched, inlaid lid, $375-475.

h.   Mettlach 2959, .5L, etched, inlaid lid, $375-475; 1.0L, $500-600.

a. Mettlach 2238, .5L, etched, 7th Regiment Armory stein, inlaid lid, $900-1200.

b. Mettlach 2373, .5L, etched, *St. Augustine* (Florida) stein, inlaid lid, $500-600.

c. Mettlach 2871, 1.0L, etched, *Cornell University* stein, inlaid lid, $750-950.

d. Mettlach 3135, .5L, etched, American Flag stein, inlaid lid, $950-1200.

e. Mettlach 2282, .5L, etched, inlaid lid, $450-550.

f. Mettlach 2285, .5L, etched, inlaid lid, $425-525.

g. Mettlach 2301, .5L, etched, inlaid lid, $500-600.

h. Mettlach 2324, .5L, etched, inlaid lid, $1500-1800.

a.   Mettlach 2089, .5L, etched, inlaid lid, $600-700.

b.   Mettlach 2090, .5L, etched, inlaid lid, $475-575.

c.   Mettlach 2091, .5L, etched, inlaid lid, $700-850.

d.   Mettlach 2092, .5L, etched, inlaid lid, $600-700.

e.   Mettlach 2231, .5L, etched, inlaid lid, $450-550.

f.   Mettlach 2640, .5L, etched, inlaid lid, $450-550.

g.   Mettlach 2693, .5L, etched, inlaid lid, $575-675.

h.   Mettlach 2780, .5L, etched, inlaid lid, $450-550; 1.0L, $625-725.

a.   Mettlach 2528, .5L, etched, inlaid lid, $900-1100.

b.   Mettlach 2582, .5L, etched, Jester stein, inlaid lid, $650-750; 1.0L, $750-875.

c.   Mettlach 2716, .5L, etched, inlaid lid, $500-600; 1.0L, $650-750.

d.   Mettlach 3220, .5L, etched, inlaid lid, $500-600.

e.   Mettlach 2044, .5L, etched, inlaid lid, $550-650.

f.   Mettlach 2051, .5L, etched, inlaid lid, $500-600.

g.   Mettlach 2532, .5L, etched, inlaid lid, $450-550.

h.   Mettlach 2520, .5L, etched, inlaid lid, $575-675; 1.0L, $700-800.

a. Mettlach 1379, .5L, etched, Architect stein, inlaid
    lid, $550-650.

b. Mettlach 1724, .5L, etched, Fireman stein, inlaid
    lid, $1500-1800.

c. Mettlach 1914, .5L, etched, 4F stein, inlaid lid,
    $500-600.

d. Mettlach 2049, .5L, etched, Chess stein, inlaid lid,
    $2200-2600.

e. Mettlach 1856, .5L, etched & glazed, Postman
    stein, inlaid lid, $1500-1900; 1.0L, $1800-2200.

f. Mettlach 2075, .5L, etched & glazed, Telegrapher
    stein, inlaid lid, $1500-1900.

g. Mettlach 2082, .5L, etched, William Tell stein,
    inlaid lid, $1000-1200; 1.0L, $1700-2100; .3L,
    $1000-1200.

h. Mettlach 2083, .5L, etched, Board Hunt stein,
    inlaid lid, $1000-1200; 1.0L, $1700-2100; .3L,
    $1000-1200.

a.   Mettlach 1732, .5L, etched, inlaid lid, $700-850.

b.   Mettlach 1934, .5L, etched, inlaid lid, $750-850.

c.   Mettlach 2030, .5L, etched, inlaid lid, $850-1000.

d.   Mettlach 2031, .5L, etched, inlaid lid, $850-1000.

e.   Mettlach 1725, .5L, etched, inlaid lid, $425-525;
     .25L, $250-325.

f.   Mettlach 2235, .5L, etched, inlaid lid, $550-650;
     1.0L, $750-950.

g.   Mettlach 2599, 1.0L, etched, inlaid lid, $900-1100.

h.   Mettlach 2768, .5L, etched, inlaid lid, $550-650.

a. Mettlach 2727, .5L, etched & glazed, inlaid lid, Printer occupation, $1800-2200.

b. Mettlach 2728, .5L, etched & glazed, inlaid lid, Brewer occupation, $1300-1600.

c. Mettlach 2729, .5L, etched & glazed, inlaid lid, Blacksmith occupation, $2100-2500.

d. Mettlach 2730, .5L, etched & glazed, inlaid lid, Butcher occupation, $2000-2400.

e. Mettlach 2833B, .5L, etched, inlaid lid, $400-500.

f. Mettlach 3000, .5L, etched, pewter lid, $300-400; 1.0L, $400-500.

g. Mettlach 3001, .5L, etched, pewter lid, $300-400.

h. Mettlach 3250, .5L, etched, inlaid lid, $400-500.

a. Mettlach 5013, 1.0L, faience type, Rothenburg, pewter lid, $1000-1300.

b. Mettlach 5019, 1.0L, faience type, pewter lid, $700-900.

c. Mettlach 5023, 1.0L, faience type, pewter lid, $1500-1900.

d. Mettlach 5024, 1.0L, faience type, pewter lid, $1100-1400.

e. Mettlach 5013, .5L, faience type, *München*, pewter lid, $500-600.

f. Mettlach 5189, .5L, Delft type, pewter lid, $350-450.

g. Mettlach 5190, .5L, Delft type, pewter lid, $400-500.

h. Mettlach 5191, .3L, Delft type, pewter lid, $350-450.

a. Mettlach 2790/6135, .5L, Rookwood type, pewter lid, $325-425.

b. Mettlach 2790/6146, .5L, Rookwood type, pewter lid, $325-425.

c. Mettlach 2790/6147, .5L, Rookwood type, pewter lid, $325-425.

Opposite top:

a. Mettlach 2038, 3.8L, decorated relief, inlaid lid, $3200-3800.

b. Mettlach 2076, 1.85L, relief, inlaid lid, $225-325.

c. Mettlach 2085, 4.1L, relief, inlaid lid, $225-325.

Opposite bottom:

d. Mettlach 1739, 3.3L, relief, inlaid lid, $500-650.

e. Mettlach 1169, 2.5L, relief, inlaid lid, $500-650.

f. Mettlach 2284, 3.9L, relief, inlaid lid, $475-575.

d. Mettlach 2783/6139, 4.8L, Rookwood type, pewter lid, $700-850.

Opposite:

a.   Mettlach 1578, 4.5L, etched, pewter lid, $1300-1700.

b.   Mettlach 2524, 4.2L, etched, pewter lid, $2400-2900.

c.   Mettlach 1690, 4.5L, etched, inlaid lid, $1900-2300.

a.   Mettlach 6, 1.6L, relief, inlaid lid, $175-250.

b.   Mettlach 171, 3.2L, relief, pewter lid, $225-300.

c.   Mettlach 409, 2.7L, relief, inlaid lid, $350-425.

d.   Mettlach 1200(2893), 3.25L, PUG, pewter lid, $300-400.

e.   Mettlach 954(2176), 2.1L, PUG, pewter lid, $500-700.

f.   Mettlach 1075(2384), 2.25L, PUG, pewter lid, $600-750.

d. Mettlach 1940, 3.0L, etched, inlaid lid, $900-1100.

e. Mettlach 2428, 2.75L, etched, inlaid lid, $900-1100.

f. Mettlach 2692, 3.0L, etched, inlaid lid, $1100-1400.

a. Mettlach 1469, 6.0L, etched, inlaid lid, $2200-2600.

b. Mettlach 1818, 6.2L, etched, pewter lid, $1600-2000.

c. Mettlach 2205, 5.2L, etched, inlaid lid, $2100-2500.

10. Other Etched Ceramics

It is clear that the success of the Villeroy & Boch, Mettlach *etched* steins attracted the interest of many of the stein factories. The first Mettlach steins to use the *inlaid clays* etched technique were made around 1879. They immediately captured the Grand Prizes at the world trade fairs. The Mettlach technique was often advertised as *secret*, which added to the public interest in these steins, and thus stimulated the interest of other manufacturers.

It is not known which competitor was first to follow Mettlach's lead in the etched steins, but it had certainly occurred by about 1890. In fact, by 1900 there were etched steins by Simon Peter Gerz, Marzi & Remy, J.W. Remy, A.J. Thewalt, Merkelbach & Wick, Matthias Girmscheid, and HR.

All of these factories had one thing in common: they produced etched steins in the same way, and it was not the Mettlach method. Rather than painting the colored slips *into* molds, these other factories had their decorators paint the colored slips directly onto the *outside* of their molded steins. The results lack the uniformity, clarity, and soft finish of the Mettlach etched steins.

It was obviously *easier* to decorate these steins from the outside, but not all of these manufacturers were looking to capture the *low end* of the etched stein market. In fact, original price lists of HR etched steins show them at *higher* prices than the Mettlach etched steins. Some of these manufacturers were apparently trying to appeal to the *special order* market.

The Steinzeugwerke, or literally Stoneware Works, was a consortium of several factories that banded together around 1900 and lasted until about 1910. The major factories that joined the Steinzeugwerke were Reinhold Merkelbach, Simon Peter Gerz, and Marzi & Remy, all from the Höhr-Grenzhausen area. Collective marketing seems to have been the primary purpose of the consortium.

The Steinzeugwerke had no separate trademark, and the only way its members have been identified has been through the examination of a catalog that shows their steins. This catalog shows that it was possible to purchase these steins plain, blue or brown saltglazed, sparsely painted, or fully painted.

For some of the individual companies in the consortium, as well as other stein factories, catalogs have also been found. These show many etched and character steins that have yet to be found. They provide a good indication of how exciting searching for steins can be, as well as an indication of how much damage there was to steins during the two World Wars.

The end of Section 2 shows the marks and dates of these etched stein factories. Books and articles about individual factories are listed in the bibliography, Section 18.

a.   Marzi & Remy, #1765, .5L, pottery, etched, c.1900,
     inlaid lid, $300-400.

b.   Marzi & Remy, #1764, .5L, pottery, etched, c.1900,
     inlaid lid, $300-400.

c.   Marzi & Remy, #1615, .5L, pottery, etched, c.1900,
     inlaid lid, $250-350.

d.   Marzi & Remy, #1768, .5L, pottery, etched, c.1900,
     inlaid lid, $300-400.

e.   Marzi & Remy, #1619, 1.0L, pottery, etched,
     c.1900, inlaid lid, $350-450.

f.   Marzi & Remy, #1620, 1.0L, pottery, etched,
     c.1900, inlaid lid, $350-450.

g.   Marzi & Remy, #1629, 1.0L, pottery, etched,
     c.1900, inlaid lid, $300-400.

h.   Marzi & Remy, #1618, 1.0L, pottery, etched,
     c.1900, inlaid lid, $300-400.

a.   Marzi & Remy, #1621, .5L, pottery, etched, c.1900, inlaid lid, $300-400.

b.   Marzi & Remy, #1614, .5L, pottery, etched, c.1900, inlaid lid, $300-400.

c.   Marzi & Remy, #1622, .5L, pottery, etched, c.1900, inlaid lid, $350-450.

d.   Marzi & Remy, #1767, .5L, pottery, etched, c.1900, inlaid lid, $300-400.

e.   Marzi & Remy, #1653, .5L, pottery, etched, c.1900, inlaid lid, $350-450.

f.   Marzi & Remy, #1613, .5L, pottery, etched, c.1900, inlaid lid, $300-400.

g.   Marzi & Remy, #1644, .5L, pottery, hand-painted scene of Heidelberg, c.1900, pewter lid, $250-350.

a.   Marzi & Remy, #1637, .5L, pottery, etched, c.1900, inlaid lid, $350-450.

b.   Marzi & Remy, #1688, .5L, pottery, etched, c.1900, inlaid lid, $350-450.

c.   Marzi & Remy, #6044, .5L, pottery, etched, *Souvenir of Florida*, (St. Augustine), c.1900, inlaid lid, $200-300.

d.   Marzi & Remy, #972, .5L, pottery, etched, c.1900, inlaid lid, $300-400.

e.   Marzi & Remy, #1644, .5L, pottery, etched, hand-painted scene, c.1900, pewter lid, $250-350.

f.   Gerz, #1420, .5L, pottery, etched, c.1900, inlaid lid, $250-350.

g.   Gerz, #1210, .5L, pottery, etched, c.1900, inlaid lid, $200-300.

h.   Gerz, #1314B, .5L, pottery, etched, c.1900, inlaid lid, $200-300.

a.   Marzi & Remy, #1635, .5L, pottery, etched, c.1900, inlaid lid, $150-225.

b.   Marzi & Remy, #1636, .5L, pottery, etched, c.1900, inlaid lid, $125-200.

c.   Marzi & Remy, #1617, .5L, pottery, etched, c.1900, inlaid lid, $125-200.

d.   Gerz, #1220, .5L, pottery, etched, c.1900, inlaid lid, $125-200.

e.   Gerz, #1334, 1.0L, pottery, etched, c.1900, pewter lid, $175-275.

f.   Gerz, #1326, 1.0L, pottery, etched, c.1900, inlaid lid, $250-350.

g.   Matthias Girmscheid, #1085, .5L, stoneware, etched, c.1900, stoneware lid, $125-200.

h.   Steinzeugwerke, #1851, 1.0L, pottery, etched, early 1900's, inlaid lid, $150-250.

a.   Gerz, #1423, .5L, pottery, etched, *Parsival Acts 1, 2, and 3*, c.1900, inlaid lid, $250-350.

b.   Gerz, #1428, .5L, pottery, etched, *Siegfried*, c.1900, inlaid lid, $250-350.

c.   Gerz, #1421, .5L, pottery, etched, *Siegfried*, c.1900, inlaid lid, $250-350.

d.   Gerz, #1422, .5L, pottery, etched, *Lohengrin*, c.1900, inlaid lid, $250-350.

e.   Gerz, #1216, .5L, pottery, etched, c.1900, pewter lid, $150-225.

f.   Gerz, #1265, .5L, pottery, etched, hunter and dogs, c.1900, pewter lid, $150-225.

g.   Gerz, #1254, .5L, pottery, etched, c.1900, inlaid lid, $200-300.

h.   Gerz, #1210, .5L, pottery, etched, c.1900, inlaid lid, $200-300.

a.   Gerz, #1345BI, .4L, pottery, etched, sleigh ride, c.1900, inlaid lid, $150-250.

b.   Gerz, #1209, .4L, pottery, etched, c.1900, inlaid lid, $100-175.

c.   Gerz, #1219, .5L, pottery, etched, c.1900, pewter lid, $100-175.

d.   Gerz, #1214B, .3L, pottery, etched, c.1900, inlaid lid, $100-175.

e.   Gerz, #1215, 1.0L, pottery, etched, c.1900, inlaid lid, $250-350.

f.   Gerz, #1318, 1.0L, pottery, etched, c.1900, inlaid lid, $250-350.

g.   Gerz, #1388, 1.0L, pottery, etched, c.1900, inlaid lid, $250-350.

h.   Gerz, #1389, 1.0L, pottery, etched, c.1900, inlaid lid, $250-350.

a. J.W. Remy, #1221, .5L, pottery, etched, c.1900, inlaid lid, $125-200.

b. J.W. Remy, #1493, .5L, pottery, etched, c.1900, inlaid lid, $125-200.

c. J.W. Remy, #884, .5L, pottery, etched, c.1900, inlaid lid, $100-175.

d. J.W. Remy, #883, .5L, pottery, etched, c.1900, inlaid lid, $100-175.

e. J.W. Remy, #1333, 1.0L, pottery, etched, c.1900, inlaid lid, $150-250.

f. J.W. Remy, #1222, 1.0L, pottery, etched, c.1900, inlaid lid, $150-250.

g. J.W. Remy, #829, .5L, pottery, etched, c.1900, inlaid lid, $125-200.

h. J.W. Remy, #828, .5L, pottery, etched, c.1900, inlaid lid, $150-250.

a. J.W. Remy, #1227, .5L, pottery, etched, c.1900, inlaid lid, $125-200.

b. Pottery, #1227, .5L, etched, marked TP, same mold as preceding stein, c.1900, inlaid lid, $125-200.

c. Pottery, #1411, 1.0L, etched, marked TP, c.1900, inlaid lid, $250-350.

d. J.W. Remy, #1409, .5L, pottery, etched, c.1900, inlaid lid, $150-250.

e. J.W. Remy, #907, .4L, pottery, etched, c.1900, inlaid lid, $100-175.

f. J.W. Remy, #1291, .5L, pottery, etched, c.1900, inlaid lid, $100-175.

g. J.W. Remy, #1294, .5L, pottery, etched, c.1900, inlaid lid, $100-175.

h. J.W. Remy, #1334, .4L, pottery, etched, c.1900, inlaid lid, $100-175.

a.   Pottery, #1227, .5L, etched, marked TP, c.1900, inlaid lid, $125-200.

b.   Pottery, #1218, .5L, etched, marked TP, c.1900, inlaid lid, $125-200.

c.   Pottery, #1410, .5L, etched, marked TP, c.1900, inlaid lid, $200-300.

d.   J.W. Remy, #954, .5L, pottery, etched, c.1900, inlaid lid, $250-350.

e.   Pottery, .5L, unmarked, etched, c.1900, inlaid lid, $100-175.

f.   Pottery, #1013, .5L, etched, c.1900, inlaid lid, $100-175.

g.   Pottery, #1360, .3L, etched, marked Coblenz Rheinland, c.1900, inlaid lid, $75-125.

h.   Pottery, #1263, .5L, etched, marked Reinhold Hanke, c.1900, inlaid lid, $100-175.

a. Pottery, #1453, .5L, etched, bicycles, c.1900, inlaid lid, $400-550.

b. Steinzeugwerke, #1720, .5L, pottery, etched, signed R.D., early 1900's, inlaid lid, $125-200.

c. Pottery, #1512, .5L, etched, duck run over by car, early 1900's, inlaid lid, $200-300.

d. Pottery, #1513, .5L, etched, speeding car, early 1900's, inlaid lid, $200-300.

e. J.W. Remy, #1394, .5L, pottery, etched, c.1900, inlaid lid, $300-400.

f. J.W. Remy, #1393, .5L, pottery, etched, c.1900, inlaid lid, $300-400.

g. Merkelbach & Wick, #1175A, .5L, pottery, etched, c.1900, pewter lid, $150-250.

h. A.J. Thewalt, #474, .5L, pottery, etched, c.1900, inlaid lid, $125-200.

a. Matthias Girmscheid, #1088, 1.0L, stoneware, etched, c.1900, pewter lid, $100-175.

b. Gerz, #1709, 1.0L, pottery, etched, c.1900, pewter lid, $200-300.

c. Merkelbach & Wick, 1.0L, etched, c.1900, inlaid lid, $200-300.

d. Pottery, #1284, 1.0L, etched, c.1900, inlaid lid, $125-200.

a.   Pottery, #1693, .5L, etched, c.1900, pewter lid, $100-175.

b.   Pottery, #155, .5L, etched, c.1900, pewter lid, $150-250.

c.   Pottery, #768, .5L, etched, c.1900, pewter lid, $100-175.

d.   Matthias Girmscheid, #843, .5L, stoneware, etched, c.1900, pewter lid, $100-175.

Opposite:

e.   Pottery, .5L, unmarked, etched, c.1900, inlaid lid, $125-200.

f.   Pottery, .5L, unmarked, etched, c.1900, inlaid lid, $150-250.

g.   Pottery, .5L, unmarked, etched, c.1900, pewter lid, $100-175.

h.   Matthias Girmscheid, #963, .5L, stoneware, etched, c.1900, pewter lid, $125-200.

e.   Steinzeugwerke, #1714, .5L, pottery, etched, Lawyer Book stein, early 1900's, inlaid lid, $300-400.

f.   Steinzeugwerke, #1714, .5L, pottery, etched, Doctor Book stein, early 1900's, inlaid lid, $300-400.

a.   Merkelbach & Wick, #1171, .5L, pottery, etched,
     c.1900, pewter lid, $150-250.

b.   Merkelbach & Wick, .5L, pottery, etched, c.1900,
     pewter lid, $150-250.

c.   Pottery, #1581, .5L, etched, c.1900, inlaid lid,
     $100-175.

d.   Pottery, #848, .5L, etched, bawdy house scene,
     c.1900, inlaid lid, $250-350.

e.   Pottery, #1555, .5L, etched, c.1900, pewter lid,
     $100-175.

f.   Pottery, #1553, .5L, etched, c.1900, pewter lid,
     $100-175.

g.   Pottery, #1551, .5L, etched, c.1900, pewter lid,
     $100-175.

h.   Pottery, #1514, .5L, etched, c.1900, pewter lid,
     $100-175.

a. A.J. Thewalt, #407, 1.0L, pottery, etched, c.1900, inlaid lid, $150-250.

b. Merkelbach & Wick, #3002B, .5L, pottery, etched, c.1900, pewter lid, $200-300.

c. Pottery, #334, .5L, etched, c.1900, inlaid lid, $150-250.

d. Pottery, #327, .5L, etched, c.1900, inlaid lid, $150-250.

e. Pottery, .3L, unmarked, etched, c.1900, inlaid lid, $125-200.

f. Pottery, #1434, .3L, marked TP, etched, c.1900, inlaid lid, $100-175.

g. HR, #502, .25L, pottery, etched, c.1900, pewter lid, $150-250.

h. HR, #500, .25L, pottery, etched, c.1900, pewter lid, $150-250.

a. HR, #510, .5L, pottery, etched, c.1900, inlaid lid, $250-350.

b. HR, #162, .5L, stoneware, etched, c.1900, pewter lid, $100-175.

c. HR, #156, .5L, pottery, etched, c.1900, pewter lid, $150-250.

d. HR, #157, .5L, stoneware, etched, c.1900, pewter lid, $100-175.

e. HR, #158, .5L, stoneware, etched, c.1900, pewter lid, $100-175.

f. HR, #163, .5L, stoneware, etched, c.1900, pewter lid, $100-175.

g. HR, #167, .5L, stoneware, etched, c.1900, pewter lid, $100-175.

a. HR, #421, .5L, pottery, etched, c.1900, pewter
    lid, $225-325.

b. HR, #436, .5L, pottery, etched, c.1900, pewter
    lid, $225-325.

c. HR, #426, .5L, pottery, etched, c.1900, pewter
    lid, $250-350.

d. HR, #405, .5L, pottery, etched, c.1900, inlaid lid,
    $250-350.

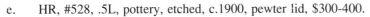

e. HR, #528, .5L, pottery, etched, c.1900, pewter lid, $300-400.

f. HR, #408, .5L, pottery, etched, c.1900, pewter lid, $275-375.

g. HR, #482, .5L, pottery, etched, c.1900, pewter lid, $150-250.

h. HR, #216, .5L, pottery,
    etched, c.1900, pewter
    lid, $125-200.

a. HR, #441, .5L, pottery, etched, c.1900, pewter
    lid, $250-350.

b. HR, #444, .5L, pottery, etched, c.1900, inlaid lid,
    $300-400.

c. HR, #443, .5L, pottery, etched, c.1900, pewter
    lid, $250-350.

d. HR, #161, .5L, pottery, etched, c.1900, pewter
    lid, $250-350.

e. HR, #429, .5L, pottery, etched, c.1900, pewter
    lid, $250-350.

f. HR, #439, .5L, pottery, etched, c.1900, pewter
    lid, $275-375.

g. HR, #417, .5L, pottery, etched, Lohengrin, c.1900,
    pewter lid, $250-350.

h. HR, #418, .5L, pottery, etched, Lohengrin, c.1900,
    pewter lid, $250-350.

a.   HR, #427, .5L, pottery, etched, c.1900, pewter lid, $225-325.

b.   HR, #411, .5L, pottery, etched, c.1900, pewter lid, $200-300.

c.   HR, #437, .5L, pottery, etched, c.1900, pewter lid, $200-300.

d.   HR, #494, .5L, pottery, etched, c.1900, pewter lid, $250-350.

e.   HR, #175, .5L, pottery, etched, c.1900, pewter lid, $200-300.

f.   HR, #489, .5L, pottery, etched, c.1900, pewter lid, $225-325.

g.   HR, #428, .5L, pottery, etched, c.1900, pewter lid, $225-325.

h.   HR, #413, .5L, pottery, etched, c.1900, pewter lid, $225-325.

a.   HR, #203, .5L, pottery, etched, c.1900, pewter lid with relief scene of Fraü Helvetia, $250-350.

b.   HR, #407, .5L, pottery, etched, c.1900, pewter lid, $225-325.

c.   HR, #425, .5L, pottery, etched, c.1900, pewter lid, $225-325.

d.   HR, #160, .5L, porcelain, etched, c.1900, pewter lid, $200-300.

e.   HR, #424, .5L, pottery, etched, *Heidelberg*, c.1900, pewter lid, $200-300.

f.   HR, #531, .5L, pottery, etched, *Nürnberg*, c.1900, pewter lid, $200-300.

g.   HR, #522, .5L, pottery, etched, c.1900, pewter lid, $225-325.

h.   HR, #476, .5L, pottery, etched, c.1900, pewter lid, $200-300.

a. HR, #1001, .5L, pottery, etched, c.1900, pewter lid, $1000-1400.

b. HR, #1002, .5L, pottery, etched, c.1900, pewter lid, $350-450.

c. HR, #1004, .5L, pottery, etched, c.1900, pewter lid, $350-450.

d. HR, #446, .5L, pottery, etched, c.1900, pewter lid, $200-300.

e. HR, #520, .5L, pottery, etched, c.1900, pewter lid, $250-350.

f. HR, #1005, .5L, pottery, etched, c.1900, pewter lid, $300-400.

g. HR, #166, .5L, pottery, etched, c.1900, pewter lid, $500-700.

h. HR, #438, .5L, pottery, etched, c.1900, pewter lid, $500-700.

a.   HR, #431, 1.0L, pottery, etched, c.1900, pewter
     lid, $250-350.

b.   HR, #514, 1.0L, pottery, etched, c.1900, pewter
     lid, $250-350.

c.   HR, #434, 2.0L, pottery, etched, c.1900, pewter   e.   HR, #435, 2.0L, pottery, etched, c.1900, pewter
     lid, $400-500.   lid, $450-550.

d.   HR, #433, 2.0L, pottery, etched, c.1900, pewter
     lid, $450-550.

a.   J.W. Remy, #962, 2.0L, pottery,
     etched, c.1900, inlaid lid, $300-400.

b.   J.W. Remy, #847, 2.0L, pottery,
     etched, c.1900, inlaid lid, $300-400.

c.   Steinzeugwerke, #1664, 1.0L, pottery, etched, early 1900's, inlaid lid, $150-250.

d.   Steinzeugwerke, #1316, 1.5L, pottery, etched, early 1900's, inlaid lid, $200-300.

e.   Merkelbach & Wick, #3002, 2.0L, pottery, etched, c.1900, inlaid lid, $200-300.

Opposite Top:

a.   Marzi & Remy, #1682, 3.0L, pottery, etched, c.1900, inlaid lid, $450-600.

b.   Marzi & Remy, #1518, 1.5L, pottery, etched, c.1900, inlaid lid, $400-500.

c.   Merkelbach & Wick, 1.5L, pottery, etched, c.1900, inlaid lid, $200-300.

d.   Pottery, 1.5L, unmarked, etched, signed GK, c.1900, inlaid lid, $200-300.

a.   Gerz, #1235, 2.0L, pottery, etched, c.1900, pewter lid, $300-400.

b.   A.J. Thewalt, #391, 3.0L, pottery, etched, c.1900, pewter lid, $250-350.

c.   Marzi & Remy, #1681, 3.0L, pottery, etched, c.1900, inlaid lid, $450-600.

Opposite Bottom:

e.   A.J. Thewalt, #411, 3.0L, pottery, etched, c.1900, pewter lid, $250-350.

f.   Pottery, #1638, 2.0L, etched, c.1900, pewter lid, $300-400.

g.   Pottery, 2.0L, unmarked, etched, c.1900, inlaid lid, $300-400.

a.   Pottery, #1612, 2.0L, etched, c.1900, inlaid lid, $350-450.

b.   J.W. Remy, #848, 3.0L, pottery, etched, c.1900, inlaid lid, $350-450.

11. Other Pottery and Stoneware

This section covers the post-1850 ceramic steins that are not etched (Section 10) or made by Mettlach (Section 9). Most of this section's steins are *relief* types, but there are also some steins that have been *transfer-decorated* or *hand-painted* onto smooth bodies. There is not as much information available on these steins as one might suspect. The production techniques are known, but the identity of the manufacturers of many of these steins is unknown. In the instance where good records and other information about one of these manufacturers are available, it is generally because original stein catalogs from that company have been discovered. Often these have been reproduced, and Section 18 lists these excellent resources for collectors particularly interested in these steins.

11.1 History

The earliest steins which fall into the category of this section are a direct consequence of the tastes of the Historicism, or neo-Renaissance, period. They are a revival of the 1500's Siegburg style: undecorated gray stoneware with relief scenes. However, unlike the Siegburgs, the relief scenes are usually *genre* (realistic everyday themes), they are squat half-liters, and the lids have brightly decorated porcelain inlays. The clay is the white-to-grayish, or so-called *Rhenish* clay, found from Höhr-Grenzhausen to Cologne. It is uncertain who manufactured these steins.

It is worth noting that personal steins were (and in some areas still are) kept at the neighborhood tavern. Regular customers thus had a fresh draught of beer served to them almost as soon as they arrived. Oil paintings from the period show these customers' steins stored along a high shelf, *upside-down* with the lid open and over the edge of the shelf. This practice makes it clear why so much attention was paid to the decoration of the porcelain inlays, and why they often depict portraits, occupations, or some other important remembrance or preference with which the stein's owner wished to be associated.

In the early 1860's, Reinhold Hanke turned his attention to the resurrection of the *lost* art of producing fine, *cobalt-glazed*, stoneware steins. Hanke worked hard to make the mass-production methods of his day work as well as possible in copying the Renaissance styles. This meant that *molds* had to be used, but Hanke insisted that these molds be of outstanding craftsmanship. The shapes of these steins ranged from small cylindricals to large jugs, just as were common in the 1500's and 1600's. Decorations were also in the Renaissance style, but toward the 1890's, they changed to genre scenes, which continued to be produced into the 1900's by the Hanke firm.

In 1869, Peter Dümler began working for Hanke; his specialty was making copies of Renaissance stoneware designs. In 1883, he left that firm and joined with an in-law to begin a new stoneware manufacturer, Dümler & Breiden.

Unfortunately, it is not possible to relate here the stories of all of the stein factories. Records indicate that at one time, in the Höhr-Grenzhausen region alone, there were more than 600 factories. Most of the pre-World War I stein makers began their businesses in the short time between the opening of Hanke's factory and that of Dümler. Some of these include: Simon Peter Gerz in 1862, Merkelbach & Wick in 1872, and Marzi & Remy in 1879. A couple of firms, J.W. Remy (1830) and Reinhold Merkelbach (1849), were started earlier, but did not produce steins until after Hanke. Other firms were relative latecomers, such as A.J. Thewalt in 1893, Eckhardt & Engler in 1898, and H.R. (probably Hauber & Reuther), in 1876. All of these companies, with the exception of Hauber & Reuther, were located in Höhr-Grenzhausen or nearby.

The 1880's were apparently tough times for stein makers, at least relief-decorated stein makers. Dümler wrote in his notebooks that "after running like a dog" through the streets of Cologne trying to sell steins, he "didn't want to see another piece of stoneware." But great numbers of steins were being made, and it wasn't until about 1909 that economic conditions slowed the stein industry to a near stop.

After World War I, business in relief, hand-painted, and transfer-decorated steins rebounded, perhaps more so than any other stein type. And the same rebound occurred after World War II. In fact, it rebounded so much that, beginning in the 1950's, hand-painted relief steins began achieving a dominance of the stein market that they still hold today.

11.2 Production

Pottery (*Steingut*) has a porous structure; stoneware (*Steinzeug*) is solid. Sometimes, since the same variety of colors of clay and glazes are used on each, weight is the easiest way to tell them apart; pottery is substantially lighter than stoneware. Common usage has led to all gray ceramics being called stoneware and all tan ceramics being called pottery, including tan *steinzeug* (stoneware).

The recipe for pottery can vary from a rather ordinary clay, to a complex and expensive mixture of clay, quartz, feldspar, kaolin (fine white clay), and whiting (chalk). Pottery is usually fired at a lower temperature than stoneware, but occasionally will be fired at about the same temperature, 1200°C (2100°F).

Because of the porous structure of pottery it is important for it to be *glazed* so that it will be waterproof. It is possible to find some *lead-glazed* pottery steins that were being made up to the 1870's. Thereafter, however, only the *glass-based* glazes were being used, to protect against the detrimental effects of lead on one's health.

The making of *stoneware* is described in Section 3, and the common ways of using pottery and stoneware to make steins has been explained in Section 2, so these will not be repeated here; this just leaves the subject of *decorations.*

The relief steins were almost always decorated by hand. The steins with smooth surfaces could have been decorated in several ways. Hand-painted designs are quite common, especially on steins from around 1900 and before. Occasionally, especially on these older steins or on Regimentals, a metal-plate engraving was used to *print* a decal, which was then transferred to the stein and then touched up, or colored in, by hand. A few of the decals were *silk-screened,* but the detail on these was not as precise as could be achieved with engraved plates, especially those that were prepared by photographic reductions. Most modern steins are decorated solely with decals, using no hand work. It is not very difficult to determine which decorating technique has been used. Hand-painted areas of steins can be recognized because they don't feel as *smooth* as decal, or transfer-decorated areas.

11.3 Collecting

These relief, hand-painted and transfer-decorated steins are the styles most frequently seen for sale. Their tremendous variety opens up many avenues for collecting strategies. *Topical* specialties on which some collectors concentrate include steins decorated with: a Munich Child, scenes from Defregger paintings, playing cards, frogs, dwarfs, eagles, and military themes, designs by Franz Ringer, occupationals (covered in Section 12), hunting, sports, and many others. Other than specializing in certain types of *decorations,* there are several other themes collectors may pursue, such as steins with music boxes, ornate/heavy pewter lids, inlaid lids, very deep relief, pottery figural lids, early gray relief stoneware, or from specific factories, and so on.

When put together in a display these fine steins greatly enhance each others' attractiveness. Recently the demand for these old pottery and stoneware steins has increased significantly.

a. Pottery, .5L, swirled, brown, blue, green, white & tan, inlaid lid, dwarf thumblift, $250-400.

a. Thewalt & HR, #131, .5L, pottery, relief, c.1900, pewter lid, $100-160.

b. Pottery, .5L, relief, c.1900, pewter lid, $80-120.

c. Pottery, #300, .5L, relief, c.1900, pewter lid, $50-80.

d. Pottery, .5L, relief, *B.P.O.E.*, ELKS, c.1900, inlaid lid, $50-80.

e. Pottery, #1232, .5L, relief, c.1900, pewter lid, $150-225.

f. Pottery, #34, .5L, relief, c.1900, pewter lid, $50-80.

g. Pottery, #874, .5L, marked D.R.G.M., relief, early 1900's, pewter lid, $80-120.

h. Merkelbach & Wick, .5L, pottery, relief, c.1900, pewter lid, $50-80.

a.   Rosskopf & Gerz, .5L, relief & transfer, early
     1900's, pewter lid, $60-90.

b.   Pottery, #662, .5L, relief & transfer, *Reichenhall*,
     c.1900, pewter lid, $60-90.

c.   Pottery, #1542, relief, horses jumping fences,
     c.1900, pewter lid, $140-200.

d.   Pottery, #37, 1.0L, etched & low relief, three
     panels, singing, drinking, lovers, c.1900, pewter
     lid, $200-300.

e.   Pottery, .5L, relief, c.1900, pewter lid, $50-80.

f.   Pottery, .5L, relief, c.1900, pewter lid, $60-90.

g.   Pottery, #11045, 1.0L, relief, c.1900, pewter lid,
     $50-80.

h.   Pottery, 1.0L, relief, c.1900, pewter lid, $100-160.

a. Pottery, #1234, 1.0L, relief, c.1900, pottery lid, $100-160.

b. Pottery, #67, 1.0L, relief, c.1900, pewter lid, $60-90.

c. Pottery, #240, .5L, relief, c.1900, pewter lid, $60-90.

d. Thewalt, #315, .5L, relief, *Heidelberg*, c.1900, pewter lid, $90-130.

e. Pottery, .5L, relief, Saarguemines, c.1900, pottery lid, $150-250.

f. Steinzeugwerke, #1401, .5L, pottery, relief, early 1900's, pewter lid, $100-175.

g. Steinzeugwerke, #1279, .5L, pottery, relief, composers, early 1900's, inlaid lid, $150-225.

h. Steinzeugwerke, #1278, .5L, pottery, relief, composers, early 1900's, inlaid lid, $150-225.

a. Steinzeugwerke, #1272, .5L, pottery, relief, early
    1900's, inlaid lid, $150-225.

b. Steinzeugwerke, #1272, .5L, pottery, relief, early
    1900's, pewter lid, $75-125.

c. Pottery, #368, .5L, relief, c.1900, inlaid lid,
    $150-225.

d. Gerz, #1109, .5L, pottery, relief, c.1900, pewter
    lid, $125-200.

e. Pottery, #68, .5L, relief, c.1900, pewter lid,
    $120-180.

f. Pottery, #67, .5L, relief, c.1900, pewter lid,
    $120-180.

g. Dümler & Breiden, #547, 1.0L, pottery, relief,
    c.1900, pewter lid, $140-200.

h. Dümler & Breiden, #682, 1.0L, pottery, relief,
    c.1900, pewter lid, $120-180.

a. Pottery, 1.0L, relief, soccer game, c.1900, pottery lid, $120-180.

b. Pottery, #1541, .5L, relief, c.1900, pewter lid, $100-160.

c. Pottery, #1269, .5L, relief, c.1900, pewter lid, $150-225.

d. Pottery, #1266, .5L, relief, *Rear Admiral W.S. Schley, U.S.N.*, early 1900's, pewter lid, $100-160.

e. Pottery, #1408, .75L, relief, Wilhelm II, c.1910, pewter lid, $250-375.

f. Pottery, #1274, .5L, relief, c.1900, pewter lid, $120-180.

g. Pottery, #583, 1.0L, relief, c.1900, pewter lid, $140-200.

h. Merkelbach & Wick, 1.0L, stoneware, relief, blue & purple saltglaze, c.1900, pewter lid with carved horn, carved horn thumblift, $175-250.

a. Pottery, .5L, transfer, early 1900's, metal lid, $60-90.

b. Pottery, .5L, transfer, early 1900's, pewter lid, $70-100.

c. Pottery, .5L, transfer, early 1900's, pewter lid with relief scene of Munich, $80-120.

d. Pottery, .25L, transfer, early 1900's, pewter lid with relief scene of Munich, $60-90.

e. Pottery, #1164A, 2.0L, relief, c.1900, pewter lid, $100-160.

f. Pottery, #1044, 2.0L, relief, c.1900, pewter lid, $100-160.

g. Pottery, 1.5L, relief, c.1900, pewter lid, $90-140.

a.   Pottery, #653, 2.5L, relief, c.1900, pewter lid, $150-250.

b.   Pottery, #1066, 1.5L, relief, c.1900, pottery lid, $200-300.

c.   Pottery, #1008, 2.5L, relief, c.1900, pottery lid, $200-300.

d.   Pottery, #156, 2.5L, relief, c.1900, pottery lid, $200-300.

e.   Pottery, .5L, marked Rookwood Pottery, (Cincinnati, Ohio), hand-painted & relief, dated 1895, made for *Commercial Club of Cincinnati*, pewter lid, $1800-2300.

a.   Pottery, .5L, relief, *Washington Monument, Washington, D.C.*, early 1900's, pewter lid, $60-90.

b.   Pottery, .5L, relief, *Atlantic City, N.J.*, early 1900's, pewter lid, $50-80.

c.   Pottery, .5L, relief, *Lee Monument, New Orleans*, early 1900's, inlaid lid, $50-80.

d.   Pottery, .5L, relief, *Capitol, Washington, D.C.*, early 1900's, inlaid lid, $70-100.

e.   Pottery, .5L, relief, *St. Louis Exposition, 1904*, pewter lid, $100-160.

f.   Pottery, .5L, relief, *Union Station, St. Louis*, early 1900's, pewter lid, $60-90.

g.   Pottery, .5L, relief, *State Capital, Pheonix, Arizona*, early 1900's, pewter lid, $50-80.

h.   Pottery, .5L, relief, *Mt. Clemens, Michigan Court House*, early 1900's, pewter lid, $50-80.

a. Pottery, #838, .5L, relief, c.1900, figural lid, $100-160.

b. Pottery, .5L, relief, c.1900, inlaid figural lid, $90-130.

c. Pottery, #2, .5L, relief, c.1900, figural lid, $120-180.

d. Pottery, #1200, .5L, relief, c.1900, figural lid, $100-160.

e. Reinhold Hanke, #1150, .5L, stoneware, relief, *Christoph Columbus*, c.1900, inlaid lid, $350-500.

f. Gerz, #27, .5L, stoneware, relief, c.1900, pewter lid, $80-120.

g. Merkelbach & Wick, .5L, stoneware, relief, c.1900, pewter lid with small inlaid glass, $60-100.

h. HR, #152, .5L, stoneware, relief & threading, c.1900, pewter lid, $80-120.

a.   Reinhold Hanke, #320, 1.0L, stoneware, relief, c.1900, pewter lid, $80-120.

b.   Stoneware, 1.0L, relief, c.1900, pewter lid, $60-100.

c.   Reinhold Merkelbach, #33, 1.0L, stoneware, relief, c.1900, pewter lid, $60-100.

d.   Marzi & Remy, 1.0L, stoneware, relief, dwarfs & verse, c.1900, porcelain inlaid lid, $100-160.

e.   Stoneware, .5L, relief, with music box, c.1900, pewter lid, $70-100.

f.   Gerz, .5L, stoneware, relief, with music box, c.1900, pewter lid, $70-100.

g.   Stoneware, #207, .5L, relief, Wilhelm I, Wilhelm II, Bismarck, Von Moltke, Frederich III, early 1900's, pewter lid, $140-200.

h.   Gerz, #968B, .4L, stoneware, relief, c.1900, inlaid lid, $40-60.

a.   Stoneware, 1.0L, relief, Gambrinus, brown/gray color, late 1800's, pewter lid, $80-120.

b.   Stoneware, 1.25L, relief, Gambrinus, brown/gray color, late 1800's, pewter lid, $100-160.

c.   Stoneware, .5L, relief, Ludwig, brown/gray color, late 1800's, pewter lid, $70-100.

d.   Pottery, .5L, relief, anti-Semitic scenes, early 1900's, inlaid lid, $500-700.

e.   Marzi & Remy, #1543, .5L, pottery, relief, c.1900, pewter lid, $100-160.

f.   Merkelbach & Wick, 1.0L, pottery, transfer, c.1900, silver on copper lid, $120-180.

g.   Stoneware, .5L, marked L.B.&C., transfer, c.1900, inlaid figural lid, $140-200.

a. Pottery, .5L, marked Saarguemines, hand-painted enamel, c.1900, pewter lid, $100-160.

b. Pottery, .5L, marked Nesselsdorf, relief & hand-painted enamel, c.1900, pewter lid, $140-200.

c. Pottery, .5L, relief, c.1900, inlaid lid, $140-200.

d. Pottery, #7127, .5L, relief, glazed, Art Nouveau, inlaid lid, $150-250.

e. Marzi & Remy, #2323, .5L, stoneware, relief, c.1900, pewter lid, $120-180.

f. Marzi & Remy, #1802, .5L, stoneware, relief, c.1900, pewter lid, $120-180.

g. Marzi & Remy, #1800, .5L, stoneware, relief, c.1900, pewter lid, $120-180.

h. Marzi & Remy, #1848, .4L, stoneware, relief, c.1900, pewter lid, $120-180.

a. Stoneware, #1202, .5L, incised & enameled, red/
    brown, marked TS (possibly A. Shäfer) c.1930,
    pewter lid, $100-160.

b. Stoneware, .5L, relief, 4F, c.1900, pewter lid,
    $50-80.

c. Gerz, .5L, stoneware, relief, golfers, early 1900's,
    pewter lid, $300-500.

d. Rosskopf & Gerz, #647, 1.0L, stoneware, relief,
    early 1900's, pewter lid, $140-200.

e. Rosskopf & Gerz, #780, 1.0L, stoneware, relief
    & etched, early 1900's, pewter lid, $175-250.

f. Dumler & Breiden, .5L, pottery, relief, c.1900,
    pewter lid, $80-120.

g. Reinhold Merkelbach, 1.0L, pottery, low relief,
    Art Nouveau, c.1900, pewter lid, $120-180.

Courtesy of Cypress Antiques

a. Saargemund, 1.0L, relief, Darmstadt crest, c.1900, pewter lid, $400-550.

b. Saargemund, 1.0L, relief, Imperial Eagle, c.1900, pewter lid, $550-750.

c. Saargemund, 1.0L, relief, c.1900, dog handle, pewter lid, $400-550.

d. Saargemund, #2668, 1.0L, relief, c.1900, cat handle, pewter lid, $400-550.

Courtesy of Cypress Antiques

e. Saargemund, #2784, 1.0L, relief, Munich Child, c.1900, pewter lid, $550-750.

f. Saargemund, #2783, 1.0L, relief, c.1900, fox handle, pewter lid, $400-550.

g. Saargemund, #2888, 1.0L, relief, c.1900, pewter lid, $450-600.

h. Saargemund, #2717, 1.0L, relief, c.1900, monkey handle, pewter lid, $350-500.

a.   HR, #459, .5L, pottery, relief, c.1900, pewter lid, $250-350.

b.   HR, #458, .5L, pottery, relief, c.1900, pewter lid, $80-120.

c.   HR, #454, 1.0L, pottery, relief, c.1900, pewter lid, $120-180.

d.   HR, #452, 1.0L, pottery, relief, c.1900, pewter lid, $90-140.

e.   HR, #451, .5L, pottery, relief, c.1900, pewter lid, $80-120.

f.   HR, #455, .5L, pottery, relief, c.1900, pewter lid, $80-120.

g.   HR, #457, .5L, pottery, relief, full color, c.1900, pewter lid, $120-180.

h.   HR, #453, .5L, pottery, relief, full color, c.1900, pewter lid, $120-180.

a.   Pottery, .5L, hand-painted, bicycle rider, early 1900's, pewter lid, $275-375.

b.   Pottery, #6049, .5L, relief & hand-painted, alligator handle, c.1910, inlaid lid, $80-120.

c.   Pottery, .5L, transfer, c.1900, pewter lid, $60-90.

d.   Pottery, .5L, hand-painted, c.1900, pewter lid with relief scene of Munich, $120-180.

e.   Pottery, .5L, transfer, music box, early 1900's, pewter lid, $100-160.

f.   Merkelbach & Wick, .5L, pottery, transfer, c.1900, pewter lid, $60-90.

g.   Pottery, .5L, transfer, c.1900, pewter lid, $60-90.

h.   Pottery, .5L, transfer, c.1900, pewter lid, $100-160.

a. Dorfner Brothers, .5L, pottery, transfer, c.1900, pewter lid, $50-80.

b. Dorfner Brothers, 1.0L, pottery, transfer, c.1900, pewter lid, $60-90.

c. Rosskopf & Gerz, #570, .5L, pottery, relief & transfer, early 1900's, pewter lid, $60-90.

d. Rosskopf & Gerz, #384, .5L, pottery, relief & transfer, early 1900's, pewter lid, $60-90.

e. Dorfner Brothers, 1.0L, pottery, transfer, c.1900, pewter lid, $120-180.

f. Reinhold Merkelbach, .5L, pottery, transfer, bicycle rider, early 1900's, pewter lid with relief scene of bicycle rider, $275-375.

g. Reinhold Hanke, #563, .5L, pottery, mold 1090, transfer, c.1900, pewter lid, $75-125.

h. Reinhold Hanke, #565, .5L, pottery, mold 1090, transfer, c.1900, pewter lid, $75-125.

a.   Merkelbach & Wick, .5L, pottery, transfer, 4F, early 1900's, pewter lid, $70-100.

b.   Stoneware, .5L, transfer, 4F, early 1900's, pewter lid, $70-100.

c.   Stoneware, .5L, transfer, 4F, *11. Deutsches Turnfest, Frankfurt 1908*, pewter lid, $100-160.

d.   Stoneware, .5L, transfer, 4F, early 1900's, pewter lid, $80-120.

e.   Stoneware, 1.0L, hand-painted, dated 1893, pewter lid has relief boar, $275-375.

f.   Wick-Werke, 1.0L, hand-painted, pewter lid with carved horn dachshund, lid dated 1928, $275-375.

g.   Gerz, 1.0L, transfer, *Münchener Kunstausstelhung*, early 1900's, pewter lid with relief Munich Child, $200-300.

h.   Stoneware, 1.0L, transfer, *Prinz-Regent Luitpold von Bayern*, c.1912, pewter lid with relief city crests, $150-250.

a. Stoneware, .5L, transfer, early 1900's, pewter lid with relief scene of Munich, $120-180.

b. Merkelbach & Wick, .5L, stoneware, transfer, early 1900's, pewter lid with relief mountain climbing tools, $120-180.

c. Eckhardt & Engler, .5L, stoneware, transfer, *Hofbrauhaus*, early 1900's, pewter lid with relief scene of Munich, $100-160.

d. Merkelbach & Wick, .5L, stoneware, transfer, early 1900's, pewter lid, $80-120.

e. Stoneware, 1.0L, transfer, design by Franz Ringer, early 1900's, pewter lid with embossed heart, $300-400.

f. Stoneware, 1.0L, transfer, design by Franz Ringer, early 1900's, pewter lid, $300-400.

g. Stoneware, 1.0L, transfer, design by Franz Ringer, early 1900's, pewter lid with relief Hofbrauhaus, $300-400.

h. Stoneware, 1.0L, transfer, design by Franz Ringer, *15. Deutsch Bundesschießen, München, 1906*, pewter lid with relief Munich Child, $350-450.

a. Merkelbach & Wick, .5L, stoneware, transfer, *Prinz Rupprecht, 20. Inft. Regt. Lindau*, c.1910, pewter lid, $150-225.

b. Stoneware, .5L, transfer, *München Hofbräuhaus*, early 1900's, pewter lid with relief *HB*, $100-160.

c. Stoneware, .5L, transfer, early 1900's, Art Nouveau, pewter lid, $100-160.

d. Stoneware, #1492, .5L, relief, c.1900, pewter lid, $120-180.

e. Wick-Werke, 1.0L, stoneware, transfer, 1920's, pewter lid, $50-80.

f. Marzi & Remy, 1.0L, stoneware, hand-painted, c.1900, pewter lid with relief tavern scene, $175-250.

g. Stoneware, 1.0L, transfer, *American Society of Mechanical Engineers, München, 7 Juli, 1913*, pewter lid, $300-400.

h. Marzi & Remy, 1.0L, transfer, 1920's, pewter lid, $100-160.

a. Stoneware, .5L, transfer, design by Franz Ringer, *12. Deutsches Turnfest, Liepzig, 1913*, pewter lid with relief 4F, $350-450.

b. Stoneware, .5L, transfer, design by Franz Ringer, *11. Deutsches Turnfest, Frankfurt, 1908*, pewter lid with relief scene of Frankfurt, $300-400.

c. Stoneware, .5L, transfer, design by Franz Ringer, *16. Deutsches Bundesschießen, Hamburg, 1909*, pewter lid with relief scene of Hamburg, $350-450.

d. Stoneware, .5L, transfer, design by Franz Ringer, *15. Deutsches Bundesschießen, München, 1906*, pewter lid with relief Munich Child, $300-400.

e. Marzi & Remy, #5, 1.0L, stoneware, transfer, c.1900, pewter lid, $80-120.

f. Merkelbach & Wick, 1.0L, stoneware, transfer, c.1900, pewter lid, $80-120.

g. Stoneware, 1.0L, transfer, c.1900, pewter lid, $80-120.

h. Stoneware, 1.0L, transfer, c.1900, pewter lid, $70-100.

a.   Stoneware, .5L, transfer, blue on gray, design by Franz Ringer, early 1900's, Art Nouveau, pewter lid, $200-300.

b.   Stoneware, .5L, transfer, blue on gray, design by Franz Ringer, early 1900's, Art Nouveau, pewter lid, $150-225.

c.   Stoneware, .5L, transfer, blue on gray, design by Franz Ringer, early 1900's, Art Nouveau, pewter lid, $175-250.

d.   Stoneware, .5L, transfer, blue on gray, design by Franz Ringer, early 1900's, Art Nouveau, pewter lid, $200-300.

e.   Rosskopf & Gerz, .5L, stoneware, transfer, *Nürnberg*, early 1900's, pewter lid with relief Denkmal Nürnberg, $60-90.

f.   Stoneware, .5L, transfer, early 1900's, pewter lid with relief crest, $60-90.

g.   Stoneware, .5L, transfer, early 1900's, pewter lid, $70-100.

h.   Stoneware, .5L, transfer, early 1900's, pewter lid, $70-100.

a.   Stoneware, .5L, transfer, 1920's, pewter lid, $40-60.

b.   Stoneware, .5L, transfer, early 1900's, pewter lid, $40-60.

c.   Pottery, .5L, transfer, 1920's, pewter lid, $40-60.

d.   Pottery, .5L, transfer, 1920's, pewter lid, $40-60.

e.   Wick-Werke, .5L, stoneware, transfer, 1920's, pewter lid, $40-60.

f.   Stoneware, .5L, transfer, pewter lid, $50-80.

g.   Gerz, .5L, stoneware, transfer, early 1900's, pewter lid with relief leaf, $50-80.

h.   Stoneware, .5L, transfer, *14. Oberbayrisches Berzirksturnfest, 1914*, pewter lid, $100-160.

a. Thewalt, .5L, stoneware, transfer, design by Franz Ringer, early 1900's, pewter lid, $250-350.

b. Stoneware, .5L, transfer, design by Franz Ringer, early 1900's, pewter lid, $250-350.

c. Stoneware, .5L, transfer, design by Franz Ringer, early 1900's, metal lid, $225-325.

d. Stoneware, .5L, transfer, design by Franz Ringer, early 1900's, pewter lid, $250-350.

e. Earthenware, 1.0L, faience style, enameled, design by Franz Ringer, early 1900's, pewter lid, $500-700.

f. Reinhold Merkelbach, 1.0L, stoneware, threading, Art Nouveau, early 1900's, pewter lid, $120-180.

g. Rosskopf & Gerz, #437, .5L, relief, early 1900's, pewter lid, $120-180.

a. Stoneware, .5L, transfer, German Engineers Society, Munich, 1903, design by Franz Ringer, pewter lid, $250-350.

b. Stoneware, .5L, transfer, *1909, Deutschen Brau v. Malz Meisterbund*, design by Franz Ringer, pewter lid with relief Munich Child, $300-400.

c. Stoneware, .5L, transfer, *8. Deutsches Sängerbundes Fest Nürnberg 1912*, design by Franz Ringer, pewter lid with relief scene of Nürnberg, $250-350.

d. Stoneware, .5L, transfer, design by Franz Ringer, pewter lid, $225-325.

e. Stoneware, 1.0L, transfer, design by Franz Ringer, early 1900's, pewter lid, $250-350.

f. Stoneware, 1.0L, transfer, design by Franz Ringer, early 1900's, pewter lid, $250-350.

g. Stoneware, 1.0L, transfer, design by Franz Ringer, early 1900's, pewter lid, $350-450.

h. Merkelbach & Wick, 1.0L, stoneware, transfer, design by Franz Ringer, early 1900's, pewter lid, $300-400.

a.   Eckhardt & Engler, #1417, .5L, stoneware, blue glaze, c.1925, Art Nouveau, pewter lid, $60-90.

b.   Stoneware, #1650, .5L, blue glaze, c.1925, Art Nouveau, pewter lid, $70-100.

c.   Stoneware, #1702, .5L, blue glaze, c.1925, Art Nouveau, pewter lid, $70-100.

d.   Stoneware, #3203, .5L, blue & brown glazes, c.1925, Art Nouveau, pewter lid, $70-100.

e.   Marzi & Remy, #1919, 1.0L, stoneware, blue & gray saltglaze, c.1908, Art Nouveau, pewter lid, $80-120.

f.   Marzi & Remy, #2012, 1.0L, stoneware, blue & gray saltglaze, c.1908, Art Nouveau, pewter lid, $100-150.

g.   Marzi & Remy, #2201, 1.0L, stoneware, blue & gray saltglaze, c.1908, Art Nouveau, pewter lid, $100-150.

h.   Marzi & Remy, #2106, 1.0L, stoneware, brown saltglaze, c.1908, Art Nouveau, pewter lid, $80-120.

a. Reinhold Merkelbach, #2311, .5L, stoneware, blue & green glazes, design by Bruno Mauder, c.1910, Art Nouveau, metal lid, $80-120.

b. Reinhold Merkelbach, #2196, .5L, stoneware, blue glaze, design by Paul Neu, c.1910, Art Nouveau, pewter lid, $100-150.

c. Reinhold Merkelbach, #2215, .5L, stoneware, blue glaze, design by Paul Neu, c.1910, Art Nouveau, pewter lid, $100-150.

d. Reinhold Merkelbach, #3267, .5L, stoneware, blue & green glazes, design by Karl Mehlem, c.1922, Art Nouveau, pewter lid, $100-150.

e. Reinhold Merkelbach, #3226, .5L, stoneware, blue & green glazes, c.1910, Art Nouveau, pewter lid, $70-100.

f. Stoneware, #2235, .5L, incised, blue glaze, early 1900's, Art Nouveau, pewter lid, $100-150.

g. Marzi & Remy, #1779, .5L, stoneware, blue, brown & black glaze, early 1900's, Art Nouveau, inlaid lid, $100-150.

h. Eckhardt & Engler, .5L, stoneware, blue glaze, c.1925, Art Nouveau, pewter lid, $50-80.

a. Stoneware, #105, .5L, brown saltglaze, c.1910, Art Nouveau, metal lid, $60-90.

b. Otto Blum, #154, .5L, stoneware, blue & green saltglaze, c.1910, Art Nouveau, pewter lid, $60-90.

c. Otto Blum, .5L, stoneware, blue & gray saltglaze, c.1910, Art Nouveau, pewter lid, $60-90.

d. Otto Blum, #140, .5L, stoneware, blue & gray saltglaze, c.1910, Art Nouveau, pewter lid, $60-90.

e. Merkelbach & Wick, .5L, pottery, green & brown glaze, c.1904, Art Nouveau, pewter lid, $50-80.

f. Wick-Werke, #2119, .5L, stoneware, blue glaze, c.1904, Art Nouveau, pewter lid, $80-120.

g. Wick-Werke, .5L, stoneware, blue glaze, c.1910, Art Nouveau, pewter lid, $70-110.

h. Merkelbach & Wick, #1169A, .5L, stoneware, blue & purple glazes, c.1902, Art Nouveau, pewter lid, $90-130.

12. Occupational

It's understandable that many stein purchasers of previous centuries, when choosing a theme for the decoration of their personal stein, decided on their *occupation*. In fact, that was such a common theme that there are those who now specialize only in the collection of these so-called *occupational* steins.

There is a predictable pattern to the occupations that are most often depicted on steins. Merchants, tradesmen, public servants, and professionals are the most common categories, including occupations such as tailors, butchers, bakers, brewers, shoemakers, blacksmiths, locksmiths, teamsters, machinists, dairy workers, farmers, carpenters, firemen, postmen, soldiers, and toward the end of the 1800's, doctors and lawyers.

Rarely depicted occupations can perhaps be explained by three factors:

1. There may have been too little money for a stein or too little pride in some occupations, for example, in the case of servants, grave diggers, or street crews.
2. Prudence may have played a role in making some occupationals scarce, such as teachers, clergy, or judges.
3. Finally, some occupations would obviously have had very few members: goldsmiths, street car operators, or circus performers.

The representation of the occupation is usually obvious, even to the untrained modern observer. The decoration on the body, lid, and/or thumblift usually shows the worker in *action* or in *uniform*, or the *products* or *tools* of his occupation. Some tools that may at first viewing be difficult to recognize are the *bucket, stirrer, and scoop in a barrel* of the brewer, or the *scissors and divider* of the tailor. *Oxheads* and *pretzels* are occasionally used rather casually as symbols of butchers and bakers, respectively. Steins in the form of *books* or sets of books often indicate professional occupations and can be identified by examining the titles of the books.

When a famous craftsman is depicted, the fact that the stein is an occupational may be overlooked. The most common examples are the poet Hans Sachs, a shoemaker, and the Hapsburg double-headed eagle, which was the symbol of the first *printer*, Johann Gutenberg.

Occupational steins can be found from all eras and in all materials (with the possible exception of ivory), from the incised stoneware of the 1600's to glass from the 1800's and porcelain from the 1900's. Occupational stein collectors, however, rarely concentrate on acquiring the rarer forms of occupational steins, unless they happen to depict their own occupation. The most commonly collected occupationals are those from around 1900 that have steepled pewter lids and porcelain or stoneware bodies, as are shown in the remainder of this Section.

a.   Postal Service worker, .5L, porcelain, lithophane, dated 1915, Cassel, pewter lid, $400-500.

b.   Wagon driver, .5L, porcelain, lithophane, "Frankfurter Eiswerke - Morsch", c.1900, pewter lid, $350-450.

c.   Lumber wagon driver, .5L, porcelain, lithophane, c.1900, pewter lid, $350-450.

d.   Flösser (moves lumber on raft), .5L, porcelain, lithophane, c.1900, pewter lid, $350-450.

e.   Blacksmith, .5L, porcelain, lithophane, dated 1916, Stuttgart, pewter lid, $250-350.

f.   Farmer, .5L, porcelain, lithophane, c.1900, pewter lid, $225-325.

g.   Stonecutter, .5L, porcelain, lithophane, c.1900, pewter lid, $350-450.

h.   Butcher, .5L, porcelain, lithophane, dated 1916, pewter lid, $250-350.

a. Coach driver, .5L, porcelain, lithophane, c.1900, pewter lid, $300-400.

b. Dairy farmer, .5L, porcelain, lithophane, c.1900, pewter lid, $250-350.

c. Construction carpenter, .5L, porcelain, lithophane, c.1900, pewter lid, $250-350.

d. Butcher, .5L, porcelain, lithophane, dated 1909, pewter lid, $250-350.

e. Miner, .5L, porcelain, lithophane, c.1900, pewter lid, $400-500.

f. Wagon driver (beer barrels), .5L, porcelain, lithophane, c.1900, pewter lid, $300-400.

g. Construction carpenter, .5L, porcelain, lithophane, c.1900, pewter lid, $250-350.

h. Farmer, .5L, porcelain, lithophane, c.1900, pewter lid, $200-300.

a. Newspaper deliverer, 1.0L, porcelain, lithophane, dated 1906, pewter lid, $500-700.

b. Blacksmith, .5L, porcelain, lithophane, dated 1910, pewter lid, $250-350.

c. Brewmaster, .5L, porcelain, lithophane, c.1900, pewter lid, $250-350.

d. Cheese maker, .5L, porcelain, lithophane, c.1900, pewter lid, $250-350.

e. Cheese maker, .5L, porcelain, lithophane, c.1900, pewter lid, $250-350.

f. Miller, .5L, porcelain, lithophane, c.1900, pewter lid, $225-325.

g. Farrier (graduate of veterinary college), .5L, porcelain, lithophane, dated 1903, prism lid, $350-450.

h. Butcher, .5L, porcelain, lithophane, c.1900, pewter lid, $225-325.

a. Farmer, .5L, porcelain, lithophane, c.1900, pewter lid, $225-325.

b. Electrician, .5L, porcelain, lithophane, c.1900, pewter lid, $350-450.

c. Cooper (barrel maker), .5L, porcelain, lithophane, c.1900, pewter lid, $300-400.

d. Horse trader, .5L, porcelain, lithophane, c.1900, pewter lid, $350-450.

e. Postman, 1.0L, stoneware, dated 1913, pewter lid, $400-500.

f. Eisenbahner, 1.0L, stoneware, c.1900, pewter lid, $400-500.

g. Carpenter, .5L, stoneware, dated 1914, pewter lid, $275-375.

h. Locksmith, .5L, porcelain, lithophane, c.1900, pewter lid, $250-350.

a.   Baker, .5L, porcelain, lithophane, dated 1909, pewter lid, $250-350.

b.   Baker, .5L, porcelain, lithophane, c.1900, pewter lid, $250-350.

c.   Farmer, .5L, porcelain, lithophane, c.1900, pewter lid, $200-300.

d.   Cabinet maker, .5L, stoneware, c.1900, pewter lid, $250-350.

Side scenes from stein b., above, Baker occupational stein.

e.   Hotel Hausmeister Sterben (Concierge), .5L, porcelain, lithophane, Hotel Glocke & Krone, c.1900, pewter lid, $500-700.

f.   Hoteldiener (Bellhop), .5L, porcelain, lithophane, Hotel Bayer Hof, c.1900, pewter lid, $500-700.

13. Regimentals

Steins have served as souvenirs of military service ever since the 1600's. Regimental, or perhaps more accurately *Reservist*, steins have had some resurgence of popularity since 1950. These modern era souvenirs very often have no lid, and thus are *mugs*, and have simple decal-transferred decorations that make them less interesting to most collectors. The Regimental steins that have generated the most interest, outside of a few scattered between the 1860's and the 1940's, have been the great number of steins made as souvenirs of service in the German Imperial Armies in the period from 1890 to 1918. These are the steins briefly described and pictured in this section. Some excellent reference books exist in this specialty, and they are listed in Section 18.

13.1 History of Regimentals

With an upsurge of nationalism, pride in the success of the Franco-Prussian War, and a young, popular Emperor, Kaiser Wilhelm II, Germany began an expansion of its military system in 1888.

Military service was obligatory for men 17 to 45 years old, the primary exceptions being criminals or others without civil rights. The tour of active duty was three years for cavalry and navy and two years for others, with the exception of one year for certain professionals or volunteers. Upon completion of their active duty these men became *reservists*. It is the reservists, and not the career soldiers, who ordered souvenirs, such as steins, pipes, flasks, beakers, cups, swords, and many other items.

All reservists reported to their units in October and all graduated with the same *class* in September. The cost of Regimental steins, deducted automatically from wages, was very high, generally about two or three times the cost of a Mettlach stein. But pride in their class and in their unit was enormous; some cases have been recorded in which *all* the reservists in a given company ordered steins.

There were several branches of the Armies: infantry, cavalry, artillery, *Pionier* (engineering), *Jäger* (hunter or rifleman), and the military train. There were also technical service units such as railway (*Eisenbahn*), telegraph, aviation, and airship (*Luftschiffer*). Volunteers from all of these units were provided for the colonial troops (*Schutztruppen*). The Navy was separate from the Armies, but had all the same types of souvenirs.

13.2 Production

Regimental steins were usually produced in porcelain, though occasionally they were of pottery or stoneware, or, rarely, glass or pewter. A few *character* Regimentals exist, such as skulls, sailors, or soldiers, but most Regimentals have *vertical* sides, a built-up base, and raised frieze bands above and below the main decorations.

The decorations were hand-painted on early Regimentals. The later steins were primarily transfer-decorated; that is, the designs were printed or silk screened onto a decal that was put on the body, touched up and augmented, then fired.

These decorations generally depicted typical training scenes, portraits, or, rarely, combat scenes. The glazes on these steins included great varieties of *color* and *brilliance* that were made with formulas that have mostly been lost and cannot easily be duplicated.

Rosters can be found, usually near the handle, on most steins except the early Regimentals. Where rosters are not included on later steins, it is speculated that steins were ordered on an individual basis, following discharge.

The pewterwork on most Regimental steins is both elaborate and meaningful.

Some of the varieties of **lids** include:

steeples	usually early date
fuses	field or foot artillery
prisms over scenes	usually southern German
flat relief	usually Bavarian or Saxony
crowns	used on some Bavarian units
helmets	used on infantry, artillery, or mounted
screw-off lids	mostly southern German
finial-type lid	all types of units

The **finials** are also informative:

field guns	artillery
locomotives	Eisenbahn
machine guns	machine gun companies
tschako	Jäger
horse and rider	most often cavalry but could be other types
eagle	mostly Prussian
seated or standing soldiers	almost any type of unit

Different types of **thumblifts** tend to be more indicative of the region of the unit, but occasionally they represent different types of units. Examples include:

eagle	Prussian
lion	Bavarian or Hessen
griffin	Baden
bird	Ulm
St. Barbara	artillery
St. Hubertus	Jäger
engineering implements	Pionier

Villeroy and Boch of Mettlach produced many Regimental steins, for a great number of different units. They all have print under glaze (PUG) decoration, usually of several soldiers in a single scene. The lids are flat domes, as were used on most of the Mettlach PUG steins.

13.3 Collecting Regimentals

The collecting strategy of many Regimental collectors is to seek the beautiful, the unusual, and the *rare*. Some of the *predictably* rarer Regimentals include those: from units started after 1912; in sizes other than .5L and 1.0L; and, of course, those for small or specialty units. Unfortunately, there is also a great deal of *unpredictable* rarity in Regimental steins, such as larger units for which no steins have been *found*. An understanding of Regimentals thus requires some study of collections and prices - the following picture section will provide a very good start.

Reproductions of Regimentals have been manufactured at least since the 1950's. Reproductions have generally been made of porcelain with finial-type lids. They can usually be identified by examining the historical accuracy of the information, decoration and lid, but this knowledge may be beyond that which has been accumulated by the casual collector. So here are some production clues to the identification of reproductions.

Original Regimentals dated after 1900 almost never had *tapered* bodies; reproductions frequently do. Some reproductions have flimsy *stamped* lids, rather than carefully cast ones as the originals have. Reproductions often have an *uncrowned*, rampant lion for a thumblift. And finally, lithophanes of nudes, dancing girls, or girls in suggestive poses, are definitely reproductions; originals usually had lithophanes of a soldier and girl, home scenes, nature and outdoor scenes, busts of King Ludwig or Kaiser Wilhelm II, and military scenes. Examples of new or reproduction Regimental steins can be found in Section 17.

The Military Glossary that follows provides the meanings of many of the foreign words and abbreviations used in the following picture captions. For the most part the segments of the caption listed in *italics* have come directly from the stein; only a few obvious errors or important inconsistencies have been changed. Because many of the military names originated with Napoleon, the unit names on the steins are a difficult combination of French, German and Germanized-French words. Hopefully, this confusion will be outweighed by the convenience of having these unit names listed as they actually appear on the steins.

Evaluation Information
The value range for the steins illustrated in this chapter reflects the normal price that can be expected from a knowledgeable dealer selling to a serious collector in the United States. Prices can vary in other countries. Prices can and will change in the United States to reflect both price changes in West Germany and other countries, as well as changes in currency exchange rates.

Military Glossary

Abteilung, Abtl., Abt.: detachment
Armee-Korps: Army Corps
Armierungs: armament
Artillerie: artillery
Bäckerie: bakery unit
Bataillon, Batl., Bat.: battalion
Batterie, Battr., Batt.: artillery battery
Bayr.: Bavarian
Bekleidung:: uniforms
Bespannungs: draft horse
Betriebs: railway traffic
Bezirkskommando: district headquarters
Chevauleger: Bavarian light cavalry
Comp., Komp.: company
Dragoner: Dragoon
Einjähr. Freiwilliger: one year volunteer
Eisenbahn: railway
Eskadron, Eskr., Esk.: squadron
Fahrer: driver
Feld: field
Flieger: Airman, lowest rank in airforce unit
Freiwilliger: volunteer
Fusilier: fusilier
Fuss: foot
Garde: guard
Garnison: garrison
Gefreiter: Private First Class
Grenadier: grenadier
Handwerker: tailor or shoemaker
Hornist: bugler (foot troops)
Husar(en): Hussar
Infanterie: infantry
Jäger: rifleman, hunter
Jäger zu Pferde: mounted rifleman
Kanonier: gunner
Kavallerie: cavalry
Kompagnie, Komp.: company

Kraftfahr: motor vehicle unit
Krankenträger:stretcher bearer
Krankenwärter: medical assistant, attendant
Kürassier: cuirassier
Lazarett: hospital
Lehr-: instruction, training
Lehrschmiede: blacksmith school
Leib: life or personal
Leib-Garde: body guard unit
Leichte: light (weight)
Luftschiffer: airshipper
Marine: Naval
Maschinengewehr: machine gun
Matrose: Seaman, lowest rank in naval units
Militärbäcker: military baker
Musketier: Musketeer, infantry soldier
Nr., No.: number
Pferde: horse
Pferdewärter: horse groom
Pionier: engineer or technician
Radfahrer: bicyclist
Regiment, Regt., Rgt.: regiment
Reiter: rider
Reservist: soldier who served minimum service time
Sanitätsgefreiter: Medical Private or Medical Corporal
Schule: school
Schütze: sharpshooter
Schutztruppen: Colonial troops
Schwadron: squadron (cavalry)
Schwer: heavy
See-Bataillon: sea battalion, Naval infantry, marines
S.M.S.: ship
Tambour: drummer
Train: supply
Trompeter: trumpeter (mounted troops)
Tschako: head gear for Jäger regiments
Ulan(en): lancer
Versuchs: experimental or testing
Verkehrstruppen: technical troops

It was the German success in the Franco-Prussian War of 1870-1871 that boosted nationalism and resulted in the proud reservist system. Here, the artillery at Gravelotte.

a.   *Bayr. Infanterie Leib Regt., München, 1904-1906,
     .5L, porcelain, $325-425.*

b.   *Bayr. 9. Infanterie Regt., Würzburg, 1900-1902, .5L,
     porcelain, $300-400.*

c.   *Bayr. 6. Infanterie Regt., Amberg, 1896-1898, .5L,
     porcelain, $250-325.*

d.   *Bayr. 8. Infanterie Regt., Metz, 1909-1911, .5L,
     porcelain, $350-450.*

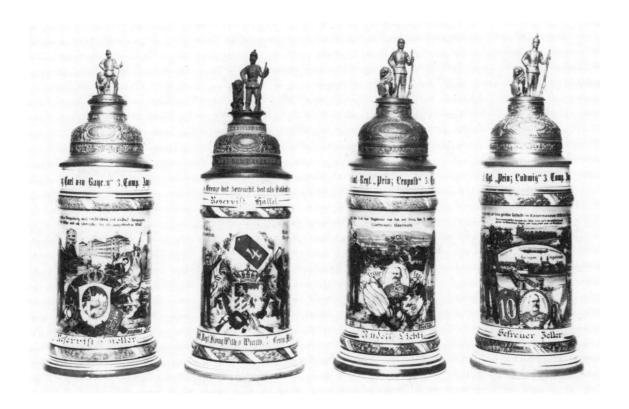

a. *Bayr. 3. Infanterie Regt., Augsburg, 1905-1907, .5L,*
   porcelain, $275-350.

b. *Bayr. 4. Infanterie Regt., Metz, 1903-1905, .5L,*
   porcelain, $275-350.

c. *Bayr. 7. Infanterie Regt., Bayreuth, 1906-1908, .5L,*
   porcelain, $300-375.

d. *Bayr. 10. Infanterie Regt., Ingolstadt, 1908-1910,*
   .5L, porcelain, $300-375.

Opposite:

e. *Bayr. Infanterie Leib Regt., München, 1912-1914,*
   .5L, porcelain, 100 year commemorative, lid
   unscrews to reveal prism, $550-700.

f. *Bayr. 4. Infanterie Regt., Metz, 1905-1907, .5L,*
   porcelain, 200 year commemorative, $350-450.

g. *Bayr. 4. Infanterie Regt., Metz, 1904-1906, .5L,*
   porcelain, 200 year commemorative, $350-450.

h. *Bayr. 12. Infanterie Regt., Neu-Ulm, 1912-1914,*
   .5L, stoneware, 100 year commemorative, lid
   unscrews to reveal portrait of Prinz Arnulf,
   $550-700.

Opposite:

a. *Bayr. Infanterie Leib Regt., München, 1909-1911,*
    .5L, porcelain, 1909 King's Prize, $450-550.

b. *Bayr. 13. Infanterie Regt., Ingolstadt, 1904-1906,*
    .5L, stoneware, 100 year commemorative, unusual
    lid, $475-600.

c. *Bayr. 21. and 23. Infanterie Regts., Eichstatt* and
    Germersheim, 1912-1914, .5L, porcelain, finial
    unscrews to reveal owner's photo, $550-700.

d. *Infanterie Regt. Nr. 111, Rastatt, 1906-1907,* and
    Infanterie Schiess Schule (Marksmanship School),
    Spandau-Rühleben, 1907-1908, .5L, porcelain,
    $650-800.

a. *Infanterie Regt. Nr. 101, Dresden, 1904-1906,* .5L,
    porcelain, $350-450.

b. *Infanterie Regt. Nr. 103, Bautzen, 1908-1910,* .5L,
    porcelain, $375-475.

c. *Infanterie Regt. Nr. 104, Chemnitz, 1904-1906,* .5L,
    porcelain, $350-475.

d. *Infanterie Regt. Nr. 105, Straßburg, 1903-1905,* .5L,
    porcelain, $325-425.

Opposite:

e. *Infanterie Regt. Nr. 88, Mainz, 1897-1899,* .5L,
    porcelain, thumblift is bust of Wilhelm II,
    $425-525.

f. *Infanterie Regt. Nr. 112, Mülhausen, 1906-1907,*
    and *Infanterie Schiess Schule* (Marksmanship
    School), *Spandau, 1907-1908,* .5L, porcelain,
    $650-800.

g. *Bayr. 15. Infanterie Regt., Neuberg, 1904-1906,* .5L,
    porcelain, unusual lid, thumblift is large soldier
    shooting through wall, $600-800.

h. *Bayr. 13. Infanterie Regt., Eichstätt, 1911-1913,*
    .5L, porcelain, named to *Pferdewarter,* has two
    side scenes grooming horses, prism lid, $500-700.

a. *Infanterie Regt. Nr. 20, Wittenberg, 1901-1903, .5L,*
   porcelain, $275-375.

b. *Infanterie Regt. Nr. 80, Bad Homburg, 1902-1904,*
   .5L, porcelain, $275-350.

c. *Infanterie Regt. Nr. 167, Cassel, 1903-1905, .5L,*
   porcelain, $300-400.

d. *Infanterie Regt. Nr. 172, Neubreissach, 1909-1911,*
   .5L, porcelain, $275-350.

a. *Infanterie Regt. Nr. 110, Mannheim, 1911-1913,*
    .5L, porcelain, $450-600.

b. *Infanterie Regt. Nr. 113, Freiburg, 1908-1910,* .5L,
    porcelain, $300-400.

c. *Infanterie Regt. Nr. 119, Stuttgart, 1912-1914,* .5L,
    porcelain, lid unscrews to reveal prism, finial
    unscrews, $600-750.

d. *Infanterie Regt. Nr. 121, Ludwigsburg, 1906-1908,*
    .5L, porcelain, $300-400.

Opposite:

e. *Infanterie Regt. Nr. 109, Karlsruhe, 1897-1899,* .5L,
    porcelain, $250-325.

f. *Infanterie Regt. Nr. 113, Freiburg, 1898-1900,* .5L,
    porcelain, $250-325.

g. *Infanterie Regt. Nr. 126, Straßburg, 1902-1904,* .5L,
    porcelain, $275-350.

h. *Infanterie Regt. Nr. 169, Lahr, 1904-1906,* .5L,
    porcelain, $275-350.

a. *Infanterie Regt. Nr. 92, Braunschweig, 1904-1906,* .5L, pottery, $450-600.

b. *Garde Grenadier Regt. Nr. 1, Berlin, 1907-1909,* .5L, pottery, $500-650.

c. *Garde Grenadier Regt. Nr. 2, Charlottenburg, 1904-1906,* .5L, porcelain, $550-750.

d. *Infanterie Regt. Nr.87, Mainz, 1907-1909,* 100 year commemorative, .5L, porcelain, $350-475.

a.   *Infanterie Regt. Nr. 162, Lübeck, 1907-1909*, .5L, pottery, $400-500.

b.   *Infanterie Regt. Nr. 68, Koblenz, 1905-1907*, .5L, pottery, $400-500.

c.   *Infanterie Regt. Nr. 79, Hildesheim, 1903-1905*, .5L, pottery, Gibraltar banner, inscription for Gibraltar campaign, $450-600.

d.   *Infanterie Regt. Nr. 91, Oldenburg, 1904-1906*, .5L, pottery, unusual lid with owner's photo under glass, $350-450.

Opposite:

e.   *Infanterie Regt. Nr. 40, Rastatt, 1909-1911*, .5L, porcelain, $325-425.

f.   *Infanterie Regt. Nr. 167, Kassel, 1906-1908*, .5L, porcelain, $300-400.

g.   *Infanterie Regt. Nr. 170, Offenburg, 1904-1906*, .5L, porcelain, $400-550.

h.   *Infanterie Regt. Nr. 174, Forbach, 1911-1913*, .5L, porcelain, $325-425.

a. *Infanterie Regt. Nr. 149, Schneidemuhl, 1911-1913*, .5L, pottery, $400-500.

b. *Infanterie Regt. Nr. 82, Göttingen, 1903-1905*, .5L, pottery, $375-475.

c. *Infanterie Regt. Nr. 28, Ehrenbreitstein, 1904-1906*, .5L, pottery, $325-425.

d. *Schützen Fusilier Regt. Nr. 108, Dresden, 1902-1904*, .5L, pottery, appearance of Jäger stein, $700-900.

e. *Bayr. Infanterie Leib Regt., München, 1909-1911*, .5L, porcelain, pewter crown lid covers glass dome, under glass dome are guard house, soldier, and officer on horse, $1100-1500.

f. *Garde Regt. Zu Fuss, Leib Cp., Potsdam, 1901-1903*, .5L, porcelain, miter helmet finial, $2000-2500.

a. *Maschinengewehr Comp., Bayr. 11. Infanterie Regt., Regensburg, 1910-1912, .5L, porcelain, prism lid, $700-900.*

b. *Maschinengewehr Comp., Infanterie Regt. Nr. 83, Cassel, 1912-1914, .5L, porcelain, machine gun with crew finial, $1400-1700.*

c. *Maschinengewehr Comp., Infanterie Regt. Nr. 29, Trier, 1912-1914, 1.0L, pottery, machine gun with crew finial, $1600-2000.*

d. *Maschinengewehr Comp., Bayr. 20. Infanterie Regt., Kempten, 1912-1914, .5L, stoneware, $500-700.*

e. *Maschinengewehr Comp., Infanterie Regt. Nr. 125, Stuttgart, 1912-1914, .5L, porcelain, lid unscrews to reveal prism, finial unscrews to reveal glass jewel, $1100-1400.*

f. *Maschinengewehr Comp., Bayr. 4. Infanterie Regt., Metz, 1910-1912, machine gun and crew finial on unusual lid, $2000-2400.*

a.   *Bayr. 1. Maschinengewehr Abteilung des 1. Armee Korps, Augsburg, 1904-1906, .5L, porcelain, tschako finial, $800-1000.*

b.   *Maschinengewehr Comp., Bayr. 7 Infanterie Regt., Bayreuth, 1909-1911, .5L, porcelain, prism lid, $700-900.*

c.   *Maschinengewehr Comp., Bayr. 22. Infanterie Regt., Zweibrücken, 1912-1914, .5L, porcelain, $1100-1300.*

d.   *Maschinengewehr Comp., Infanterie Regt. Nr. 118, Worms, 1912-1914, .5L, pottery, $1200-1400.*

a. *Maschinengewehr Comp., Infanterie Regt. Nr. 111, Rastatt, 1912-1914, .5L, porcelain, $1100-1400.*

b. *Maschinengewehr Comp., Infanterie Regt. Nr. 111, Rastatt, 1909-1911, .5L, porcelain, $1100-1400.*

c. *Maschinengewehr Comp., Infanterie Regt. Nr. 121, Ludwigsburg, 1910-1912, .5L, porcelain, $1100-1400.*

d. *Maschinengewehr Comp., Infanterie Regt. Nr. 119, Stuttgart, 1911-1913, .5L, porcelain, $1100-1400.*

Opposite:

e. *Garde Maschinengewehr Abteilung Nr. 2, Gross-Lichterfelde, 1907-1909, .5L, porcelain, $1500-1800.*

f. *Maschinengewehr Comp., Infanterie Regt. Nr. 106, Leipzig, 1909-1911, .5L, porcelain, named to Waffenmeister, $1400-1700.*

g. *Maschinengewehr Abteilung Nr. 3, Bitsch und Straßburg, 1905-1907, .5L, pottery, $1400-1700.*

h. *Maschinengewehr Comp., Bayr. 3, Infanterie Regt., Augsburg, 1908-1910, .5L, stoneware, $1100-1400.*

a.   *Garde Schützen Bataillon, Gr. Lichterfelde, 1909-1911, .5L, pottery, $1000-1200.*

b.   *Jäger Bataillon Nr. 4, Bitsch, 1903 1905, .5L, porcelain, $1000-1200.*

c.   *Jäger Bataillon Nr. 10, Bitsch, 1906-1908, .5L, porcelain, $1000-1200.*

d.   *Bayr. 2. Jäger Bataillon, Aschaffenburg, 1907-1909, carved horn on lid, tschako finial, $800-1000.*

a.   *Bayr. 1. Jäger Bataillon, Straubing, 1898-1900*, .5L, porcelain, $500-700.

b.   *Bayr. 2. Jäger Bataillon, Aschaffenburg, 1900-1902*, .5L, porcelain, $600-800.

c.   *Bayr. 2. Jäger Bataillon, Aschaffenburg, 1902-1904*, .5L, porcelain, $700-900.

d.   *Jäger Bataillon Nr. 8, Schlettstadt, 1899-1901*, .5L, porcelain, $800-1000.

Opposite:

e.   *Bayr. 2. Jäger Bataillon, Aschaffenburg, 1908-1910*, .5L, pottery, King's Prize, tschako finial, $1000-1200.

f.   *Jäger Bataillon Nr. 4, Bitsch, 1903-1905*, .5L, porcelain, $1000-1200.

g.   *Jäger Bataillon Nr. 12, Freiberg, 1905-1907*, .5L, porcelain, King's Prize, tschako finial, $1100-1300.

h.   *Jäger Bataillon Nr. 13, Dresden, 1909-1910*, .5L, stoneware, King's Prize, one year volunteer, tschako finial, $700-900.

a. *Garde Schützen Bataillon, Gr. Lichterfelde, 1903-1905*, .5L, porcelain, tschako finial, $1100-1300.

b. *Garde Jäger Bataillon, Potsdam, 1904-1906*, .5L, pottery, $1000-1200.

c. *Jäger Bataillon Nr. 11, Marburg, 1901-1903*, .5L, porcelain, $1000-1200.

d. *Bayr. 2. Jäger Bataillon, Aschaffenburg, 1899-1901*, .5L, porcelain, 1899 Shooting Prize, roster has names of volunteers who went to China for Boxer Rebellion, $900-1100.

e. *Jäger Bataillon Nr. 8, Schlettstadt, 1905-1907*, .5L, pottery, $1100-1400.

f. *Jäger Bataillon Nr. 9, Ratzeburg, 1910-1912*, .5L, pottery, $1500-2000.

a. *Bayr. 2. Pionier Bataillon, Speyer, 1901-1903,*
    .5L, porcelain, $450-575.

b. *Pionier Bataillon, Nr. 11, Mainz, 1899-1901,*
    .5L, porcelain, $450-575.

c. *Pionier Bataillon Nr. 14, Kehl, 1902-1904, .5L,*
    porcelain, $500-650.

d. *Pionier Bataillon Nr. 22, Riesa, 1902-1904, .5L,*
    porcelain, $550-700.

e. *Armierungs Bataillon Nr. 14, 1916-1918, .5L,*
    porcelain, $1800-2200.

f. *Bayr. 3. Pionier Bataillon, Ingolstadt, 1912-*
    1914, Scheinwerferzug, .5L, porcelain, side
    scene depicts Pioniers using search lights,
    prism lid, $1400-1800.

Opposite:

a. *Pionier Bataillon Nr. 3, Spandau, 1907-1909*, .5L, porcelain, $650-800.

b. *Pionier Bataillon Nr. 4, Magdeburg, 1910-1912*, .5L, porcelain, finial unscrews, $650-800.

c. *Pionier Bataillon Nr. 20, Metz, 1908-1910*, .5L, porcelain, $550-700.

d. *Pionier Bataillon Nr. 21, Mainz-Kastel, 1908-1910*, .5L, porcelain, $600-750.

a. *Bayr. 1. Pionier Bataillon, Ingolstadt, 1909-1911*, .5L, porcelain, finial unscrews, $500-650.

b. *Pionier Bataillon Nr. 7, Köln-Riehl, 1909-1911*, .5L, pottery, $500-650.

c. *Pionier Bataillon Nr. 11, Hannover-Münden, 1910-1912*, .5L, porcelain, $550-700.

d. *Pionier Bataillon Nr. 16, Metz, 1906-1908*, .5L, porcelain, $500-650.

Opposite:

e. *Pionier Bataillon Nr. 9, Harburg, 1912-1913* and *Militartubar Akademie, Berlin, 1913-1914*, .5L, pottery, $1200-1500.

f. *Pionier Bataillon Nr. 25, Mainz-Kastel, 1909-1911*, .5L, pottery, $575-725.

g. *Pionier Bataillon Nr. 14, Kehl, 1904-1906*, .5L, porcelain, $475-625.

h. *Pionier Bataillon Nr. 21, Mainz-Kastel, 1909-1911*, .5L, porcelain, $475-625.

a. *Bayr. 2. Pionier Bataillon, Speyer, 1904-1906, .5L, porcelain, prism lid, $450-600.*

b. *Bayr. 3. Pionier Bataillon, München, 1904-1906, .5L, porcelain, prism lid, $450-600.*

c. *Pionier Bataillon Nr. 12, Dresden, 1909-1911, .5L, porcelain, $450-600.*

d. *Pionier Bataillon Nr. 24, Köln-Riehl, 1911-1912, and Pionier Versuchs Kompagnie, Berlin, 1912-1913, .5L, porcelain, $1300-1700.*

a.   *Bayr. Eisenbahn Batl., 2. Comp., München, 1911-*
     1913, .5L, stoneware, $600-800.

b.   *Bayr. Eisenbahn Batl., 2. Comp., München, 1908-*
     1910, .5L, stoneware, $900-1100.

c.   *Eisenbahn Regt. Nr. 2, 3. Comp., Berlin-Schöneberg,*
     1904-1906, .5L, porcelain, $600-750.

d.   *Eisenbahn Regt. Nr. 3, 1. Comp., Hanau, 1912-*
     1914, .5L, porcelain, $700-900.

Opposite:

e.   *Eisenbahn Regt. Nr. 1, 8. Comp., Berlin, 1910-*
     1912, .5L, porcelain, $1000-1300.

f.   *Eisenbahn Regt. Nr. 2, 7. Comp., Berlin, 1904-*
     1906, .5L, porcelain, $600-750.

g.   *Eisenbahn Regt. Nr. 3, 3. Comp., Hanau a.M.,*
     1911-1913, .5L, pottery, $1100-1400.

h.   *Bayr. Eisenbahn Batl., 1. Comp., München, 1902-*
     1904, .5L, porcelain, $600-800.

a. *Eisenbahn Regt. Nr. 3, 4. Comp., Berlin, 1903-1905, .5L, pottery, $800-1000.*

b. *Eisenbahn Regt. Nr. 2, 2. Comp., Berlin-Schöneberg, 1903-1905, .5L, pottery, $600-800.*

c. *Eisenbahn Regt. Nr. 1, 3. Comp., Berlin, 1899-1901, .5L, pottery, $600-800.*

d. *Eisenbahn Regt. Nr. 2, 3. Comp., Berlin, 1905-1907, .5L, pottery, $1000-1200.*

a.   Mettlach, 790(2140), .5L, PUG, *2. Garde Feld Artillerie Regt.*, c.1900, pewter lid, $500-600.

b.   Mettlach, 825(2140), .5L, PUG, *Infanterie Regt. Nr. 141*, c.1900, pewter lid, $425-525.

c.   Mettlach, 786(2140), .5L, PUG, *Eisenbahn Regt. Nr. 3*, c.1900, pewter lid, $475-575.

d.   Mettlach, 775(2140), .5L, PUG, *Garde Kürassier*, c.1900, pewter lid, $550-700.

Opposite:

e.   *Eisenbahn Regt. Nr. 3, 8. Comp., Berlin-Schöneberg, 1908-1910*, .5L, pottery, $1100-1400.

f.   *Eisenbahn Regt. Nr. 3, 4. Comp., Hanau, 1910-1912*, .5L, pottery, $1200-1500.

g.   *Betriebs Abteilung Eisenbahn Brigade, Schöneberg-Berlin, 1900-1902*, .5L, pottery, $1100-1400.

Opposite:

a. *Feld Artillerie Regt. Nr. 10, Hannover, 1902-1905,* .5L, pottery, $450-550.

b. *Feld Artillerie Regt. Nr. 10, Hannover, 1902-1904,* .5L, pottery, $400-500.

c. *Feld Artillerie Regt. Nr. 34, Metz, 1910-1912,* 1.0L, pottery, horse and rider thumblift, $550-700.

d. *Feld Artillerie Regt. Nr. 10, Hannover, 1911-1912,* and *Feld Artillerie Regt. Nr. 80, Hagenau, 1912-1913,* 1.0L, pottery, horse and rider thumblift, $550-700.

a. *Bayr. 1. Fuss Artillerie Regt., Bespannungs Abtl., 1. Fahr. Batt., Neu-Ulm, 1908-1910,* .5L, porcelain, $550-750.

b. *Fuss Artillerie Regt. Nr. 2, Emden-Borkum, 1911-1913,* .5L, porcelain, $500-650.

c. *Feld Artillerie Regt. Nr. 55, Naumburg, 1911-1913,* .5L, porcelain, $450-575.

d. *Feld Artillerie Regt. Nr. 9, Itzehue, 1903-1905,* .5L, porcelain, porcelain inlaid lid, $700-1000.

Opposite:

e. *Feld Artillerie Regt. Nr. 15, Mörchingen, 1911-1913,* .5L, porcelain, $425-525.

f. *Feld Artillerie Regt. Nr. 26, Verden, 1907-1909,* .5L, porcelain, $450-550.

g. *Feld Artillerie Regt. Nr. 63, Mainz, 1910-1912,* .5L, porcelain, $450-550.

h. *Bayr. 2. Feld Artillerie Regt., Würzburg, 1901-1903,* .5L, porcelain, porcelain inlaid lid, $600-800.

a. *Feld Artillerie Regt. Nr. 11, Cassel, 1902-1904, .5L,
    porcelain, $325-425.*

b. *Feld Artillerie Regt. Nr. 48, Dresden, 1902-1904,
    .5L, porcelain, $375-475.*

c. *Feld Artillerie Regt. Nr. 49, Ulm, 1899-1901, .5L,
    porcelain, $250-350.*

d. *Feld Artillerie Regt. Nr. 66, Lahr, 1902-1903, .5L,
    porcelain, $325-425.*

a. *Garde Feld Artillerie Regt. Reitende Batterie, Berlin, 1906-1909*, .5L, porcelain, $500-650.

b. *Garde Fuss Artillerie Regt., Spandau, 1906-1908*, .5L, porcelain, $500-650.

c. *Fuss Artillerie Regt. Nr. 8, Bespannungs Abtl., Metz, 1904-1906*, .5L, porcelain, $500-700.

d. *Bayr. Feld Artillerie Regt. Nr. 8, Nürnberg, 1910-1912*, and *Oberfeuerverlasschule, München, 1912*, .5L, stoneware, pewter crown lid covers glass dome, under glass dome is cannon and crew, $1200-1500.

Opposite:

e. *Garde Fuss Artillerie Regt., Spandau, 1903-1905*, .5L, porcelain, one large scene wraps around entire stein, $550-750.

f. *3. Garde Feld Artillerie Regt., Berlin, 1904-1906*, .5L, porcelain, $450-550.

g. *Feld Artillerie Regt. Nr. 70*, and *Schiess-Schule, Jüterbog, 1906-1908*, .5L, porcelain, $450-600.

h. *Feld Artillerie Regt. Nr. 29, Ludwigsburg, 1905-1907*, .5L, porcelain, $350-450.

Opposite:

a. *Telegraphen Batl. Nr. 4, Funker Abteilung, Karlsruhe, 1911-1913*, .5L, stoneware, $400-600.

b. *1. Komp. Telegraphen Detachement, München, 1908-1910*, .5L, stoneware, $600-800.

c. *Bayr. 2. Telegraphen Batl., 2 (Funker) Comp., München, 1912-1914*, .5L, porcelain, lid unscrews to reveal scene of Munich in pewter, $1800-2200.

a. *Telegraphen Batl. Nr. 1, Berlin, 1906-1908*, .5L, porcelain, $1200-1400.

b. *Telegraphen Batl. Nr. 2, Frankfurt, 1905-1907*, .5L, porcelain, $1300-1600.

c. *Telegraphen Batl. Nr. 3, Coblenz, 1899-1901*, .5L, porcelain, $1400-1700.

d. *Telegraphen Batl. Nr. 5, 4. (Funker) Comp., 1911-1913*, .5L, porcelain, $1500-1900.

Opposite:

d. *Telegraphen Batl. Nr. 3, Coblenz, 1900-1902*, .5L, pottery, $1100-1300.

e. *Telegraphen Batl. Nr. 3, Coblenz, 1905-1907*, .5L, pottery, $1400-1700.

f. *Telegraphen Batl. Nr. 4, Karlsruhe, 1907-1909*, .5L, porcelain, $1300-1600.

Opposite:

a. *Leib Garde Husaren Regt., Leib Esk., Potsdam, 1904-1907*, .5L, pottery, $900-1100.

b. *2. Leib Husaren Regt., Posen* and *Danzig-Langfuhr, 1896-1899*, .5L, porcelain, $1100-1400.

c. *Husaren Regt. Nr. 3, Rathenow, 1908-1911*, .5L, pottery, $700-900.

d. *Husaren Regt. Nr. 4, Ohlau, 1910-1913*, .5L, porcelain, $900-1100.

a. *Husaren Regt. Nr. 8, Paderborn, 1900-1903*, .5L, porcelain, $600-800.

b. *Husaren Regt. Nr. 12, Torgau, 1906-1909*, .5L, porcelain, $550-700.

c. *Husaren Regt. Nr. 13, Mainz, 1900-1903*, .5L, porcelain, $550-700.

d. *Husaren Regt. Nr. 15, Wandsbeck, 1904-1907*, .5L, porcelain, $600-800.

e. *Husaren Regt. Nr. 7, Bonn, 1908-1910*, .5L, pottery, $700-900.

f. *Husaren Regt. Nr. 9, Straßburg, 1909-1912*, .5L, pottery, $750-1000.

g. *Husaren Regt. Nr. 11, Krefeld, 1908-1911*, .5L, pottery, $800-1100.

h. *Husaren Regt. Nr. 16, Schleswig, 1904-1907*, .5L, pottery, $700-900.

a.   *Dragoner Regt. Nr. 5, Hofgeismar, 1910-1913,* .5L, pottery, $700-950.

b.   *Dragoner Regt. Nr. 13, Metz, 1908-1911,* 1.0L, pottery, $650-850.

c.   *Dragoner Regt. Nr. 14, Colmar i. Els,* 1.0L, pottery, $700-900.

d.   *Dragoner Regt. Nr. 15, Hagenau, 1907-1910,* .5L, pottery, $650-850.

e.   *Husaren Regt. Nr. 17, Braunschweig, 1908-1911,* .5L, pottery skull, $1600-1900.

a.   *Dragoner Regt. Nr. 6, Mainz, 1907-1910, .5L,*
     porcelain, $550-750.

b.   *Dragoner Regt. Nr. 9, Metz, 1906-1909, .5L,*
     porcelain, $550-750.

c.   *Dragoner Regt. Nr. 21, Schwetzingen, 1910-1913,*
     .5L, porcelain, $550-750.

d.   *Dragoner Regt. Nr. 22, Mülhausen, 1904-1907, .5L,*
     porcelain, $550-750.

e.   *1. Garde Dragoner Regt., Berlin, 1903-1906, .5L,*
     pottery, $1000-1300.

f.   *2. Garde Dragoner Regt., Berlin, 1909-1912, .5L,*
     pottery, $1100-1400.

a. *Dragoner Regt Nr. 7, Saarbrücken, 1904-1907, .5L,*
   pottery, $600-800.

b. *Dragoner Regt. Nr. 13, Metz, 1904-1908, .5L,*
   porcelain, $600-750.

c. *Dragoner Regt. Nr. 15, Hagenau, 1910-1913, .5L,*
   porcelain, $600-750.

d. *Dragoner Regt. Nr. 9, Metz, 1902-1905, .5L,*
   pottery, $600-800.

e. *Dragoner Regt. Nr. 23, Darmstadt, 1907-1910, .5L,*
   porcelain, $600-800.

a. *Bayr. 2. Chevaulegers Regt., Dillingen-Regensburg, 1908-1911*, .5L, porcelain, finial unscrews to reveal photo locket, $600-750.

b. *Bayr. 3. Chevaulegers Regt., Dieuze, 1909-1912*, .5L, porcelain, $650-850.

c. *Bayr. 5. Chevaulegers Regt., Saargemund, 1909-1912*, .5L, porcelain, $475-625.

d. *Bayr. 8. Chevaulegers Regt., Dillingen, 1911-1914*, .5L, porcelain, lid unscrews to reveal prism, finial unscrews to reveal photo locket, $750-1000.

e. *Bayr. 1. Schweres Reiter Regt., München, 1916-1919*, .5L, porcelain, $500-700.

f. *Bayr. 1. Schweres Reiter Regt., München, 1910-1913*, .5L, porcelain, finial unscrews to reveal photo of owner, $550-750.

Opposite:

a. *Ulanen Regt. Nr. 20, Ludwigsburg, 1910-1913,* .5L, porcelain, $600-750.

b. *Ulanen Regt. Nr. 21, Chemnitz, 1908-1911,* .5L, porcelain, $700-900.

c. *Bayr. 1. Ulanen Regt., Bamberg, 1903-1906,* .5L, porcelain, $500-700.

d. *Bayr. 2. Ulanen Regt., Ansbach, 1911-1914,* .5L, porcelain, lid unscrews to reveal relief pewter scene, $600-800.

a. *Ulanen Regt. Nr. 5, Düsseldorf, 1906-1909,* .5L, pottery, $600-750.

b. *Ulanen Regt. Nr. 7, Saarbrücken, 1904-1907,* .5L, pottery, $600-800.

c. *Ulanen Regt. Nr. 11, Saarburg, 1902-1905,* .5L, pottery, $600-750.

d. *Ulanen Regt. Nr. 15, Saarburg, 1906-1909,* .5L, pottery, $600-750.

Opposite:

e. *1. Garde Ulanen Regt., Potsdam, 1909-1912,* 1.0L, pottery, $1100-1400.

f. *2. Garde Ulanen Regt., Berlin, 1905-1908,* .5L, pottery, $800-1000.

g. *3. Garde Ulanen Regt., Potsdam,* undated, .5L, porcelain, $800-1000.

h. *Ulanen Regt. Nr. 1, Militsch, 1901-1904,* .5L, porcelain, $900-1100.

Opposite:

a. *Sächsisches Karabinier Regt., Borna, 1908-1911,* .5L, porcelain, $1400-1700.

b. *Sächsisches Garde Reiter Regt., Dresden, 1901-1904,* .5L, pottery, $1400-1700.

c. *Regiment der Gardes du Corps, Potsdam, 1907-1910,* .5L, pottery, $1000-1200.

d. *Kürassier Regt. Nr. 5, Riesenburg, 1896-1899,* .5L, pottery, $1000-1300.

a. *Jäger Regt. zu Pferde, Nr. 3, Colmar, 1908-1911,* 1.0L, porcelain, $1200-1500.

b. *Jäger Regt. zu Pferde, Nr. 4, Graudenz, 1909-1912,* .5L, pottery, $1200-1500.

c. *Jäger Regt. zu Pferde, Nr. 7, Trier, 1913-1914* and *Ulanen Regt. Nr. 13, Hannover, 1911-1913,* .5L, pottery, $1200-1500.

d. *Jäger Regt. zu Pferde, Nr. 13, Saarlouis* and *Dragoner Regt. Nr. 22, Mülhausen, 1911-1914,* .5L, porcelain, $1100-1400.

Opposite:

e. *Garde Kürassier Regt., Berlin, 1900-1903,* .5L, pottery, $900-1100.

f. *Kürassier Regt. Nr. 2, Pasewalk, 1911-1914,* 1.0L, pottery, $1400-1700.

g. *Kürassier Regt. Nr. 4, Munster, 1909-1912,* .5L, pottery, $1000-1200.

h. *Kürassier Regt. Nr. 5, Riesenburg, 1909-1912,* 1.0L, pottery, $1300-1600.

Opposite:

a. *Jäger Regt. zu Pferde, Nr. 8, Trier, 1913-1915*, and *Husaren Regt. Nr. 14, Cassel, 1912-1913*, .5L, pottery, $1300-1700.

b. *Jäger Regt. zu Pferde, Nr. 2, Langensalza, 1911-1914*, .5L, porcelain, $1000-1200.

c. *Jäger Regt. zu Pferde, VI Armee Korps, Posen, 1901-1904*, .5L, porcelain, $900-1100.

d. *Eskadron Jäger zu Pferde, XII Armee Korps, Dresden, 1899-1902*, .5L, porcelain, $1200-1500.

a *Infanterie Regt. Nr. 134, Plauen, 1906*, and *Militär Bäcker Abteilung des 2. Armeekorps Nr. 19, Riesa*, .5L, porcelain, $1000-1300.

b. *Militärbäckerie, Ulm, 1907-1909*, .5L, porcelain, $800-1000.

c. *Militär Bäcker Abteilung, Darmstadt, 1895-1897*, .5L, porcelain, $700-900.

Opposite:

e. *Garde Eskadron Jäger zu Pferde, Potsdam, 1900-1903*, .5L, porcelain, $1200-1500.

f. *Meldereiter Detachement XI Armee Korps, Langensalza, 1900-1903*, .5L, porcelain, $900-1200.

g. *Jäger Regt. zu Pferde, Nr. 5, Mülhausen* and *Husaren Regt. Nr. 3, Rathanow, 1906-1909*, .5L, porcelain, $1100-1400.

h. *Jäger Regt. zu Pferde, Nr. 11, Tarnowitz, 1913-1915*, and *Husaren Regt. Nr. 12, Torgau, 1912-1913*, .5L, pottery, $1200-1500.

a.   *Luftschiffer Abteilung, München, 1904-1906, .5L,
     stoneware, $2500-3000.*

c.   *Luftschiffer Abteilung, München, 1906-1908, .5L,
     stoneware, $2800-3400.*

b.   *Luftschiffer Abteilung, München, 1901-1903, .5L,
     stoneware, $2500-3000.*

d.   *Luftschiffer u. Kraftfahr Bataillon,
     München Kraftfahr Komp. Reserve, 1912-
     1914*, .5L, stoneware, $1600-2000.

e.   *Luftschiffer Batl., 2. Comp., Berlin, 1901-
     1903*, .5L, pottery, $2600-3200.

a.   *Bayr. 20. Infanterie Regt., Radfahr Detach., München, 1899*, .5L, porcelain, $3500-4500.

b.   *Infanterie Regt. Nr. 145, Kraftfahrer Abteilung, Metz, 1910-1912*, .5L, porcelain, $3500-4500.

c.   *Bayr. 10. Infanterie Regt. Ingolstadt* and *Bezirk-skomando, Dillingen*, undated, .5L, porcelain, $1100-1400.

d.   *Bekleidungsamt XI Armeekorps, Handwerker Abtl., Cassel, 1901-1903*, .5L, porcelain, $800-1100.

e.   *Bezirkskomando, Heidelberg, 1912-1914*, .5L, pottery, $1400-1800.

a. *Bayr. 13. Infanterie Regt., Ingolstadt, 1904-1906,* named to *Sanitätsgefreiter*, .5L, stoneware, one side has medical scene, $1500-2000.

b. *Garnisons Lazarett, Bamberg, 1912-1914,* .5L, porcelain, $1100-1400.

c. *Bayr. Infanterie Regt. Nr. 3, Augsburg, 1903-1905,* named to *Sanitätsgefreiter*, .5L, porcelain, medical scene on one side and under prism, $1200-1600.

d. *Bayr. 15. Infanterie Regt., Neuburg, 1900-1902,* named to *Sanitätsgefreiter*, .5L, porcelain, two medical scenes in side panels, $1600-2200.

a. *97. Lehrgang der Heeres Lehrschmiede, München, undated, c.1905, .5L, porcelain, $700-900.*

b. *Infanterie Regt. Nr. 181, Chemnitz, 1911-1912, named to Krankentrager, .5L, porcelain, $700-1000.*

c. *Garnisons Lazarett, III Armeekorps, Erlangen, 1912-1914, .5L, porcelain, medical scenes in side panels and under prism, $1400-1700.*

d. *Kaiserlichen Schutztruppe Deutsch Sud West Afrika, 1904-1906, Feldzug, .5L, porcelain, $3500-4500.*

e. *Armierungs Bn., Bayr. III Armeekorps, 4. Komp, Ingolstadt, 1914-1915, .5L, porcelain, $1600-2000.*

f. *Bespannungs Abteilung d. Kgl. Bayr. Verkehrstruppen, München, 1910-1912, .5L, porcelain, $1800-2200.*

a.   *S.M.S. Drache, 1908-1911*, .5L, porcelain,
$900-1100.

c.   *S.M.S. Kaiser Wilhelm der Grosse*, undated, .5L,
porcelain, $800-1000.

b.   *S.M.S. Wettin, 1905-1908*, .5L, porcelain,
$900-1100.

d.   *S.M.S. Niobe, 1905-1908*, .5L, porcelain,
$850-1100.

a.   *Matrosen Artillerie, Tsingtau, 1910-1913*, 1.0L,
     pottery, $2400-3000.

b.   *S.M.S. Kaiser Friedrich III, 1901-1904*, .5L, pottery,
     $650-850.

c.   *5. Matrosen Artillerie Abteilung, Helgoland, 1911-
     1914*, .5L, porcelain, lid unscrews to reveal
     porcelain with scene of Helgoland, $2000-2500.

d.   *Telegraphen Zug, II See Bataillon, Wilhelmshaven,
     1910-1913*, .5L, porcelain, $1800-2200.

Opposite:

e.   *S.M.S. Westfalen, 1911-1914*, 1.0L, pottery,
     $1100-1400.

f.   *S.M.S. Hessen* and *S.M.S. Nassau, 1908-1911*,
     1.0L, pottery, $1000-1300.

g.   *S.M.S. Hamburg, 1906-1909*, 1.0L, pottery,
     $900-1200.

h.   *II See Bataillon, Wilhelmshaven, 1907-1910*, .5L,
     pottery, $1800-2300.

Opposite:

a. *S.M.S. Oldenburg* and *S.M.S. Schlesien, 1910-1913*, 1.0L, pottery, $1200-1500.

b. *S.M.S. Pommern, 1912-1915*, 1.0L, pottery, $1300-1600.

c. *S.M.S. Helgoland, 1912-1915*, 1.0L, pottery, lid unscrews to reveal porcelain with scene of Helgoland, $1300-1600.

d. *S.M.S. Frederich Karl, 1910-1913*, 1.0L, pottery, $1100-1400.

a. *S.M.S. Hohenzollern, 1907-1910*, 1.0L, pottery, $1000-1300.

b. *S.M.S. Kaiser Barbarossa, 1905-1908*, .5L, pottery, $800-1000.

c. *S.M.S. Braunschweig, 1906-1908*, .5L, pottery, $800-1000.

d. *S.M.S. Pfeil, 1906-1909*, .5L, pottery, unusual front scene, $1100-1400.

Opposite:

e. *S.M.S. Schleswig Holstein, 1910-1913*, 1.0L, pottery, $1000-1300.

f. *S.M.S. Nassau, 1909-1912*, 1.0L, pottery, $1000-1300.

g. *S.M.S. Kaiser Karl der Grosse, 1908-1909* and *S.M.S. Braunschweig, 1909-1911*, 1.0L, pottery, $1000-1300.

h. *S.M.S. Rheinland, 1909-1912*, 1.0L, pottery, $950-1250.

a.   *Maschinengewehr Zug, II See Bataillon, Wilhelmshaven, 1911-1914*, .5L, porcelain, $1800-2200.

b.   *S.M.S. Gneisenau, 1909-1912*, 1.0L, pottery, Neptune figural lid, $2000-2400.

c.   *S.M.S. Stuttgart, 1909-1912*, 1.0L, porcelain, $1400-1800.

14. Military

The history of the military steins covered in this chapter begins on June 28, 1914, when Archduke Francis Ferdinand of Austria-Hungary and his wife were murdered in Bosnia, triggering events leading to World War I.

World War I steins, as covered in this chapter, are of two general types. The first type are commemorative, mostly made in 1914 when the war was going well for Germany. These steins usually feature an Iron Cross. The second type are military steins for a specific unit, often dated with *Weihnachten* (Christmas). World War I steins were generally much simpler in style than the previous Imperial Reservist steins. The production costs of those tall porcelain steins was just too high. The most common steins were smaller stoneware steins with print-under-glaze *decals,* steins that were generally from the Höhr-Grenzhausen area factories. With the German defeat, and the revolt against the Imperial system, it is not surprising that relatively few German wartime souvenirs were generated in the postwar era.

The Reichswehr (German military 1919-1935) Army steins are also frequently found with a Christmas date, and are occasionally marked with twelve-year service intervals. Single date and undated versions also exist that were used for birthdays, anniversaries, weddings, and other occasions during the service period. These steins are usually ivory stoneware or gray salt-glazed stoneware, produced mainly in the Westerwald region. They are mostly 0.4 or 0.5 liter, with print-under-glaze decorations, and pewter or nickel-plated lids. Some steins during this period were made as commemorative pieces for Imperial or World War I veterans' organization meetings. These veterans'

meetings were held beginning in about 1920 and ending in 1933, when they were declared to be illegal by the government.

With regard to steins, it is important to note that on March 16, 1935 there was an official name change from the Reichswehr Army to the *Deutsche Wehrmacht,* or Nazi army. With the increased national pride at this time there was an increase in the production of military steins, usually of the smaller stoneware types. From 1936 to 1939, the most prolific production of military steins of any period between 1914 and 1945 took place. Most of these were of the 0.5 liter size and were made from stoneware. Those that are found to have manufacturers' marks are usually from Wick-Werke, Merkelbach, and Marzi & Remy. The Mettlach factory produced a few commemorative military steins during this period.

Then, beginning in September 1939, and while the war was expanding, the production of steins was greatly reduced. That there were any steins produced at all shows that they were considered to be important morale boosters. There are even fewer examples of steins dated in the period from 1941 through 1944 that still exist today. One can only speculate, however, on how many were actually produced. Most soldiers who were among the invading forces have recalled that Nazi and other steins too large to pocket as souvenirs, were methodically destroyed wherever they were encountered.

From 1918 through the early 1920's, and again from 1945 through the early 1960's, American soldiers purchased steins as souvenirs of their service. While the porcelain 0.5 liter steins of the 1950's are fairly common, earlier military steins are fairly hard to find.

a. Stoneware, .5L, marked Marzi & Remy, #2962, relief, blue glaze, airplanes, Nazi swastika markings on planes, c.1936, metal lid, $450-550.

b. Stoneware, .5L, marked #2882, relief, blue glaze, *Mit Gott für König und Vaterland*, pewter lid with relief Iron Cross, 1914, $200-300.

c. Stoneware, .5L, enameled, German & Austrian Alliance, pewter lid with relief Iron Cross, 1914, $250-350.

d. Stoneware, .5L, enameled, *Treu und Fest, in Ost und West*, pewter lid with relief Iron Cross, 1914, $200-300.

e. Stoneware, 1.0L, transfer, *Nachrichten Abt. 7, Weichnachten 1921*, pewter lid, $300-400.

f. Stoneware, 1.0L, transfer and enameled, Wilhelm II, German, Austrian, Turkish Alliance, *1914-1916*, pewter lid with relief Iron Cross, $300-400.

g. Pottery, 1.0L, transfer, Wilhelm I and Wilhelm II, German and Austrian eagles, *1914-1915*, pewter lid with relief Iron Cross, $250-350.

h. Porcelain, .5L, transfer, General *v. Hindenburg*, lithophane, Iron Cross, 1914, pewter lid, $150-250.

a. Stoneware, .5L, transfer, *Geb. Jäger Regt. 99, 16. (E.M.G.) Komp. Sonthofen*, c.1936, pewter lid with relief helmet with swastika, $450-550.

b. Pottery, .5L, marked Marzi & Remy, transfer, *12. (M.G.) Komp. Inf. Rgt. Lübeck*, c.1937, pewter lid with relief helmet with swastika, $450-550.

c. Pottery, .5L, transfer, *Uffz. Corps d. 5. (S.) Schwd. Reit Rgt. Brieg, 16.12.1934*, pewter lid with helmet finial, $400-500.

d. Porcelain, .5L, marked Bauscher, *7. Komp., I.R. Regensburg*, c.1937, pewter lid with impressed eagle & swastika, $250-350.

e. Stoneware, .5L, transfer, *Pferde Lazarett 107, Sonthofen, 1939-1940* (horse hospital), pewter lid with relief helmet with swastika, $450-600.

f. Pottery, .5L, transfer, *1.252., 1934-1935, Königstein*, labor service, metal lid with relief worker, $200-300.

g. Pottery, .5L, transfer, *Unteroffizier Korps der 1. Kompanie der 1. (preuß.) Kraftfahr Abteilung*, c.1932, pewter lid, $400-500.

h. Porcelain, .5L, transfer, *Reichsparteitag, Nürnberg, 1938*, pewter lid with relief scene of Nürnberg, $250-350.

a. Pottery, .5L, relief, *Army of Occupation, 148. F.A., Army Artillery*, c.1919, no lid, $80-120.

b. Pottery, .5L, transfer, *First Division Circus, Montabaur Germany, July 11 & 12, 1919*, no lid, $60-90.

c. Pottery, .125L, transfer, *2nd. Bataillon Radio Detail, Souvenir of Hoehr Germany, 1919*, no lid, $30-50.

d. Pottery, .5L, *440 th. AAABN, On the Rhine in 1945*, no lid, $80-120.

e. Pottery, .5L, transfer, *110th Infantry Regiment, Ulm/Donau, 1951-1952*, pewter lid with relief combat infantry badge, army eagle thumblift, $150-250.

f. Porcelain, .5L, American military, *Naval Air Facility, Naples Italy*, 1950's, pewter lid, $40-70.

g. Porcelain, .5L, American military, *Headquarters Twelfth Air Force, Germany, 1956-1959*, pewter lid, $40-70.

15. Characters

A *character* stein is a stein with a shape designed to represent an object, person, or animal. So, like occupationals and Regimentals it is a *style* category, as opposed to the *materials* categories described in most of the other sections.

15.1 History and Production

Although figural vessels date back to several centuries before the Greeks, true character steins had to await the development of the hinged lid, in the early 1500's. And, in fact, there *are* stoneware character steins that date from about that period, generally in the form of owls or seated bears, but they are quite rare.

One can only speculate as to why there are so few character steins that pre-date the late 1800's. One theory is that the odd shapes were too whimsical to be socially acceptable in earlier times. The other popular theory is that there was just too much effort required to produce these *statuettes* before the introduction, in the late 1800's, of molds that could more easily accommodate such shapes, such as the slip molds described in Subsection 2.3.

Some of the character steins that appeared around the 1850's were dull-finished bisque porcelain pieces that were made in slip molds. Among the most common are various varieties of skulls, purchased by medical students, secret societies, and some fraternities, among others. Many have been identified as having been made by *E. Bohne Söhne* of the Thuringen region, a factory that started in 1854. This factory, along with others in Plaue are believed to be responsible for much of the initial manufacture of character steins.

Beginning in the 1870's, several other factories that produced character steins were *founded*, but they probably did not actually begin *production* of character steins until the 1880's. Some of these include: Merkelbach & Wick, Dümler & Breiden, Reinhold Merkelbach, Simon Peter Gerz, and Marzi & Remy. The Villeroy & Boch factory at Mettlach began producing character steins around 1892. Marks from these factories are shown at the end of Section 2.

The commonly seen *hash* or *cross hatch* mark was used by the Porzellanmanufaktur Plaue (C.G. Schierholz & Söhn). It often is accompanied by *MUSTERSCHUTZ*, which conveys the same meaning as a copyright mark. The cross hatch is most often seen in green, *MUSTERSCHUTZ* in blue.

The Plaue factory has long been associated with *lithophane* manufacture, which deserves a word here. Lithophanes are the panels, occasionally found in the bottom of porcelain steins, that show a picture when put up to a source of light. The darker or lighter areas are accomplished with thicker or thinner areas of porcelain.

Lithophanes were designed by first putting a layer of translucent beeswax on a pane of glass with a light underneath. The wax was carved until the desired scene was completed, then the wax was used to make the plaster mold for the base of the stein. On rare occasions, steins can be found on which colored glazes have been used to tint the outside of the lithophane, which then shows a subtly colored scene when viewed.

While many character steins are made of porcelain there are also other important materials. Next to porcelain the most common is stoneware, often also slip molded, but occasionally stoneware steins are seen that were pressed into molds. These stoneware steins were mostly decorated with blue or purple saltglazes, or a kind of blackish combination. Brown and green saltglazes were also known in the late 1800's, and are sometimes seen on stoneware character steins.

Various kinds of pottery, earthenware, and pewter round out the character stein materials that are occasionally encountered.

Many of the *porcelain* character steins can be found with more than one distinct coloring pattern. The most common example is a tan and brown stein that is frequently known to exist in a full color version and in blues. The blue and white versions are sometimes thinner and may have been produced with a slightly different porcelain recipe. Some of these are so delicate that it is easy to imagine that they were intended only as decorative items.

15.2 Collecting Characters

Unlike many occupational steins, individual character steins were often produced in such numbers that a collector can often seek out and find a particular stein. This affects collecting strategies.

For one thing it makes *condition* more important on the *common* steins. When an example is known to be available in better condition, the price of less perfect ones often has to be discounted more in order to make a transaction.

In addition, with several of the same stein available, a market price establishes itself for specific character steins. And it is not a market that lends itself to any kind of formulas. *Rarity* is probably the most important determinant of this market price, but rarity cannot be determined by looking at a character stein. Even the absurd looking steins, like the radishes, can be relatively common.

Aesthetic appeal, although it can be judged by looking at a stein, is not always a good indicator of high market price. In fact, it sometimes seems that the most attractive character steins are often relatively common, and thus lower in price.

Guide to photos:

	Page	
Faces of people		278 to 284
Figures of people		285 to 302
Radishes & Skulls		303 to 305
Animal faces		306 to 307
Animal figures		308 to 318
Athletic items		319 to 323
Miscellaneous		322 to 327
Barrels		325
Towers		328 to 331
Monks, Nuns, Munich Child		331 to 336

a. Von Moltke, .5L, porcelain, marked MUSTER-SCHUTZ (Schierholz), tan colors, c.1900, $900-1300.

b. Soldier, .5L, porcelain, marked MUSTER-SCHUTZ (Schierholz), tan colors, c.1900, $900-1300.

c. Soldier, .5L, porcelain, marked MUSTER-SCHUTZ (Schierholz), tan colors, c.1900, $1000-1400.

d. Chinese-German Soldier, .5L, porcelain, marked MUSTERSCHUTZ (Schierholz), tan colors, c.1900, $1800-2300.

a. Wilhelm I, .5L, porcelain, marked MUSTER-
    SCHUTZ (Schierholz), tan colors, c.1900,
    $900-1300.

b. Wilhelm II, .5L, porcelain, marked MUSTER-
    SCHUTZ (Schierholz), tan colors, c.1900,
    $1500-2000; full color version, $4000-5000.

c. Wilhelm II, .5L, porcelain, marked MUSTER-
    SCHUTZ (Schierholz), tan colors, c.1900,
    $900-1300.

d. Frederich III, .5L, porcelain, marked MUSTER-
    SCHUTZ (Schierholz), tan colors, c.1900,
    $2000-2500.

e. Bismarck, .4L, stoneware, by Whites of Utica,
    blue saltglaze, c.1900, $350-450.

f. Bismarck, .5L, porcelain, marked with cross hatch
    mark, full color, c.1950, $200-300.

g. Bismarck, .5L, porcelain, marked MUSTER-
    SCHUTZ (Schierholz), tan colors, c.1900,
    $500-650; .3L, $400-500; .5L, marked MUSTER-
    SCHUTZ, full color version, $4000-5000; .5L,
    blue & white, $700-900.

h. Bismarck in Retirement, .5L, porcelain, marked
    MUSTERSCHUTZ (Schierholz), tan colors,
    c.1900, $900-1300.

a. Soldier, .5L, porcelain, marked #1932, full color, c.1900, $1000-1400.

b. Soldier, .5L, porcelain, unmarked, full color, various colors exist to depict different regiment uniforms, c.1900, $1000-1400.

c. Student Duelist, .5L, porcelain, marked Brüder Traubnauber, München, full color, lithophane, c.1900, $1100-1500.

d. Alpine Man, .5L, porcelain, unmarked, full color, lithophane, c.1900, $700-1000.

e. Man in the Moon, .5L, porcelain, marked E. Bohne Söhne, tan colors, c.1900, $700-1000; .4L, $700-1000; .3L, $600-750.

f. Target Lady, .5L, porcelain, unmarked, reddish brown & white, c.1900, $800-1100.

g. Von Zeppelin, .5L, porcelain, unmarked, full color, c.1900, $1500-2000.

h. Black Man, 1.0L, porcelain, unmarked, full color, c.1900, $1000-1400; .5L version with different lid, $1000-1400.

i. English Sailor, .125L, porcelain, unmarked, full color, c.1900, $700-1000.

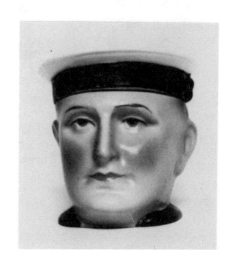

a. Father Jahn, 1.0L, porcelain, marked MUSTER-SCHUTZ (Schierholz), tan colors, c.1900, $1200-1600; .5L, $1000-1400; 1.0L, blue & white version, $1500-2000.

b. Father Jahn, .5L, porcelain, marked MUSTER-SCHUTZ (Schierholz), tan colors, c.1900, $1000-1400.

c. Masquerade Lady, .5L, porcelain, marked MUSTERSCHUTZ (Schierholz), tan colors, c.1900, $2600-3400.

d. Uncle Sam, .5L, porcelain, marked MUSTER-SCHUTZ (Schierholz), tan colors, c.1900, $1400-1800; full color version, $4000-5000.

e. Heidelberg Teacher, .5L, porcelain, marked MUSTERSCHUTZ (Schierholz), tan colors, c.1900, $1100-1500; .5L, with music box, $1200-1600.

f. Heidelberg Student, .5L, porcelain, marked MUSTERSCHUTZ (Schierholz), tan colors, c.1900, $1100-1500; .5L, with music box, $1200 - 1600.

g. Pixie, .5L, porcelain, marked MUSTERSCHUTZ (Schierholz), tan colors, c.1900, $700-900; .5L, with music box base, $900-1300.

h. Judge, .5L, porcelain, marked MUSTERSCHUTZ (Schierholz), tan colors, platinum colored lid, c.1900, $600-800.

a. Hops Lady, .5L, porcelain, marked MUSTER-
    SCHUTZ (Schierholz), tan colors, c.1900,
    $600-750; blue & white version, $800-1100.

b. Caroline, .5L, porcelain, marked MUSTER-
    SCHUTZ (Schierholz), tan colors, c.1900,
    $600-750; full color version, $1400-1800.

c. Chinaman, .5L, porcelain, marked MUSTER-
    SCHUTZ (Schierholz), tan colors, c.1900,
    $600-800; .3L, $450-600.

d. Chinaman, .5L, porcelain, marked J. Reinemann,
    München, yellow, red & black, lithophane, c.1900,
    pewter lid, $500-650.

a. Scotsman, .5L, stoneware, marked LB&C, blue saltglaze, c.1900, $600-800.

b. Swiss Soldier, .5L, stoneware, marked LB&C, blue saltglaze, c.1900, $600-800.

c. Russian Soldier, .5L, stoneware, marked LB&C, blue saltglaze, c.1900, $600-800.

d. Knight, .5L, stoneware, unmarked, blue & purple saltglazes, c.1900, $500-700; tan version, $400 - 600.

Opposite middle:

e. Potato Head, .5L, porcelain, marked MUSTER-SCHUTZ (Schierholz), full color, c.1900, $1800-2300.

f. Smiling Woman, .5L, porcelain, marked MUSTERSCHUTZ (Schierholz), full color, c.1900, $2000-2600.

g. Woodsman, .5L, porcelain, marked MUSTERSCHUTZ (Schierholz), brown & gray, c.1900, $1200-1600.

h. Racing Driver, .5L, porcelain, bisque glaze probably by E. Bohne Söhne, gray & orange, glass eyes, c.1900, $800-1100; .3L, $600-800; 1.0L, $1000-1400.

Opposite bottom:

i. Indian Chief, .5L, porcelain, bisque glaze, marked E. Bohne Söhne, full color, c.1900, $600-750.

j. Indian Chief, .25L, porcelain, bisque glaze, marked E. Bohne Söhne, full color, c.1900, $400-500.

k. Devil, .5L, porcelain, bisque glaze, marked E. Bohne Söhne, full color, c.1900, $600-750; .25L, $400-500.

l. Tipsy Monk, .5L, porcelain, bisque glaze, marked E. Bohne Söhne, full color, c.1900, $700-900; .25L, $500-650.

e. Woman, .5L, pottery, marked D.R.G.M. (Diesinger), #702, full color, early 1900's, $250-350.

f. Student, .5L, pottery, marked D.R.G.M. (Diesinger), #704, full color, early 1900's, $250-350.

a. Hops Lady, .5L, pottery, marked #1424 (by Steinzeugwerke), full color, early 1900's, pewter lid, $120-180.

b. Man with Duck in Mouth, .5L, pottery, marked #692, probably by Diesinger, full color, early 1900's, $250-350.

c. Student, .5L, pottery, marked Eckhardt & Engler, full color, 1920's, $250-350; version marked #426 (by Rosskopf & Gerz), early 1900's, $275-375.

d. Mother-in-Law, .5L, pottery, marked #1457 (by Steinzeugwerke), full color, early 1900's, pewter lid, $175-275.

Above:

e. Egyptian, .5L, pottery, marked #431 (by Rosskopf & Gerz), full color, early 1900's, $250-350. A later version made by Eckhardt & Engler.

f. Uncomfortable Burger, .5L, pottery, marked #1426 (by Steinzeugwerke), full color, early 1900's, pewter lid, $150-225.

g. Man with Pipe, .5L, pottery, marked #1425 (by Steinzeugwerke), full color, early 1900's, pewter lid, $140-200.

h. Man with Pipe, .5L, pottery, marked #1459 (by Steinzeugwerke), full color, early 1900's, pewter lid, $150-250.

a. Sea Captain, .5L, porcelain, marked MUSTER-
    SCHUTZ (Schierholz), tan colors, c.1900,
    $800-1100.

b. Alpine Man, .5L, porcelain, marked MUSTER-
    SCHUTZ (Schierholz), tan colors, c.1900,
    $900-1200; full color version, $2000-2600.

c. Barmaid, .5L, porcelain, marked MUSTER-
    SCHUTZ (Schierholz), tan colors, c.1900,
    $1200-1600.

d. Turkish Man, .5L, porcelain, marked MUSTER-
    SCHUTZ (Schierholz), tan colors, c.1900,
    $800-1100; full color version, $2000-2600.

e. Judge, .5L, porcelain, marked MUSTERSCHUTZ
    (Schierholz), tan colors, jester thumblift, c.1900,
    $1000-1400; blue & white version, $1300-1700.

f. Burgermeister, .5L, porcelain, marked MUSTER-
    SCHUTZ (Schierholz), tan colors, c.1900,
    $700-1000.

g. Landlord, .5L, porcelain, unmarked, tan colors,
    c.1900, $700-900; full color version, $900-1200.

h. Perkeo, .5L, porcelain, unmarked, full color, c.1900,
    $700-1000.

Opposite:

i. Man, .5L, pottery, marked Eckhardt & Engler,
    #428, red, green & brown, c.1900, $300-400;
    earlier version by Rosskopf & Gerz

j. Woman, .5L, pottery, marked Eckhardt & Engler,
    #429, tan, brown & yellow, c.1900, $300-400;
    earlier version by Rosskopf & Gerz.

a.   Schoolteacher, .5L, porcelain, marked M. Pauson, München, full color, bisque glaze, lithophane, c.1900, $1100-1400.

b.   Schoolteacher, .5L, porcelain, marked M. Pauson, München, full color, bisque glaze, lithophane, c.1900, $1100-1400.

c.   Falstaff, 1.0L, porcelain, unmarked, tan colors, c.1900, $700-900; full color version, $900-1200.

d.   Sleepy Hunter, .5L, porcelain, unmarked, full color, c.1900, $900-1200; tan color version, $700-900.

e.   Dutch Girl, .5L, porcelain, marked MUSTER-SCHUTZ (Schierholz), blue & white, c.1900, $700-1000; full color version, $1300-1700.

f.   Dutch Boy, .5L, porcelain, marked MUSTER-SCHUTZ (Schierholz), blue & white, c.1900, $700-1000; full color version, $1200-1600.

g.   Moneybags, .5L, porcelain, marked #403, H. Hutschenreuther, full color, c.1912, $400-550.

h.   Baby, .25L, porcelain, unmarked, full color, c.1900, $1000-1300; .5L, $1200-1600; .125L, $700-1000.

a. Gooseman of Nürnberg, .5L, porcelain, marked MUSTERSCHUTZ (Schierholz), tan colors, lithophane, c.1900, $800-1100.

b. Gooseman of Nürnberg, .5L, porcelain, unmarked, full color, lithophane, c.1900, $450-600.

c. Gooseman of Nürnberg, .5L, porcelain, unmarked, full color, bisque glaze, c.1900, $1200-1600; .25L, $900-1200.

d. Gooseman of Nürnberg, .5L, porcelain, unmarked, green/bronze color, c.1900, $700-900; .25L, $500-700.

e. Heidelberg Black Student, .5L, porcelain, unmarked, full color, lithophane, c.1900, $350-500.

f. Heidelberg Student, .5L, porcelain, marked with cross hatch mark, full color, c.1950, $250-350.

g. Student, .5L, pottery, marked #425 (by Rosskopf & Gerz), full color, c.1900, $200-300; later version by Eckhardt & Engler.

h. Wizard, .5L, pottery, marked #389, Merkelbach & Wick, black, blue & brown, early 1900's, $250-350.

a. Bismarck, .5L, porcelain, unmarked, full color, white coat, lithophane, c.1900, $700-900.

b. Bismarck, .5L, stoneware, marked Merkelbach & Wick, purple saltglaze, early 1900's, $400-500.

c. Bismarck, .5L, pottery, unmarked, by Dümler & Breiden, black, red & green, c.1900, $400-500.

d. Ludwig II, .5L, pottery, marked #935 (by Marzi & Remy), brown, black & tan, c.1900, $450-600.

e. Wilhelm I, .5L, stoneware, marked #809 (by Marzi & Remy), blue & purple saltglazes, c.1900, $450-550.

f. Wilhelm I, .5L, stoneware, unmarked, by Marzi & Remy, blue & purple saltglazes, c.1900, $500-600.

g. Wilhelm I, .5L, stoneware, marked #583 (by Reinhold Hanke), blue saltglaze, c.1900, $450-550.

h. Wilhelm I, .5L, pottery, marked #13, brown, black & tan, c.1900, $450-550.

Above, top row, left to right:

a.   Wilhelm I, .5L, porcelain, marked MUSTERSCHUTZ (Schierholz), c.1900, $900-1300.

b.   Sea Captain, .5L, porcelain, marked MUSTER-SCHUTZ (Schierholz), c.1900, $800-1100.

c.   King Ludwig II, .5L, porcelain, unmarked, c.1900, $3000-4000.

d.   Owl, .5L, porcelain, by E. Bohne Söhne, c.1900, $1100-1400.

e.   Wrap around Alligator, .5L, porcelain, by E. Bohne Söhne, c.1900, $600-750.

Above, bottom row, left to right:

f.   Bird, .5L, porcelain, marked E. Bohne Söhne, c.1900, $1500-2000.

g.   Gentleman Rabbit, .5L, porcelain, marked MUSTERSCHUTZ (Schierholz), c.1900, $2600-3200.

h.   Umbrella Men, .5L, porcelain, unmarked, lithophane, c.1900, pewter lid, $800-1000.

i.   Barmaid, .5L, porcelain, marked MUSTERSCHUTZ (Schierholz), c.1900, $1200-1600.

j.   Munich Tower, .5L, porcelain, marked Josef Mayer, lithophane, c.1900, $1200-1600.

Opposite, left to right:

a. Black Man, .5L, porcelain, marked MUSTER-SCHUTZ (Schierholz), c.1900, $2200-2800.

b. Monkey, .5L, porcelain, marked E. Bohne Söhne, c.1900, $2000-2500.

c. Gentleman Boar, .5L, porcelain, marked MUS-TERSCHUTZ (Schierholz), c.1900, $3400-4000.

d. Bison, .5L, porcelain, by E. Bohne Söhne, c.1900, $1600-2000.

e. Mephisto, .5L, porcelain, marked MUSTERSCHUTZ (Schierholz), c.1900, $1800-2400.

Above, top row, left to right:

a. Radish Lady, .5L, porcelain, marked MUSTER-SCHUTZ (Schierholz), c.1900, $1600-2200.

b. Newspaper Lady, .5L, porcelain, marked MUSTERSCHUTZ (Schierholz), c.1900, $1600-2200.

c. Mushroom Lady, .5L, porcelain, marked MUSTERSCHUTZ (Schierholz), c.1900, $1600-2200.

d. Mushroom Lady, .5L, porcelain, marked MUSTERSCHUTZ (Schierholz), c.1900, $1600-2200.

e. Mushroom Man, .5L, porcelain, marked MUSTERSCHUTZ (Schierholz), c.1900, $1600-2200.

Above, bottom row, left to right:

f. Dutch Boy, .5L, porcelain, marked MUSTER-SCHUTZ (Schierholz), c.1900, $1200-1600.

g. Dutch Girl, .5L, porcelain, marked MUSTER-SCHUTZ (Schierholz), c.1900, $1300-1700.

h. Gooseman of Nürnberg, .5L, porcelain, unmarked, c.1900, $1200-1600.

i. Alpine Man, .5L, porcelain, marked MUSTER-SCHUTZ (Schierholz), c.1900, $2000-2600.

j. Turkish Man, .5L, porcelain, marked MUSTER-SCHUTZ (Schierholz), c.1900, $2000-2600.

Above, top row, left to right::

f.   Monkey, .5L, porcelain, marked E. Bohne Söhne, c.1900, $1300-1700.

g.   Tyrolean Man, .5L, porcelain, by E. Bohne Söhne, c.1900, $1200-1600.

h.   Clown, .5L, porcelain, marked MUSTERSCHUTZ (Schierholz), c.1900, $2200-2800.

i.   Fisherman, .5L, porcelain, marked E. Bohne Söhne, c.1900, $1200-1600.

j.   Cross-Eyed Man, .5L, porcelain, by E. Bohne Söhne, c.1900, $1200-1600.

Above, bottom row, left to right:

k.   Snowman, .5L, porcelain, marked MUSTERSCHUTZ (Schierholz), c.1900, $1500-2000.

l.   Cat, .5L, porcelain, unmarked, c.1900, $1100-1500.

m.   Cat on the Book, .5L, porcelain, by E. Bohne Söhne, c.1900, $1800-2400.

n.   Owl, .5L, porcelain, marked E. Bohne Söhne, c.1900, $1100-1500.

o.   Cucumber, .5L, porcelain, marked MUSTER-SCHUTZ (Schierholz), c.1900, $1000-1400.

Above, top row, left to right:

a. Porcelain, .5L, Rauenstein mark, hand-painted, c.1900, inlaid lid, $300-400.

b. Porcelain, .3L, hand-painted, late 1800's, inlaid lid, $250-350.

c. Porcelain, .5L, hand-painted, c.1900, inlaid lid, $250-350.

d. Porcelain, .5L, marked Belleek, Willets, hand-painted, signed MR, silver lid, $900-1200.

e. Porcelain, .5L, marked Lenox, CAC, hand-painted, early 1900's, silver lid, $1200-1600.

Above, bottom row, left to right:

f. Porcelain, 1.0L, Meissen mark, hand-painted, porcelain lid, $450-650.

g. Porcelain, 1.0L, marked K.P.M., pewter lid & footring, $400-600.

h. Porcelain, 1.0L, Chinese Export, hand-painted, late 1600's, pewter lid, $3000-4000.

i. Porcelain, 1.0L, hand-painted, middle 1800's, porcelain lid, $600-800.

Above, top row, left to right:

a. Porcelain, .5L, marked with beehive, hand-painted, c.1900, porcelain inlaid lid, $1700-2100.

b. Porcelain, .25L, marked with beehive, hand-painted, c.1900, porcelain inlaid lid, $1300-1600.

c. Porcelain, .25L, marked with beehive, hand-painted, c.1900, porcelain inlaid lid, $1300-1600.

d. Porcelain, .25L, Meissen mark, hand-painted, late 1800's, inlaid lid, $700-1000.

e. Porcelain, .5L, marked MUSTERSCHUTZ (Schierholz), relief & hand-painted, c.1900, porcelain lid, $350-500.

f. Porcelain, .5L, marked with crown over N, Capo di Monte style, middle 1800's, inlaid lid mounted on silver, $400-600.

Above, bottom row, left to right:

g. Porcelain, .5L, marked with beehive, hand-painted, c.1900, brass mountings, $1200-1600.

h. Porcelain, 1.0L, Meissen mark, hand-painted, late 1800's, porcelain lid, $1700-2200.

i. Porcelain, .5L, hand-painted, Metal worker occupation, early 1900's, pewter lid, $300-400.

j. Porcelain, .5L, hand-painted, lithophane, c.1900, pewter lid, $100-150.

k. Porcelain, .5L, hand-painted, lithophane, c.1900, pewter lid, $150-250.

Above, top row, left to right:

a.   Mettlach 2133, .5L, etched, inlaid lid, $1600-1900.

b.   Mettlach 2093, .5L, etched, Card stein, inlaid lid, $550-700.

c.   Mettlach 1062, .5L, mosaic, inlaid lid, $550-700.

d.   Mettlach 2182, .5L, relief, inlaid lid, $200-300.

e.   Mettlach 885(2140), .5L, Dragoner Regt. Nr. 16, PUG, pewter lid, $500-650.

Avove, bottom row, left to right:

f.   Mettlach 2479, .5L, cameo, Hildebrand stein, inlaid lid, $550-750.

g.   Mettlach 2640, .5L, etched, inlaid lid, $450-550.

h.   Mettlach 3143, .5L, etched, inlaid lid, $500-650.

i.   Mettlach 1797, .5L, etched, Coin stein, inlaid lid with coins, $700-900.

j.   Mettlach 1110(1909), .5L, PUG, pewter lid, $250-350.

Above, top row, left to right:

a. Stoneware, .5L, transfer, early 1900's, pewter lid, $70-100.

b. Stoneware, .45L, hand-painted, Red Cross organization, Munich, c.1915, pewter lid, $400-600.

c. Stoneware, .5L, transfer, early 1900's, pewter lid, $70-100.

d. Stoneware, .5L, transfer, design by Franz Ringer, *12. Deutsches Turnfest, Liepzig, 1913*, pewter lid with relief 4F, $350-450.

e. Stoneware, .5L, designed by Richard Riemerschmid, made by Reinhold Merkelbach, Art Nouveau, c.1910, pewter lid, $400-600.

Above, bottom row, left to right:

f. Stoneware, #207, .5L, relief, Wilhelm I, Wilhelm II, Bismarck, Von Moltke, Frederich III, early 1900's, pewter lid, $140-200.

g. Stoneware, .5L, relief, saltglaze, early 1900's, inlaid lid, $150-250.

h. Pottery, .5L, relief, early 1900's, inlaid lid, $150-250.

i. Stoneware, 1.0L, hand-painted, *General Field Marshall v.Hindenburg, 1914 to 1916*, pewter lid with Iron Cross, $350-450.

j. Stoneware, 1.0L, hand-painted, Pionier occupation, *1900-1910, Augsburg*, porcelain inlaid lid, $250-350.

a. Munich Child, .5L, porcelain, marked Martin Pauson, lithophane, c.1900, $450-550.

b. Munich Child, .5L, porcelain, marked Josef M. Mayer, lithophane, c.1900, $400-500.

c. Cavalier, 1.0L, pottery, marked #1193, early 1900's, $1200-1600.

d. Hobo, .5L, porcelain, marked E. Bohne Söhne, c.1900, $1100-1400.

e. Coffee Girl, .5L, porcelain, unmarked, c.1900, $1500-2000.

f. Dutch Girl, .5L, porcelain, marked MUSTER-SCHUTZ (Schierholz), c.1900, $700-1000.

g. Dutch Boy, .5L, porcelain, marked MUSTER-SCHUTZ (Schierholz), c.1900, $700-1000.

h. Bismarck, .5L, porcelain, marked MUSTERSCHUTZ (Schierholz), c.1900, $700-900.

i. Bowling Pin, .5L, porcelain, marked MUSTER-SCHUTZ (Schierholz), c.1900, $600-800.

j. Seated Ram, .5L, porcelain, marked MUSTER-SCHUTZ (Schierholz), c.1900, $700-1000.

a. Bismarck, .5L, stoneware, marked #584 (by Reinhold Hanke), blue saltglaze, c.1900, $300-400.

b. Bismarck, .5L, stoneware, marked #584 (by Reinhold Hanke), blue saltglaze, c.1900, $300-400.

c. Bismarck, .5L, stoneware, unmarked, blue saltglaze, c.1900, $300-400.

d. Bismarck, .5L, stoneware, marked #801 (by Marzi & Remy), purple & black saltglazes, c.1900, $450-600.

e. Von Moltke, .5L, stoneware, marked #933 (by Marzi & Remy), purple saltglaze, c.1900, $400-500.

f. Von Moltke, .5L, stoneware, blue & purple saltglazes, c.1900, $300-400.

g. Von Moltke, .5L, pottery, marked #585 (by Reinhold Hanke), tan & brown, c.1900, $350-450; stoneware version, $350-450.

h. Wilhelm II, .5L, pottery, marked #186 (by Dümler & Breiden) brown, black & green, c.1900, $450-600.

a. Frederich III, .5L, pottery, marked Merkelbach & Wick, tan, brown & blue, early 1900's, $400-500.

b. Frederich III, .5L, stoneware, marked #932 (by Marzi & Remy), purple saltglaze, c.1900, $450-600.

c. Soldier, .5L, stoneware, marked #194, blue saltglaze, c.1900, $300-400.

d. Soldier, .5L, pottery, marked #1243, tan, c.1900, $225-325.

Above:

e. Fireman, .5L, stoneware, marked #750 (by Marzi & Remy), blue & purple saltglazes, c.1900, $300-400.

f. Fireman, .5L, stoneware, marked #237, Reinhold Merkelbach, blue saltglaze, c.1900, $350-450.

g. Funnel Man, .5L, stoneware, marked #161, blue & purple saltglazes, c.1900, $350-500.

h. Waitress, .5L, stoneware, marked #149, blue saltglaze, c.1900, $225-325.

Opposite:

f. Beer Barrel Man, .5L, pottery, marked J. Reinemann, brown, tan & green, c.1900, $250-350.

g. Beer Barrel Man, .5L, stoneware, marked J. Reinemann, blue saltglaze, c.1900, $275-375.

h. Fireman, .5L, stoneware, marked #750 (by Marzi & Remy), purple saltglaze, c.1900, $275-375.

i. Fireman, .5L, pottery, marked Merkelbach & Wick, blue, black & red, c.1900, $300-400.

a.   Sailor, .5L, pottery, marked #1821, blue, tan & black, early 1900's,
     $300-400.

b.   Black Boy, .5L, pottery, marked #737 (by Reinhold Merkelbach),
     black, tan & red, c.1900, $350-500.

c.   Funnel Man, .5L, pottery, marked #779 (by Reinhold Hanke), tan &
     brown, c.1900, $250-350; stoneware version, $300-400.

d.   Funnel Man, .5L, pottery, marked #622 (by Reinhold Hanke), tan &
     brown, c.1900, $250-350; stoneware version, $300-400.

e.   German Officer, .5L, pottery, marked #20, TW
     (Theodor Wieseler), full color, c.1900, $500-650.

a. Bartender, .5L, pottery, marked D.R.G.M. (Diesinger), #702, full color, early 1900's, $300-400.

b. Elf, .5L, pottery, marked D.R.G.M. (Diesinger), #694, full color, early 1900's, $250-350.

c. Clown, .25L, pottery, marked D.R.G.M. (Diesinger), #792, full color, early 1900's, $250-350.

d. Clown, .5L, pottery, marked D.R.G.M. (Diesinger), #747, full color, early 1900's, $300-400.

e. Clown, .5L, pottery, marked D.R.G.M. (Diesinger), #748, full color, early 1900's, $350-450.

f. Clown, .5L, pottery, marked D.R.G.M. (Diesinger), #721, full color, early 1900's, $350-450.

g. Clown, .5L, pottery, marked D.R.G.M. (Diesinger), #750, full color, early 1900's, $350-450.

h. Clown, .5L, pottery, marked D.R.G.M. (Diesinger), #749, full color, early 1900's, $350-450.

a. Trumpeter, .4L, pottery, marked #734 (by Diesinger), full color, early 1900's, $300-400.

b. Gambrinus, .5L, pottery, marked D.R.G.M. (Diesinger), #705, full color, early 1900's, $225-325.

c. Gambrinus, .25L, pottery, marked D.R.G.M. (Diesinger), #127, full color, c.1900, $250-350.

d. Gymnasium Teacher, .5L, pottery, marked D.R.G.M. (Diesinger), #697, full color, early 1900's, $250-350.

e. Man with Top Hat, .5L, pottery, marked D.R.G.M. (Diesinger), #765, full color, early 1900's, $350-450.

f. Man with Bowler Hat, .5L, pottery, marked D.R.G.M. (Diesinger), #764, full color, early 1900's, $350-450.

g. Smiling Mikado, .5L, pottery, marked #1081 (by Reinhold Hanke), tan, brown & blue, c.1900, $275-375.

h. Man with Newspaper, .5L, pottery, marked #871 (by Reinhold Hanke), tan & brown, c.1900, $200-300.

a.   Man on Barrel, .5L, pottery, marked #487, A.J. Thewalt, full color, early 1900's, $500-700.

b.   Woman on Barrel, .5L, pottery, marked #488, A.J. Thewalt, full color, early 1900's, $500-700.

Below:

c.   Man with Beret, .5L, stoneware, marked #461 (by Reinhold Hanke), blue saltglaze, c.1900, $200-300.

d.   Robust Man, .5L, stoneware, marked Merkelbach & Wick, blue & purple saltglazes, early 1900's, $200-300.

e.   Rich Man, .5L, stoneware, marked #804 (by Marzi & Remy), blue & purple saltglazes, c.1900, $225-325.

f.   Robust Man, .5L, stoneware, unmarked, by Reinhold Hanke, blue saltglaze, c.1900, $225-325.

a.   Man, .5L, pottery, marked #1045 Geschützt, full
     color, c.1900, $350-450.

b.   Man, .5L, pottery, marked #1044 Geschützt, full
     color, c.1900, $350-450.

c.   Monk, .5L, pottery, marked #138, full color,
     c.1900, $300-400.

d.   Minstrel Man, .5L, pottery, marked #1045
     Geschützt, full color, c.1900, $200-300.

e.   Jolly Fat Lady, .5L, pottery, marked #724, full
     color, c.1900, $350-450; tan & brown version,
     $150-250.

f.   Hobo, .5L, pottery, marked #723, full color, c.1900,
     $400-500; tan version, $150-250.

g.   Rich Man, .5L, pottery, marked #175, A.J. Thewalt,
     full color, c.1900, $275-375.

h.   Admiral, .5L, stoneware, marked #52, blue &
     purple saltglazes, c.1900, $400-500.

Opposite:

g.   Rich Man, .5L, pottery, marked #8669, tan &
     brown, c.1900, $225-325; saltglazed stoneware
     version, $225 -325.

h.   Woman, .5L, pottery, marked Merkelbach & Wick,
     tan, brown & pink, c.1900, $225-325; stoneware
     version, $225-325.

i.   Rich Man, .5L, pottery, unmarked, by Marzi &
     Remy, tan, brown & black, c.1900, $250-350.

j.   Rich Man, .5L, stoneware, unmarked, blue &
     purple saltglazes, c.1900, $350-450.

a.   Hunter, .5L, pottery, marked J. Reinemann, brown, tan & green, c.1900, $350-450.

b.   Miner, .5L, pottery, marked #736 (by Reinhold Merkelbach), tan, brown & black, c.1900, $350-450.

c.   Miner, .5L, pottery, marked #1241, tan, brown & black, early 1900's, $400-500.

d   Warrior, .5L, pottery, marked #1165 (probably by Steinzeugwerke), brown, green & red, early 1900's, $200-300; tan version, $150-250.

e.   Bavaria, 1.0L, pottery, marked Reinhold Merkelbach, full color, c.1900, $600-900; version with different base, $600-900.

f.   Clown, .5L, pottery, marked #987 (by Reinhold Hanke), tan & brown, c.1900, $250-350; stoneware version, $300-400.

g.   Falstaff, .5L, pottery, marked #1439 (by Steinzeugwerke), full color, early 1900's, $200-300; tan color version, $150-225.

a. Rich Lady, .5L, pottery, marked #680 (by Reinhold Merkelbach), full color, c.1900, $350-450.

b. Sailor, .5L, pottery, marked #1244, blue, white, red & black, early 1900's, $400-500.

c. Watchman, .5L, pottery, marked #1217, olive, red & green, early 1900's, $350-450.

d. Bowler, .5L, pottery, marked #1226, tan, brown & black, early 1900's, $350-450.

e. Iron Maiden of Nürnberg, .5L, stoneware, marked T.W. (Theodor Wieseler), purple saltglaze, c.1900, $350-450.

f. Barmaid (Lisl), .5L, stoneware, marked J. Reinemann, blue & purple saltglazes, c.1900, $400-500; pottery version, $400 -500.

g. Alpine Man, .5L, stoneware, marked #57, purple saltglaze, c.1900, $350-450.

h. Kellnerin, .5L, stoneware, marked #1089 (by Reinhold Hanke), blue saltglaze, c.1900, $350-450; pottery version, $300 -400.

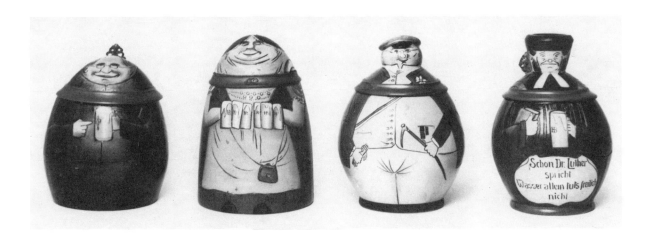

Opposite top:

a. Boy on Barrel, .5L, stoneware, marked #63, HR (Hauber & Reuther),blue & purple saltglazes, c.1900, $400-550.

b. Young Man, .5L, stoneware, marked #191 (by Reinhold Hanke), blue saltglaze, c.1900, $350-450.

c. Sea Captain, .5L, stoneware, marked #55, purple saltglaze, c.1900, $400-500.

d. Woman, .5L, stoneware, unmarked, blue, brown & green saltglazes, c.1900, $400-500.

Oppoite middle:

e. Queen, .5L, stoneware, marked J. Reinemann, München, full color, c.1900, $350-475.

f. Hanswurst, .5L, stoneware, marked J. Reinemann, München, full color, c.1900, $350-475; .25L, $300-400.

g. Old Man, .25L, stoneware, marked J. Reinemann, München, full color, c.1900, $450-575.

h. Grethl, .25L, stoneware, marked J. Reinemann, München, full color, c.1900, $300-400.

i. Little Red Riding Hood, .25L, stoneware, marked J. Reinemann, München, full color, c.1900, $300-400.

Opposite bottom:

j. Soldier, .5L, pottery, marked #1577 (by Reinhold Hanke), full color, c.1900, $350-450.

k. Woman, .5L, pottery, marked #1579 (by Reinhold Hanke), full color, c.1900, $350-450.

l. Woman with Baby, .5L, pottery, marked #1580 (by Reinhold Hanke), c.1900, $400-500.

m. Munich Child, .5L, pottery, marked J. Reinemann, München, full color, c.1900, $300-400; .25L, $250-350.

Above:

a. Monk, .5L, pottery, marked #1574 (by Reinhold Hanke), full color, c.1900, $275-375.

b. Barmaid, .5L, pottery, marked #1571 (by Reinhold Hanke), full color, c.1900, $275-375.

c. Fat Man, .5L, pottery, marked #1566 (by Reinhold Hanke), full color, c.1900, $300-400.

d. Pastor, .5L, pottery, marked #1575 (by Reinhold Hanke), full color, c.1900, $350-450.

e. Chinaman, .5L, pottery, marked Merkelbach & Wick, tan, yellow & blue, c.1900, $300-400.

f. Man on Barrel, .5L, pottery, marked #738, Reinhold Merkelbach, black, brown & green, c.1900, $350-450.

a.   Dutch Girl, .5L, pottery, marked #685, Reinhold
     Merkelbach, tan & brown, c.1900, $300-400.

b.   Gambrinus, .5L, pottery, marked #11, Reinhold
     Merkelbach, blue, brown & tan, c.1900, $350-500.

c.   Bustle Lady, .5L, pottery,
     marked #971, tan, blue & black,
     c.1900, $1800-2300.

d.   Mephistopheles Tempting the Maiden, .5L, pewter,
     unmarked, c.1900, $1800-2200.

e.   Lady with Bustle, .5L, stoneware & pewter, marked
     HR (Hauber & Reuther), blue saltglaze, c.1900,
     $1600-2000.

f.   Lady with Bustle, .5L, pewter & wood, unmarked,
     c.1900, $1300-1700.

a. Knight, .5L, stoneware, marked #448 (by Rein-
    hold Hanke), blue saltglaze, c.1900, $275-375.

b. Knight, .5L, stoneware, marked #223, purple
    saltglaze, c.1900, $300-400.

c. Knight, .5L, pottery, marked #123, blue & purple,
    c.1900, $275-375.

d. Knight, .5L, pottery, marked F. & M. N., gray,
    black & tan, c.1900, $400-500; stoneware version,
    $350-450.

e. Clown, .5L, stoneware, marked Merkelbach &
    Wick, purple saltglaze, c.1900, $400-500.

f. Jester, .5L, stoneware, unmarked, blue & purple
    saltglazes, c.1900, $350-450.

g. Lady, .5L, stoneware, marked #224, purple
    saltglaze, c.1900, $400-500.

h. Falstaff, .5L, stoneware, marked Merkelbach &
    Wick, blue & purple saltglazes, c.1900, $200-300;
    pottery version, full color, $225-325; tan color,
    $150-225.

Opposite top:

a. Clown, 2.0L, pottery, marked D.R.G.M. (Diesinger), #853, full color, c.1900, $500-700.

b. Clown, 2.0L, pottery, marked D.R.G.M (Diesinger), #752, full color, c.1900, $500-700.

c. King, 1.5L, pottery, marked D.R.G.M (Diesinger), #805, full color, c.1900, $600-800.

a. Sad Radish, .5L, porcelain, marked MUSTER-SCHUTZ (Schierholz), tan & green, c.1900, $325-425; .3L, $275-375; blue & white version, .5L, $500-700; .3L, $400-600.

b. Sad Radish, 3.0L, porcelain, marked MUSTER-SCHUTZ (Schierholz), tan & green, c.1900, $800-1100; blue & white version, $1200-1600.

c. Happy Radish, .5L, porcelain, marked MUS-TERSCHUTZ (Schierholz), tan & green, c.1900, $325-425; .3L, $275-375; blue & white version, .5L, $500-700; .3L, $400-600.

d. Bismarck Radish, .5L, porcelain, marked MUSTERSCHUTZ (Schierholz), tan & green, c.1900, $450-550; .25L, $350-450.

Opposite bottom:

d. Man, 2.0L, faience, marked ARK, blue & white, c.1900, $600-800.

e. Woman, 2.0L, faience, marked ARK, blue & white, c.1900, $600-800.

f. Knight, 1.5L, stoneware, marked #663 (by Marzi & Remy), blue saltglaze, c.1900, $400-600.

a.   Sad Radish, .5L, pottery, marked #1225, yellow, green & brown, c.1900, $200-300.

b.   Happy Radish, .4L, pottery, marked #757, tan & gray, c.1900, $200-300.

c.   Devil, .5L, stoneware, marked Merkelbach & Wick, purple saltglaze, c.1900, $225-325; light tan version, $175-250.

d.   Skull, .5L, porcelain, marked E. Bohne Söhne, tan, white & brown, bisque glaze, c.1900, $425-550; .625L, $475-600; .4L, $375-500; .3L, $325-450; .25L, $300-425; with music box base, .5L, $500-700.

e.   Skull, .5L, porcelain, unmarked, tan & black, bisque glaze, c.1900, $400-500; .4L, $350-475.

f.   Skull, .5L, porcelain, unmarked, by E. Bohne Söhne, tan & black, bisque glaze, c.1900, $350-450; .3L, $300-400; .06L, $200-300.

g.   Skull, .25L, porcelain, marked #1747, tan & black, bisque glaze, c.1900, $300-400.

a. Skull & Devil, .5L, porcelain, marked E. Bohne Söhne, tan, black & red, bisque glaze, c.1900, $600-750; .25L, $400-550.

b. Skull/Skull, .4L, porcelain, unmarked, by E. Bohne Söhne, tan & black, bisque glaze, c.1900, $500-700.

c. Skull, .5L, pottery, unmarked, by Steinzeugwerke, brown & tan, early 1900's, $200-300.

d. Skull, .5L, porcelain, unmarked, tan, white, black & red, bisque glaze, devil handle, late 1800's, $550-750.

e. Skull, .5L, porcelain, unmarked, probably by E. Bohne Söhne, tan & brown, bisque glaze, snake handle, c.1900, $550-750.

f. Skull, .5L, pottery, marked #1796 (by Marzi & Remy), tan & black, c.1900, $250-350.

a. Gentleman Boar, .5L, porcelain, marked MUSTERSCHUTZ (Schierholz), tan & brown, c.1900, $3000-3600; dark color version, $3400-4000.

b. Stag, .5L, porcelain, marked MUSTERSCHUTZ (Schierholz), tan & brown, c.1900, $3600-4200.

c. Teddy and Elephant, .5L, pottery, unmarked, gray, green & brown, Teddy Roosevelt on elephant, c.1900, $900-1200.

d. Gentleman Rabbit, .5L, porcelain, marked MUSTERSCHUTZ (Schierholz), tan, brown & green, c.1900, $2600-3200.

e. Gentleman Dog, .5L, porcelain, marked MUSTERSCHUTZ (Schierholz), tan, brown & green, c.1900, $2400-3000.

f. Gentleman Fox, .5L, porcelain, marked MUSTERSCHUTZ (Schierholz), tan, brown & green, c.1900, $2400-3000.

a. Berlin Bear, .5L, porcelain, marked MUSTER-SCHUTZ (Schierholz), tan colors, c.1900, $2000-2500; blue & white version, $2400-3000.

b. Ram, .5L, porcelain, marked MUSTERSCHUTZ (Schierholz), tan colors, c.1900, $1000-1300; with music box base, $1100-1400; blue & white version, $1300-1600.

c. Monkey, .5L, porcelain, marked E. Bohne Söhne, white & pink, bisque glaze, c.1900, $1300-1700; darker version, $1300-1700.

d. Pig, .3L, porcelain, unmarked, by E. Bohne Söhne, pink, bisque glaze, c.1900, $900-1200.

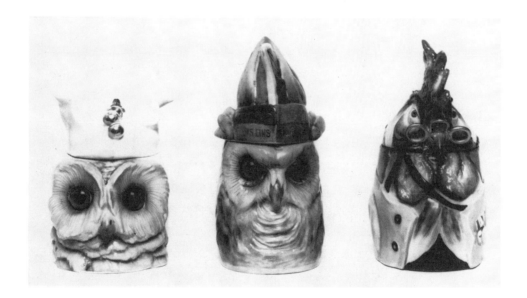

e. Owl, .5L, porcelain, marked MUSTERSCHUTZ (Schierholz), tan, white, yellow & gold, c.1900, $900-1200; blue & white version, $1200-1600.

f. Indian Chief Owl, .5L, porcelain, marked MUSTERSCHUTZ (Schierholz), tan, gray, red & blue, c.1900, $2000-2600.

g. Gentleman Rooster, .5L, porcelain, marked MUSTERSCHUTZ (Schierholz), tan, brown & red, c.1900, $1400-1800.

a.   Frog, .5L, porcelain, unmarked, probably by E. Bohne Söhne, white & green, c.1900, $800-1000; with music box base, $900-1200.

b.   Frog, .5L, porcelain, marked MUSTERSCHUTZ (Schierholz), white & green, c.1900, $900-1200.

c.   Alligator, .5L, porcelain, marked MUSTER-SCHUTZ (Schierholz), white, green & tan, c.1900, $800-1100; 1.0L, $1000-1400.

d.   Fish, .5L, porcelain, marked MUSTERSCHUTZ (Schierholz), white, gray & black, c.1900, $700-900.

e.   Frog, .5L, pottery, marked #27 (by Dümler & Breiden), tan & red, dressed as a Roman Field Commander, c.1900, $300-400; saltglazed stoneware version, $300-400.

f.   Frog, .25L, pottery, marked #849, Matthias Girmscheid, yellow & green, c.1900, $150-250.

g.   Frog, .5L, pottery, marked #825 (by Girmscheid), yellow & green, c.1900, $200-300; also later version.

h.   Frog, .5L, pottery, marked #1429, green & brown, c.1900, $200-300.

a.   Alligator, .5L, pottery, marked #1797 (by Marzi & Remy), yellow & green, c.1900, $200-300.

b.   Alligator, .125L, pottery, marked #1914, Marzi & Remy, yellow & green, c.1900, $100-160.

c.   Wrap around Alligator, .5L, porcelain, unmarked, by E. Bohne Söhne, white & green, bisque glaze, c.1900, $600-750; .25L, $450-550.

d.   Apple and Snake, .3L, porcelain, unmarked, possibly by E. Bohne Söhne, yellow & brown, c.1900, $500-700; .5L, $600-800; .125L, $300-400.

e.   Rhinoceros, .5L, porcelain, marked MUSTER-SCHUTZ (Schierholz), gray & white, c.1900, $900-1200.

f.   Elephant, .5L, porcelain, marked MUSTER-SCHUTZ (Schierholz), gray & white (or tan & brown), c.1900, $800-1100; .25L, $600-800.

g.   Student Fox, .5L, porcelain, unmarked, white, black & brown, lithophane, c.1900, $275-375.

h.   Rabbit Hunter, .5L, porcelain, marked with cross hatch mark, white & tan, probably 1920's, $400-600; version marked R.P.M., green & tan, c.1950, $250-350.

a.   Bull, .5L, pottery, marked #1453 (by Stein-
     zeugwerke), brown, early 1900's, $450-600.

b.   Bear, .5L, pottery, marked #1455 (probably by
     Steinzeugwerke), brown, early 1900's, $300-450.

c.   Bear, .5L, pottery, marked #731, Reinhold Merkel-
     bach, brown & tan, c.1900, $300-400.

d.   Elephant, .5L, pottery, marked #1447 (by Stein-
     zeugwerke), gray & black, early 1900's, $400-550.

e.   Donkey, .5L, pottery, marked #1454 (by Stein-
     zeugwerke), black & gray, early 1900's, $400-550.

f.   Eagle Owl, .5L, pottery, marked M.Sch. & Co.,
     Ulm, tan & brown, c.1900, $250-350; stoneware,
     blue saltglaze, .5L, $275-375; .3L, $225-325.

g.   Fish, .5L, pottery, marked #1152, Reinhold
     Merkelbach, tan & black, c.1900, $225-325.

h.   Rhinoceros, .5L, pottery, marked #1451 (by Stein-
     zeugwerke), dark gray, early 1900's, $350-450.

a.   Owl, 1.0L, pottery, marked #1662 (by Stein-
     zeugwerke), brown & tan, early 1900's, $400-550.

b.   Owl, .5L, pottery, marked #539 (by Reinhold
     Hanke), brown, tan & green, c.1900, $300-400.

c.   Fox, .5L, pottery, marked #827 (by M. Girmscheid),
     red, tan & green, early 1900's, $250-350.

d.   Rabbit, .5L, pottery, marked #1105, brown, tan
     & green, early 1900's, $250-350.

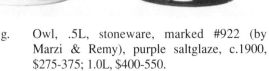

e.   Owl, .5L, stoneware, marked #64, HR
     (Hauber & Reuther), blue & purple saltglazes,
     c.1900, $350-500.

f.   Owl, .5L, stoneware, unmarked, by Reinhold
     Hanke, blue saltglaze, c.1900, $450-550.

g.   Owl, .5L, stoneware, marked #922 (by
     Marzi & Remy), purple saltglaze, c.1900,
     $275-375; 1.0L, $400-550.

h.   Owl, .5L, pottery, marked #999 (by Stein-
     zeugwerke), brown, tan & green, early 1900's,
     $200-300.

a. Berlin Bear, .5L, porcelain, marked MUSTER-SCHUTZ (Schierholz), tan colors, c.1900, $700-1000.

b. Cat with Hangover, .5L, porcelain, marked MUSTERSCHUTZ (Schierholz), tan colors, c.1900, $500-650; with music box base, $700-1000; blue & white version, $700-1000.

c. Seated Ram, .5L, porcelain, marked MUSTER-SCHUTZ (Schierholz), tan colors, c.1900, $575-625; with music box base, $700-900; blue & white version, $700-1000.

d. Drunken Monkey, .5L, porcelain, marked MUSTERSCHUTZ (Schierholz), tan colors, c.1900, $450-600; with music box base, $700-900; blue & white version, $700-1000.

e. Cat, .5L, pottery, marked #576, Reinhold Merkelbach, brown, gray & black, c.1900, $300-400.

f. Cat, .5L, pottery, marked Reinhold Merkelbach, brown, gray & black, c.1900, $300-400.

g. Cat, .5L, pottery, marked #1000 (by Steinzeugwerke), brown & black, early 1900's, $175-275.

h. Cat, .5L, pottery, marked Merkelbach & Wick, tan & black, c.1900, $225-325.

a. Cat, .5L, potttery, marked #511 (by Reinhold Hanke), tan & brown, c.1900, $275-375.

b. Cat, .5L, pottery, marked #61, Gerz, brown, tan & blue, c.1900, $200-300; .25L, $150-225; .06L, $100-150; 1.0L, marked #60, $300-400.

c. Cat, .5L, pottery, marked D.R.G.M. (Diesinger), #701, tan, brown & yellow, early 1900's, $300-400.

d. Cat, .25L, pottery, marked D.R.G.M. (Diesinger), #737, tan, brown & yellow, early 1900's, $250-350.

Below:

f. Dog, .5L, stoneware, marked #58, blue & purple saltglazes, c.1900, $450-550.

g. Cat, .5L, pottery, marked #767 (by J.W. Remy), tan, brown & black, c.1900, $275-375.

h. Dog, .5L, pottery, marked #101 (by M. Girmscheid), brown, tan & blue, c.1900, $175-275.

i. Bulldog, .5L, pottery, marked #1440 (probably by Steinzeugwerke), tan & brown, early 1900's, $275-375.

e. Cat, .5L, porcelain, marked MUSTERSCHUTZ (Schierholz), white, black & gray, c.1900, $900-1200.

a.   Poodle, .5L, pottery, marked #1452 (probably by Steinzeugwerke), tan & brown, early 1900's, $350-450.

b.   Dachshund, .5L, pottery, marked #1448 (probably by Steinzeugwerke), brown & blue, early 1900's, $400-550.

c.   Dog, .5L, stoneware, unmarked (by Gerz), blue & purple saltglazes, c.1900, $250-350.

d.   Dog, .5L, pottery, marked #768 (by J.W. Remy), brown, green & pink, c.1900, $275-375.

e.   Monkey, .5L, stoneware, unmarked, blue saltglaze, c.1900, $250-350.

f.   Monkey, .5L, stoneware, unmarked, blue & purple saltglazes, c.1900, $275-375.

g.   Ram, .5L, stoneware, marked Merkelbach & Wick, blue saltglaze, c.1900, $225-325; pottery version, $250-350.

h.   Rooster, .5L, earthenware, marked Fritz von Heider, blue, brown & green, glazed, c.1900, $300-450.

a. Fox, .5L, pottery, marked #1441 (by Stein-zeugwerke), tan & green, early 1900's, $200-300.

b. Fox, .5L, stoneware, marked #54 & #32, HR (Hauber & Reuther), tan, green, white & black, c.1900, $450-600.

c. Fox, .25L, pottery, marked D.R.G.M. (Diesin-ger), #739, yellow & brown, early 1900's, $200-300

d. Fox, .5L, stoneware, marked #54, blue & purple saltglazes, c.1900, $300-400.

e. Fox, .5L, stoneware, unmarked, by Reinhold Hanke, blue saltglaze, c.1900, $250-350.

f. Fox, .5L, stoneware, marked #806 (by Marzi & Remy), blue & purple saltglazes, c.1900, $275-375; pottery version, $250-350.

g. Student Fox, .5L, stoneware, marked Merkelbach & Wick, blue & purple saltglazes, c.1900, $275-375.

h. Fox, .5L, stoneware, marked #468 (by Reinhold Hanke), blue saltglaze, c.1900, $275-375.

a. Monkey, .5L, pottery, marked D.R.G.M. (Diesinger), #858, brown & tan, early 1900's, $350-450.

b. Monkey, .5L, pottery, marked D.R.G.M. (Diesinger), #819, brown, tan & green, early 1900's, $300-400.

c. Monkey, .5L, pottery, marked D.R.G.M. (Diesinger), #817, brown & tan, early 1900's, $300-400.

d. Military Monkey, .5L, pottery, marked #769 (by J.W. Remy), brown, black & gold, c.1900, $300-400.

e. Monkey, .5L, pottery, marked #1444 (by Steinzeugwerke), tan & brown, early 1900's, $250-350.

f. Monkey, .5L, pottery, marked #576, Reinhold Merkelbach, tan, brown & gray, c.1900, $275-375.

g. Monkey, .5L, pottery, unmarked, by Reinhold Hanke, tan, brown & black, c.1900, $275-375.

h. Monkey, .5L, pottery, marked #828 (by M. Girmscheid), tan, brown & blue, c.1900, $275-375.

a. Monkey, .5L, pottery, marked #1799 (by Marzi & Remy), tan & brown, c.1900, $225-325.

b. Monkey, .5L, pottery, marked #1088 (by Reinhold Hanke), tan, brown & black, c.1900, $275-375; with music box base, $300-400.

c. Monkey, .5L, pottery, marked #1261 (by Steinzeugwerke), tan & brown, early 1900's, $250-350.

d. Monkey, .5L, pottery, unmarked, tan & brown, c.1900, $250-350.

e. Monkey, .5L, pottery, marked #694 (by Diesinger), tan, brown & blue, c.1900, $300-400.

f. Monkey, .5L, pottery, marked #1442, tan, blue & black, c.1900, $250-350.

g. Ram, .5L, pottery, marked D.R.G.M. (Diesinger), #700, brown, tan & black, early 1900's, $250-350.

h. Ram, .25L, pottery, marked D.R.G.M. (Diesinger), #722, brown & tan, early 1900's, $200-300.

a. Pig, .5L, pottery, marked D.R.G.M. (Diesinger), #698, tan & pink, early 1900's, $300-400.

b. Pig, .5L, pottery, marked #770 (by J.W. Remy), tan, c.1900, $200-300.

c. Pig, .5L, pottery, marked #1260 (by Steinzeugwerke), tan & pink, early 1900's, $225-325.

d. Pig in a Poke, .5L, porcelain, marked #5399, H. Huschenreuther, gray & white, c.1900, $400-500.

e. Pig, .5L, pottery, marked #1116, Reinhold Merkelbach, tan, c.1900, $300-400.

f. Pig, .5L, pottery, marked #1116, Reinhold Merkelbach, tan, c.1900, $300-400.

g. Pig, .5L, pottery, marked #1116, Reinhold Merkelbach, tan, c.1900, $300-400.

h. Monkey, 1.0L, pottery, marked #1286 (by Steinzeugwerke), tan & brown, early 1900's, $300-400; gray stoneware version, $300-400.

a. Smoking Pig, .5L, porcelain, marked MUSTER-SCHUTZ (Schierholz), tan, white & pink, c.1900, $350-450; .3L, $300-400; blue & white version, .5L, $600-800.

b. Smoking Pig, .5L, porcelain, marked MUSTER-SCHUTZ (Schierholz), tan, white & pink, music box base, c.1900, $700-900.

c. Singing Pig, .5L, porcelain, marked MUSTER-SCHUTZ (Schierholz), tan, white & pink, c.1900, $350-450; .3L, $300-400; with music box base, .5L, $700-900; blue & white version, .5L, $600-800.

d. Singing Pig, .5L, porcelain, marked MUSTER-SCHUTZ (Schierholz), tan, white & pink, c.1900, $350-450; .3L, $300-400; with music box base, $700-900; blue & white version, .5L, $600-800.

e. Football, .5L, porcelain, marked T. Maddocks Sons Co., black & orange, various colleges, early 1900's, $225-325.

f. Football, 3.0L, porcelain, marked T. Maddocks Sons Co., black & orange, various colleges, early 1900's, $400-550.

g. Football, .5L, pottery, unmarked, black, orange & yellow, various colleges, early 1900's, $200-300.

h. Football, .5L, pottery, unmarked, tan, various colleges, early 1900's, $175-250.

a.   Bowling Pin, .5L, pottery, marked #1140 (by Steinzeugwerke), tan & brown, c.1900, $175-250.

b.   Bowling Pin, .5L, pottery, marked #1134 (by Steinzeugwerke), tan & brown, c.1900, $175-250.

c.   Bowling Pin, .5L, pottery, marked #1132 (by J.W. Remy), brown, blue, red & white, c.1900, $200-300.

d.   Bowling Pin, .5L, pottery, marked #1134 (by Steinzeugwerke), tan & brown, c.1900, $120-180.

e.   Bowling Pin, .5L, pottery, marked #885 (by Reinhold Merkelbach), tan & brown, c.1900, $275-375.

f.   Bowling Pin, .5L, porcelain, unmarked, tan & brown, c.1900, $300-400.

g.   Bowling Pin, .5L, porcelain, marked MUSTER-SCHUTZ (Schierholz), tan & brown, lithophane sometimes, c.1900, $400-500; blue & white version, $600-800; full color version, $600-800; with music box base, $500-600.

h.   Bowling Pin, .25L, porcelain, marked MUSTER-SCHUTZ (Schierholz), tan & brown (or light tan), c.1900, $175-275.

a. Bowling Ball, .5L, porcelain, unmarked, by H. Hutschenreuther, tan & brown, c.1900, $300-400.

b. Bowling Ball, .5L, porcelain, marked H. Hutschenreuther, gray, brown & pink, c.1900, $300-400.

c. Bowling Ball, .5L, porcelain, marked MUSTERSCHUTZ (Schierholz), tan, brown & black (or light tan), ball thumblift, c.1900, $300-400.

d. Bowling Ball, .5L, porcelain, marked MUSTERSCHUTZ (Schierholz), tan, brown & black, lithophane in color, boy thumblift, c.1900, $450-550.

e. Bowling Pins, .5L, pottery, marked #1139, tan & brown, c.1900, $120-180; 1.0L, $150-225.

f. Bowling Pins, 1.0L, pottery, marked #1266, brown & green, c.1900, $200-300.

g. Bowling Pins, 1.0L, pottery, marked #1663 (by Steinzeugwerke), brown, blue & green, c.1900, $140-200; .5L, $100-160.

Above:

a.   Soccer Ball, .5L, pottery, marked #387, brown, c.1900, $350-450.

b.   Soccer Ball, .5L, pottery, marked #1106, Rochlitz Sporthaus Charlottenburg, tan & gray, c.1900, $350-450.

c.   Weight, .5L, pottery, marked #1251 (by Steinzeugwerke), tan, black & green, early 1900's, $350-450.

d.   Lantern, .5L, pottery, unmarked, tan, gray & black, c.1900, $300-400.

Opposite top:

a.   Dice, .5L, pottery, marked #1781 (by Steinzeugwerke), tan & black, early 1900's, $300-400.

b.   Beehive, .5L, pottery, marked #1384 (by Reinhold Merkelbach), tan & red, c.1900, $200-300.

c.   League of American Wheelmen, .5L, porcelain, marked MUSTERSCHUTZ (Schierholz), tan & brown, lithophane, c.1900, $300-400; version with *All Heil* on front, $350-450.

d.   Nürnberg Trichter, .5L, porcelain, marked MUSTERSCHUTZ (Schierholz), gray, black & orange, lithophane, c.1900, $500-600; .25L, $375-475; yellow version, .5L, $600-800.

Opposite bottom:

h.   Bottle, .5L, stoneware, marked LB&C, blue saltglaze, c.1900, $250-350.

i.   Bottle, .5L, stoneware, marked LB&C, gray, brown & red, c.1900, $300-400.

j.   High Wheeler, .5L, stoneware, unmarked, blue & purple saltglazes, late 1800's, $1500-2000.

Left:

e.   Bowling Pin, 1.0L, porcelain, marked E. Bohne Söhne, tan, pink & red, c.1900, $1200-1600.

f.   Money Bag, .5L, porcelain, unmarked, probably by E. Bohne Söhne, tan & gray, music box base, c.1900, $2000-3000.

e. Barbell, .5L, pottery, marked #1227 (by Steinzeugwerke), tan & green, early 1900's, $300-400.

f. Lawn Tennis, .5L, pottery, marked #1226 (by Steinzeugwerke), tan & green, early 1900's, $350-450.

g. Soccer Game, .5L, pottery, marked #1313, tan, brown & green, c.1900, $400-500.

a. Acorn, .5L, pottery, marked #1235, brown, green & yellow, c.1900, $200-300.

b. Acorn, .5L, porcelain, marked Germany, probably by E. Bohne Soehne, tan, blue & green, c.1900, $500-700.

c. Acorn, .5L, pottery, marked #1111, tan & green, c.1900, $350-450.

d. Globe, .5L, pottery, marked #2368 (by Steinzeugwerke), brown & blue, early 1900's, $400-500; versions with Peary or Cook figure on top, $700-1000.

e. Mushroom, .5L, porcelain, marked MUSTER-SCHUTZ (Schierholz), tan & brown, c.1900, $1700-2100.

f. Target Barrel, .5L, porcelain, marked MUSTER-SCHUTZ (Schierholz), tan, brown & green, lithophane, c.1900, $800-1100.

g. Happy Radish, .5L, porcelain, unmarked, tan & green, lithophane, early 1900's, $700-900.

a.   Monkey on Barrel, .5L, porcelain, marked MUSTERSCHUTZ (Schierholz), tan & brown, c.1900, $650-850.

b.   Munich Child on Barrel, .3L, porcelain, unmarked, tan, black & blue, c.1900, $400-600.

c.   Dog in Barrel, .5L, pottery, unmarked, tan, brown & white, c.1900, $300-400.

d.   Drunken Man, .5L, pottery, unmarked, tan, black & green, c.1900, $250-350.

e.   Munich Child on Barrel, .5L, porcelain, marked MUSTERSCHUTZ (Schierholz), tan & brown, lithophane, c.1900, $700-900.

f.   Munich Child on Barrel, .5L, porcelain, marked MUSTERSCHUTZ (Schierholz), tan & brown, lithophane, c.1900, $700-900.

g.   Munich Child on Barrel, .5L, porcelain, marked MUSTERSCHUTZ (Schierholz) & Martin Pauson, tan & black, lithophane, c.1900, $700-900; 1.0L, $800-1100.

h.   Perkeo on Barrel, .5L, porcelain, marked MUSTERSCHUTZ (Schierholz), tan & brown, lithophane, c.1900, $500-700.

a.   Artillery Shell, .5L, porcelain, unmarked, blue (also other colors), lithophane, porcelain lid, early 1900's, $250-350.

b.   Artillery Shell, .5L, porcelain, unmarked, bronze & black, lithophane, pewter lid, early 1900's, $200-300.

c.   Artillery Shell, .5L, porcelain, unmarked, black & red (also other colors), porcelain lid, c.1900, $250-350.

d.   Artillery Shell, .5L, porcelain, unmarked, by E. Bohne Söhne, black, red & gold, porcelain lid, early 1900's, $350-475.

e.   Artillery Shell, .5L, pewter, unmarked, versions with various relief decorations, c.1914, $250-350.

f.   Artillery Shell, .5L, stoneware, marked #5309, gray, black & blue, c.1914-1915, $350-450.

g.   Artillery Shell, .5L, stoneware, marked #441546PA, gray, black & blue, c.1914-1915, $300-400.

h.   Artillery Shell, .5L, stoneware, marked J. Reinemann, München, gray & black, early 1900's, $250-350.

a.   Umbrella Men, .5L, porcelain, unmarked, gray, pink & red, music box base, c.1900, $1000-1300.

b.   Rook, .5L, stoneware, marked J. Reinemann, München, blue saltglaze, c.1900, $375-500.

c.   Hot Air Balloon, .75L, pottery, marked #1232, TW (Theodor Wieseler), black, green & yellow, c.1910, $800-1100; tan & brown version, $550-750.

d.   Navy Hat, .5L, porcelain, unmarked, blue, white & red (also exists white hat/blue body, all blue & all white), c.1900, $400-500.

e.   Insulator, .5L, porcelain, unmarked, white, c.1900, $400-600; blue version, $500-700.

f.   House, .5L, stoneware, marked #1777 (by Steinzeugwerke), tan, brown & red, early 1900's, $1000-1400.

Opposite top:

a. Nürnberg Tower, .1L, pewter, marked Geschütz, c.1900, $140-200.

b. Nürnberg Tower, .2L, pewter, marked D.R.G.M., c.1900, $150-225.

c. Nürnberg Tower, .125L, stoneware, unmarked, blue & purple saltglazes, c.1900, $150-225.

d. Nürnberg Tower, .125L, marked #520, F.&M.N., tan & brown, c.1900, $140-200.

e. Nürnberg Tower, .125L, marked #6183, tan & brown, no side scenes, c.1900, $140-200.

a. House, .5L, porcelain, marked M. Pauson, gray, white, red & green, lithophane, dated 1895, $900-1200; .3L, without lithophane, $700-1000.

b. East Berlin Town Hall, .5L, porcelain, unmarked, black, white & pink, lithophane, c.1900, $1000-1400.

c. Frauenkirche Tower, .5L, porcelain, marked Martin Pauson, München, red, white & green, lithophane, c.1900, $1000-1400; 1.0L, $1200-1600.

Opposite middle:

f. St. Elizabeth Church Tower (Nürnberg), .5L, stoneware, unmarked, blue saltglaze, c.1900, $300-400.

g. Frauenkirche Tower, .5L, stoneware, marked TW (Theodor Wiesler), purple saltglaze, c.1900, $175-250; .25L, $140-200; 1.0L, $250-350.

h. Tower, .5L, stoneware, marked #972, blue saltglaze, c.1900, $250-350.

i. Nürnberg Tower, .5L, stoneware, marked TW (Theodor Wiesler), blue & purple saltglazes, c.1900, $150-250; 1.0L, $200-300.

Opposite bottom:

j. Monument, .5L, pottery, unmarked, tan & brown, c.1900, $300-400.

k. Mannheimer Wasserturm, .5L, pottery, marked #097, George Leykauf, tan & black, c.1900, $600-900.

l. Nürnberg Tower, .5L, pottery, marked #131, tan & brown, c.1900, $300-400.

m. Nürnberg Tower, .5L, pottery, marked #1190, F&MN, tan & brown, c.1900, $175-250.

a. Tower, 1.0L, pewter, unmarked, c.1900, $700-1000.

b. Tower, .5L, pewter, unmarked, c.1900, $600-900.

c. Clock Tower, 1.0L, pewter, unmarked, c.1900, $1000-1500.

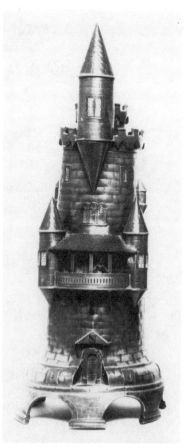

d. Zugspitze Mountain, .5L, stoneware, marked Martin Pauson, made by Merkelbach & Wick, München, gray, black & green, c.1900, $500-700.

e. Mountain, 1.0L, stoneware, unmarked, tan, gray & green, c.1900, $700-1000.

f. Wendelstein Mountain, .5L, stoneware, marked Martin Pauson, made by Merkelbach & Wick, München, gray, black & green, c.1900, $500-700.

g. Tower, 1.0L, pewter, unmarked, c.1900, $800-1100.

a.   Salzburg Tower, .5L,
     pottery, unmarked,
     tan & black, c.1900,
     $400-550.

b.   Feuerwach Thurm
     (Bad-Killingen), .5L,
     pottery, unmarked,
     tan & brown, c.1900,
     $1000-1400.

c.   Tower, .5L, pottery,
     marked #1541, tan
     & orange, c.1900,
     $500-700.

d.   Munich Child, .5L, porcelain, unmarked, black &
     yellow, lithophane, c.1900, $150-225.

e.   Munich Child, .5L, porcelain, unmarked, black &
     yellow, lithophane, c.1900, $150-225.

f.   Munich Child, .5L, porcelain, unmarked, black &
     yellow, lithophane, c.1900, $250-350.

g.   Munich Child, .5L, pottery, marked D.R.G.M.
     (Diesinger), #695, black, yellow & red, early
     1900's, $200-300.

i.   Munich Child, .1L, stoneware, marked #139,
     blue saltglaze, c.1900, $100-150.

j.   Munich Child, .1L, porcelain, unmarked, full color,
     c.1900, $200-300.

k.   Munich Child, .1L, porcelain, marked J. Reine-
     mann, München, full color, c.1900, $200-300.

l.   Munich Child, .05L, porcelain, unmarked, full
     color, c.1900, $150-225.

m.   Munich Child, .1L, porcelain, unmarked, full color,
     c.1900, $120-180.

n.   Munich Child, .02L, porcelain, unmarked, full
     color, c.1900, $150-225.

Opposite top:

a.   Munich Child, .5L, pottery, marked #1569 (probably by Steinzeugwerke), full color, early 1900's, $300-400.

b.   Munich Child, .2L, pottery, marked #1392 (probably by Steinzeugwerke), full color, early 1900's, $275-375.

c.   Munich Child, .25L, pottery, marked #1380, black & yellow, c.1900, $250-350; 1.0L, marked #1650, $300-400.

d.   Munich Child, .5L, pewter, unmarked, c.1900, $400-500.

Opposite middle:

e.   Munich Child, .5L, porcelain, unmarked, full color, c.1900, $400-500.

f.   Munich Child, .5L, porcelain, marked E. Bohne Söhne, full color, c.1900, $500-600.

g.   Munich Child, .5L, porcelain, unmarked, full color, c.1900, $500-600.

h.   Munich Child, .5L, porcelain, unmarked, red & yellow (or black & yellow), c.1900, $175-250; .25L, $150-225; .125L, $100-150.

a.   Munich Child, .5L, porcelain, unmarked, full color, lithophane, c.1900, $250-350; .25L, $200-300.

b.   Munich Child, .5L, pottery, marked #1780, full color, early 1900's, $225-325.

c.   Munich Child, .5L, pottery, marked #117, black & yellow, c.1900, $250-350.

d.   Munich Child, .5L, pottery, marked #117, black & yellow, c.1900, $250-350.

e.   Munich Child, .5L, stoneware, marked J. Reinemann, München, blue & purple saltglazes, c.1900, $300-450.

f.   Munich Child, .3L, pottery, marked Joseph Mayer, München, full color, c.1900, $300-400; .5L, $350-450.

a. Munich Child, .5L, pottery, marked J. Reinemann, München, tan & black, c.1900, $150-220;
1.0L, $250-350; .3L, $120-180; .25L, $120-180;
.125L, $100-150.

b. Munich Child, .5L, pottery, marked #323, Reinhold Merkelbach, tan & black, c.1900, $250-350.

c. Munich Child, .5L, pottery, unmarked, full color,
c.1900, $275-375; .25L, $200-300.

d. Munich Child, .5L, pottery, marked #1 (by Reinhold Merkelbach), full color, c.1900, $300-400;
.25L, $250-350.

e. Munich Child, 1.0L, pottery, marked #140, full
color, c.1900, $300-400.

f. Munich Child, 1.0L, stoneware, marked #1285
(by Steinzeugwerke), full color, early 1900's,
$300-400.

g. Munich Child, 1.0L, stoneware, marked #1285
(by Steinzeugwerke), blue saltglaze, early 1900's,
$250-350; .5L, $200-300.

h. Munich Child, .5L, stoneware, marked #314 (by
Marzi & Remy), tan & black, c.1900, $275-375.

a. Nun, .5L, porcelain, unmarked, full color, lithophane, c.1900, $150-225.

b. Monk, .5L, porcelain, unmarked, full color, lithophane, c.1900, $150-225.

c. Monk, .5L, porcelain, unmarked, full color, lithophane, c.1900, $200-275.

d. Nun, .5L, porcelain, unmarked, full color, lithophane, c.1900, $200-275.

e. Nun, .5L, stoneware, marked Merkelbach & Wick, purple saltglaze, c.1900, $175-250.

f. Monk, .5L, stoneware, marked Merkelbach & Wick, purple saltglaze, c.1900, $175-250.

g. Monk, .5L, stoneware, marked Merkelbach & Wick, purple saltglaze, c.1900, $175-250.

h. Monk, .25L, stoneware, marked #184, purple saltglaze, c.1900, $140-200.

i. Monk, .5L, stoneware, marked #14, HR (Hauber & Reuther), full color, c.1900, $500-650.

j. Nun, .5L, stoneware, marked #33, HR (Hauber & Reuther), full color, c.1900, $500-650.

a. Monk, .5L, stoneware, marked Merkelbach & Wick, purple saltglaze, c.1900, $200-275.

b. Monk, .5L, stoneware, marked #61, purple saltglaze, c.1900, $175-250.

c. Monk, .5L, stoneware, marked #61, purple saltglaze, c.1900, $175-250.

d. Monk, .5L, pewter, unmarked, c.1900, $400-500; also made currently.

e. Munich Child, 2.5L, pottery, marked #789, full color, c.1900, $500-700; 2.0L, $450-650.

f. Munich Child, 2.0L, pottery, marked D.R.G.M. (Diesinger), #729, full color, early 1900's, $500-700.

g. Munich Child, 2.0L, porcelain, marked Jos. Mayer, full color, lithophane, c.1900, $700-1000.

16. Brewery

The obvious relationship between beer steins and beer brewers naturally leads to brewery steins. While beer making implements can be found decorating steins from the 1600's and 1700's, we generally do not find the motifs of specific brewers until the late 1800's.

Brewery steins can be found for many German and American breweries and occasionally for those from other countries. The late 1800's and early 1900's saw large numbers of brewery steins produced as a promotional tool for the breweries. Due to World War I and economic conditions of the period, few brewery steins are found which were produced from 1914 through the early 1920's. During the late 1920's and 1930's, there was a resurgence in the production of brewery steins in Germany, but again production stopped with the start of WW II.

The 1960's and 1970's saw the start of production of the modern German and American brewery steins. The growth of the American brewery steins as collectibles has been phenomenal. Production of individual steins for some breweries frequently exceeds 100,000.

German brewery steins are generally pottery or stoneware. Most designs are transfer decorations. Usually they have pewter lids with relief or engraved-looking (actually impressed) designs matching the motif on the body. Undecorated glass steins with pewter lids depicting a brewery motif are sometimes found. They are generally worth much less than the pottery or stoneware steins.

American brewery steins are primarily pottery, stoneware and glass. Pottery and stoneware are ususlly relief or transfer-decorated. The glass steins are usually plain with decorated porcelain inlaid lids. Villeroy & Boch (Mettlach) made many American brewery steins. Some were etched, some print-over-glaze, but most were PUG (print under glaze).

Lids are generally an integral part of the German brewery steins. The absence of the correct lid will reduce the value to a small fraction of the lidded stein price. This will also generally be true of American brewery steins, except that many came with very simple steeple lids, or with no lid at all. For these, the absence of a lid has an insignificant influence on value.

16.1 Collecting Brewery Steins

Geographic approaches are possible with brewery stein collecting, as well as the narrower approach of collecting a specific brewery.

With antique German brewery steins, many collectors concentrate on breweries from Munich. The lack of available steins makes collecting other German cities, as a specific goal, rather difficult. It is possible to collect antique American brewery steins using the city approach, Chicago and St. Louis being prime examples of cities with many examples to collect.

Modern steins are generally easy to find, and in some cases, such as Anheuser Busch, many different steins have been made, so that a collection can easily be assembled from the steins of only one brewery. Section 17 and the color photo section also cover this subject.

a.   Stoneware, .5L, transfer, *Spaten-Bräu, München,* early 1900's, pewter lid, $150-225.

b.   Stoneware, .5L, transfer, *Spaten-Bräu, München,* early 1900's, pewter lid, $200-300.

c.   Stoneware, .5L, transfer, *Münchener Bürger-Bräu,* early 1900's, relief pewter lid, $225-325.

d.   Stoneware, .5L, transfer, *Hacker-Bräu, München,* early 1900's, relief pewter lid, $250-350.

e.   Stoneware, .5L, transfer, *Hacker-Bräu, München,* c.1904, designed by Ludwig Hohlwein, relief pewter lid, $225-325.

f.   Stoneware, .5L, transfer, *Paulanerbräu, München,* early 1900's, relief pewter lid, $150-225.

g.   Stoneware, .5L, transfer, *Paulanerbräu, München,* early 1900's, relief pewter lid, $200-300.

h.   Stoneware, .5L, transfer, *Salvatorbrauerei, München,* early 1900's, relief pewter lid, $200-300.

i.   Stoneware, .5L, transfer, *Schwabingerbräu, München,* late 1800's, relief pewter lid, $225-325.

j.   Stoneware, .5L, transfer, *Franziskaner Leistbräu, München,* early 1900's, engraved pewter lid, $140-200.

a. Pottery, .5L, transfer, *Münchener Bürger-Brau*, early 1900's, engraved pewter lid, $150-225.

b. Pottery, .5L, transfer, *Pschorr-Bräu, München*, early 1900's, engraved pewter lid, $120-180.

c. Pottery, .5L, transfer, *Pschorr-Bräu, München*, early 1900's, engraved pewter lid, $150-225.

d. Pottery, .5L, transfer, *Braverei Münchener Kindl, München*, early 1900's, relief pewter lid, $200-300.

e. Pottery, .5L, transfer, *Hacker-Bräu, München*, early 1900's, engraved pewter lid, $150-225.

f. Stoneware, .5L, transfer, *Leder Bräu, Nürnberg*, early 1900's, relief pewter lid, $90-140.

g. Stoneware, .5L, transfer, *Brauhaus Nürnberg*, early 1900's, relief pewter lid, $90-140.

h. Stoneware, .5L, transfer, *Schwanenbräu, Herbsthausen*, c.1890, relief pewter lid, $120-180.

i. Stoneware, .5L, transfer, *Brauerei z.d. 3 Kannen*, c.1890, relief pewter lid, $150-225.

j. Stonware, .5L, transfer, *Brauerei, zum Storchen, Speyer*, c.1890, pewter lid, $150-225.

a. Pottery, .5L, impressed, *Rizzi Bräu, Kulmbach*, early 1900's, pewter lid, $140-200.

b. Pottery, .5L, impressed, *Frankenbräu, Bamberg*, early 1900's, relief pewter lid, $120-180.

c. Pottery, .5L, transfer, *Hofbräu, Würzburger*, dated 1905, engraved pewter lid, $120-180.

d. Pottery, .5L, transfer, *Schloss-Bräu, Friedenfels*, early 1900's, relief pewter lid, $120-180.

e. Pottery, .5L, transfer, *Kulmbacher Rizzibräu*, early 1900's, engraved lid, $100-160.

f. Stoneware, 1.0L, transfer, *Kloster Brauerei, München*, early 1900's, relief pewter lid, $700-1000.

g. Stoneware, 1.0L, transfer, *Braeu Rosl, Pschorr-Bräu, München* on lid, early 1900's, pewter lid, $500-700.

h. Stoneware, 1.0L, transfer, *Münchener Bürger-Bräu, München*, c.1912, engraved pewter lid, $600-800.

i. Stoneware, 1.0L, transfer, *Wagner-Bräu, München*, early 1900's, relief pewter lid, $400-600.

a. Stoneware, .5L, transfer, *Stadt-Brauerei, Spalt,* early 1900's, engraved pewter lid, $100-160.

b. Stoneware, .5L, transfer, *Hechtbrauerei, Biberach,* early 1900's, relief pewter lid, $150-225.

c. Stoneware, .5L, transfer, *Stadt-Brauerei, Roth,* early 1900's, engraved pewter lid, $120-180.

d. Stoneware, .5L, transfer, *Hofbräu, A.G., Bamberg,* early 1900's, engraved pewter lid, $100-160.

e. Stoneware, .5L, transfer, *Radbier, Göppinger,* early 1900's, engraved pewter lid, $100-160.

f. Stoneware, 1.0L, impressed, *Brauerei-Bachbräu, Weilheim,* early 1900's, engraved pewter lid, $350-475.

g. Stoneware, 1.0L, transfer, *Hasenbräu, Augsburg,* early 1900's, engraved pewter lid, $175-250.

h. Stoneware, 1.0L, transfer, *Freiherrl Tucher Brauerei, Nürnberg,* early 1900's, relief pewter lid, $175-250.

i. Stoneware, 1.0L, transfer, *Stuttgarter Hofbräu,* early 1900's, engraved pewter lid, $120-180.

a. Stoneware, .125L, impressed, *HB, Hof-Bräuhaus, München*, early 1900's, relief pewter lid, $60-100.

b. Stoneware, .5L, transfer, *HB, Hof-Bräuhaus, München*, early 1900's, relief pewter lid, $80-120.

c. Stoneware, .25L, impressed, *HB, Hof-Bräuhaus, München*, early 1900's, relief pewter lid, $60-100.

d. Stoneware, 1.0L, impressed, *HB, Hof-Bräuhaus, München*, late 1800's, relief pewter lid, $150-225.

e. Stoneware, 1.0L, impressed, *HB, Hof-Bräuhaus, München*, early 1900's, relief pewter lid, $90-140.

f. Pottery, .5L, marked Reinhold Merkelbach, transfer, *John Kress Brewing Co., New York*, early 1900's, pewter lid, $150-250.

g. Pottery, .5L, transfer, *Louis Bergdall, Philadelphia, 1849-1893*, inlaid lid, $150-250.

h. Mettlach, #1909, .5L, PUG, *Pilsner Export Beer*, c.1900, pewter lid, $200-300.

i. Mettlach, #2140, .5L, PUG, *E. Tosetti Brewing Co's., Chicago*, early 1900's, pewter lid, $225-325.

a. Stoneware, 1.0L, transfer, *Lowenbraeu, München*, c.1900, engraved pewter lid, $150-225.

b. Stoneware, .5L, transfer, *Lowenbraeu, München*, c.1900, engraved pewter lid, $100-160.

c. Stoneware, 1.0L, impressed, *Lowenbräu Keller, München*, c.1900, relief pewter lid, $225-325.

d. Stoneware, .5L, impressed, *Lowenbräu, München*, c.1900, relief pewter lid, $150-225.

e. Pottery, .3L, relief, *H. Weinhard* (Brewery), *Portland, Ore.*, c.1900, no lid, $60-100.

f. Pottery, .25L, relief, *Rainier Brewery, Seattle, Wash.*, c.1900, no lid, $60-100.

g. Stoneware, .5L, relief, *Atlas Brewing Co., Chicago*, no lid, $100-160.

h. Stoneware, .5L, transfer, *Lemps Special Brew, St. Louis*, early 1900's, pewter lid, $150-250.

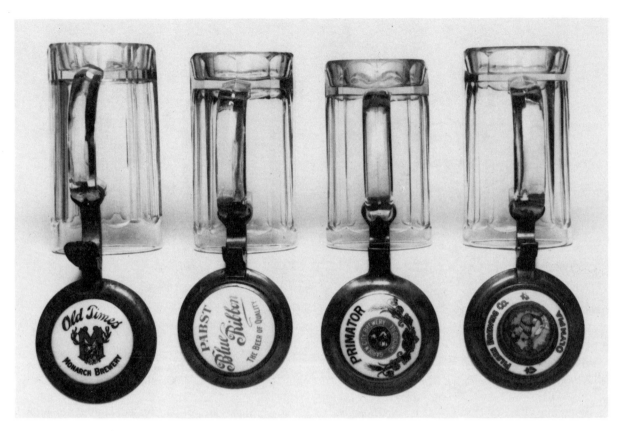

a. Glass, .5L, porcelain inlaid lid, *Old Times, Monarch Brewery*, (Chicago), $80-120.

b. Glass, .5L, porcelain inlaid lid, *Pabst Blue Ribbon* (Pabst Brewery Co.), $100-160.

c. Glass, .5L, porcelain inlaid lid, *Primator, Garden City Brewery, Chicago, Ill.*, $60-100.

d. Glass, .5L, porcelain inlaid lid, *Olympia, Pilsen Brewing Co.* (Chicago), $40-60.

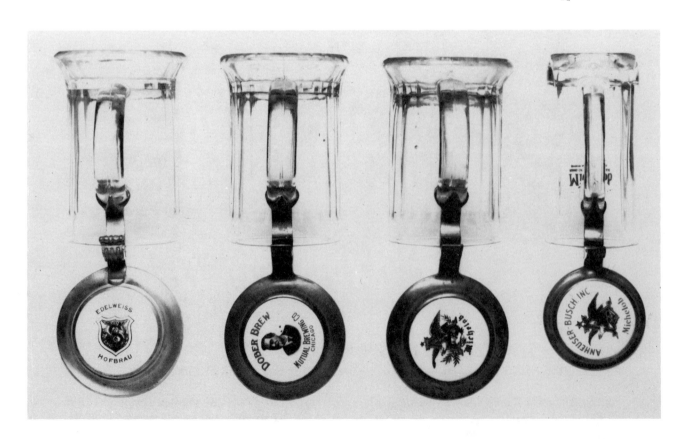

a. Pottery, .5L, transfer, *Fred Sehring Brewing Co., Joliet, Ill.*, c.1900, no lid, $50-80.

b. Mettlach, #1909, .25L, PUG, *Everett Brewing Co., Everett, Wash.*, c.1900, no lid, $150-250.

c. Mettlach, #1909, .3L, PUG, *South Bend Brewing Association*, c.1900, no lid, $50-80.

d. Mettlach, #1909, .4L, print over glaze, *Export Lager Keeley Brewing Co., Chicago, Ill.*, early 1900's, pewter lid, $120-180.

Opposite:

e. Glass, .5L, porcelain inlaid lid, *Edelweiss, Hofbrau*, early 1900's, $100-160.

f. Glass, .5L, porcelain inlaid lid, *Dober Brew, Mutual Brewing Co.*, early 1900's, $150-250.

g. Glass, .5L, porcelain inlaid lid, *Michelob* (Anheuser Busch, Inc.), early 1900's, $200-300.

h. Glass, .5L, porcelain inlaid lid, *Michelob, Anheuser Busch, Inc.*, dated 1933, $150-250.

e. Mettlach, #2303, 3" ht., PUG, *Bartholomay's Brewing Co., Rochester*, c.1900, pewter lid, $100-160.

f. Mettlach, #1909, .5L, PUG, *Bartholomay's Brewing Co., Rochester*, c.1900, inlaid lid, $150-250.

a.   Mettlach, #1997, .5L, etched & PUG, *George Ehret*, late 1800's, inlaid lid, $225-325.

b.   Mettlach, #1998, .5L, etched & PUG, *Martin Moehn Brewery, Burlington, Iowa*, late 1800's, inlaid lid, $1200-1800.

17. Post-World War II

Production of beer steins since 1945 has undergone many changes. Prior to World War I, the beer stein industry in Germany was perhaps the most significant segment of the ceramic industry in that country. From the beginning of World War I through the end of WWII, various economic as well as physical (war-time) influences significantly reduced the production and capacity of the German manufacturers.

During the first ten years following the end of World War II, beer stein production in Germany gradually revived. While most steins produced during the 1950's were reproductions of earlier designs using old molds, two notable types of new steins were produced starting in the 1950's. First are the Regimental steins which were similar to pre-1914 Imperial Regimental steins. While these are frequently referred to as reproductions, they were rarely accurate copies. Second are the souvenir steins produced for sale to U.S. military personnel, designed with military unit information applicable to the buyer. Examples of these steins can be found in Section 14.

During the 1960's and 1970's, the number of beer stein producers shrank. Now, significantly over 50% of the production of German beer steins is accounted for by only a few firms.

While some German manufacturers were slow to modernize, others such as Gerz, Thewalt and Villeroy & Boch have adopted modern manufacturing techniques. While most steins are made using all of the same procedures as steins that were made at the turn of the century, modern equipment is frequently utilized for such mundane, labor-intensive tasks as mixing, moving or carrying, cleaning, wrapping and packaging.

Historically, nearly all stein production took place in Germany and nearby areas. Ceramarte of Brazil began producing steins in the mid 1970's and during the 1980's became the largest producer of beer steins in the world, specializing in promotional products for companies and organizations. Examples of the various types of steins produced by Ceramarte can be found in the accompanying color section.

In recent years, about one-third of steins produced by German manufacturers were exported. In addition, a significant percentage of steins sold in Germany were sold to American and other tourists. Other European countries account for most of the export sales not occurring in the United States. However, in recent years, sales to Japan have been on the rise.

Factory	Current Status	Factory	Current Status
Beyer GmbH	producing	Lindner Porzellan	producing
Ceramarte (Brazil)	producing	Marzi & Remy	producing
W. Corzelius	producing	Rastal	producing
Dümler & Breiden	closed 1957	J.W. Remy	closed 1960's
Eckhardt & Engler	closed c.1971	Schierholz & Söhn	producing
Gerz GmbH	producing	A.J. Thewalt	producing
M. Girmscheid	closed c.1985	Villeroy & Boch	producing
W. Goebel	producing	Westerwald Team	producing
Kurt Hammer	producing	Wick Werke	closed 1984
Reinhold Hanke	producing, but not steins	Würfel & Müller (King)	producing
Elisabeth Liegl	producing	Zoeller & Born	producing

Some of the factories that have been producing steins during the post-World War II period.

17.1 Production

Most steins being made today use the same techniques that were developed about 100 years ago. In many cases, the same molds are being used. Companies such as Thewalt will identify with a mark that the design is from an old (original) mold. There has been a significant amount of development involving the glazes (colors) that are used on modern beer steins. The accompanying color section shows nearly all of the existing color styles, many of which were developed during the 1980's.

Villeroy & Boch (Mettlach) became famous for their etched steins. During the 1980's, this company produced many steins which closely resemble the original c.1900 etched steins. Different and secret techniques are used to make these current steins. Both Thewalt and Gerz have also produced etched type steins during the 1980's.

Porcelain steins with transfer or hand-painted decorations are produced in the same manner as c.1900 steins. Glass steins are also produced in the same way and in many of the same styles as earlier steins.

Faience steins have been produced (or reproduced) in recent years primarily as items for gift stores.

Sometimes production quality has been good enough to confuse novice collectors. Generally the quality of the newer faience steins is not the same as their two-hundred year old counterparts, but they have significant merit of their own.

Pewter relief steins are currently made in the same manner as c.1900 steins. Except for natural aging (patina), it can be difficult to distinguish the new pewter steins from the old.

17.2 Limited Editions

The 1980's saw the growth of the limited edition collectible stein. First introduced by Gerz in 1974, limited edition steins have come into popularity due to the overall increase in the popularity of beer stein collecting. Limited editions are commonly issued in quantities such as 2500, 5000, or 10,000. Occasionally, however, limited editions are issued in significantly lower, or higher, quantities.

Note: Prices indicated are original retail prices
when first sold; prices can vary for different glazes.

Faience steins, 1.0L, transfer decorations, c.1970's, pewter mounts resemble 18th century pewter, retail prices $100-200.

a.   Stoneware, .5L, relief, by King, currently available, pewter lid, $50-75.

b.   Stoneware, .5L, relief, by Gerz, c.1987, Alpine, stoneware lid, $75-100.

c.   Stoneware, .5L, relief, by Gerz, c.1985, special Opa's Haus version with fox handle, stoneware lid, $90-120.

d.   Stoneware, .5L, relief, by Beyer, c.1988, pewter lid, $75-100.

e.   Stoneware stein, .75L, Harley Davidson, 2nd Edition, limited edition of 3000, by Thewalt, c.1984, $150-200.

f.   Stoneware stein, .75L, Harley Davidson, 1st Edition, limited edition of 5000, by Thewalt, c.1983, $130-200.

a.   Stoneware, .75L, relief, by Thewalt, c.1980, Biedermeier, inlaid lid, $80-120.

b.   Stoneware, .75L, relief, by Thewalt, c.1985, traditional style, pewter lid, $100-140.

c.   Stoneware, .5L, relief, by Thewalt, c.1985, Hunting, inlaid figural lid, $90-120.

d.   Stoneware, .5L, relief, by Thewalt, c.1985, traditional style, inlaid figural lid, $90-120.

e.   Stoneware, .5L, relief, by Thewalt, c.1980, Railway, pewter lid, $60-90.

f.   Stoneware, .5L, relief, by Thewalt, c.1982, Railway, limited edition of 5000, sold out, pewter lid, $100-125.

g.   Stoneware, .5L, relief, by Thewalt, c.1982, Bicycle, limited edition of 5000, sold out, pewter lid, $100-125.

h.   Stoneware, .5L, relief, by Thewalt, c.1982, Beer Hier!, limited edition of 5000, sold out, pewter lid, $100-125.

a. Stoneware, .75L, incised, by Gerz, c.1986, St. George, limited edition of 6000, pewter lid, $125-175.

b. Stoneware, .5L, relief, by Gerz, c.1985, Altenburg Rosette, limited edition of 6000, pewter lid, $90-120.

c. Stoneware, .75L, relief, by Gerz, c.1983, Raeren, retired, pewter lid, $65-85.

d. Stoneware, .5L, relief, by Gerz, c.1984, Waldenkrug, retired, pewter lid, $65-85.

Stoneware steins, .5L, incised, by Thewalt, Mettlach style, introduced from 1978 through 1985, with pewter lid, $150-200, with inlaid lid, $140-180.

Stoneware steins, .5L, chromolith, by Villeroy & Boch, 1981 to 1984, sold by American Express and Villeroy & Boch, Fairytale series, Pinocchio, Pied Piper, Hanzel & Gretel, Peter Pan, limited edition of 10,000 each, inlaid lids, $195.

Porcelain steins, .5L, transfer, by Imagine That (U.S.A. distributor), first three are limited editions of 100 to 200, 1986, $100-150; fourth is custom design for individual firefighter, ordered with name, company, city, etc., $120-150.

Porcelain Character steins made by Porcelain Manufacturers Plaue, formerly Schierholz & Söhn, are distributed by Rastal, Höhr-Grenzhausen. Made from the same molds as the original steins and decorated with similar colors, they are marked on the base with MUSTERSCHUTZ and hash marks. Original, c.1900 steins usually have the capacity marked inside: -o,5L, while current production is marked: -0,5L; the "o" is usually slightly smaller than the "5" on c.1900 steins.

Above, left to right:

Wilhelm I, Gentleman Fox, Gooseman (factory prototype coloring), King Ludwig II (factory prototype coloring); retail prices around $400-500.

Above:

Stoneware steins made by Ceramarte of Brazil. Annual Christmas steins sold by Avon. First produced in 1976, these annual steins depict American history and daily life. Retail prices have ranged from $40-50.

C. 18

Villeroy & Boch, Mettlach, West Germany renewed stein production in the 1970's after a lapse of half a century. Chromolith type, relief and transfer decorations have been refined, placing Villeroy & Boch among the leaders in quality stein production.

Above, left:

Centennial Car Series, Rolls Royce, Mercedes Benz, Ford and Bugatti, sold by American Express, limited edition of 10,000, $195.

Above, right:

Russian Fairytale series, sold by American Express, limited edition of 10,000, $150.

Villeroy & Boch.

Above, top row, left to right:

Two porcelain steins from the Famous Sea Battles Series, $130; Summer, from the Four Seasons Series, limited edition of 10,000, $275; William Tell, $180.

Above, bottom row, left to right:

Two porcelain steins, Parsifal and Siegfried from the Wagner Series, 1985, limited edition of 10,000, sold by American Express, $150; two porcelain steins from the Game Bird Series, $120.

A.J. Thewalt GmbH, West Germany, was founded in 1893, and management still remains in the Thewalt family. They are one of the largest manufacturers of stoneware steins in West Germany. Pictured on pages c.20, c.21 and c.22, are examples of their current production. Shown are traditional steins as well as numerous new designs. Most of their steins may be obtained through retail dealers in the United States.

Above, top row, left to right:

a.   Infantry stein, .5L, transfer, decorated by Thewalt, the body is made elsewhere, one in a series of seven regimental steins, $110-135.

b.   Artillery stein, .5L, relief, hand-painted, one in a series of five regimental steins, $140-170.

c.   Castle Tower stein, .5L, relief, hand-painted, $70-90.

d.   Biedermeier stein, .75L, relief, hand-painted, one in a series of six, $100-125.

e.   Rhine stein, .5L, relief, hand-painted, one in a series of four, $110-135.

Above, bottom row, left to right:

f.   Prussian stein, .5L, incised, limited edition of 5000, one in a series of four, $130-160.

g.   Mettlach style stein, .75L, incised, one in a series of four, $130-160.

h.   Traditional stein, .5L, relief, hand-painted, one in a series of six, $70-90.

i.   Wedding stein, .5L, relief, hand-painted, limited edition of 10,000, $80-110.

j.   Bavarian stein, .5L, relief, one in a series of six, $70-90.

A.J. Thewalt GmbH.

Above, top row, left to right:

a. Traditional stein, 1.0L, relief, hand-painted, one in a series of six, $85-110.

b. Münchener Kindl stein, 1.0L, relief, hand-painted, $85-110.

c. Traditional stein, .5L, relief, hand-painted, with music box, $110-140.

d. Traditional stein, 1.0L, relief, hand-painted, one in a series of six, $85-110.

e. Fox Handle stein, .4L, relief, hand-painted, $60-75.

Above, bottom row, left to right:

f. Traditional stein, 1.0L, relief, hand-painted, one in a series of six, $105-130.

g. Lovers stein, .5L, relief, hand-painted, $110-135.

h. Crusader stein, 1.0L, relief, hand-painted, limited edition of 10,000, $180-220.

i. Navy stein, .5L, relief, hand-painted, $110-135.

j. Night Watchman stein, .5L, relief, hand-painted, $110-135.

A.J. Thewalt GmbH.

Above, top row, left to right:

a., b., c., d.   Gambrinus steins, .75L, relief, hand-painted, four differently colored versions, limited edition of 10,000, $120-200.

e.   Münchener Kindl stein, .75L, relief, hand-painted, limited edition of 10,000, $105-130.

Above, bottom row, left to right:

f.   Proletarian stein, .75L, relief, hand-painted, limited edition of 5000, $240-300.

g.   Wedding Parade stein, .75L, relief, hand-painted, limited edition of 10,000, $130-160.

h.   Crown Royalty stein, .75L, relief, hand-painted, limited edition of 10,000, $180-220.

i.   Farmer & Plow stein, .75L, relief, hand-painted, limited edition of 10,000, $95-115.

j.   Zither Player stein, .75L, relief, hand-painted, limited edition of 10,000, $130-160.

Gerz GmbH, West Germany, has been producing steins for over 100 years. Currently they are the largest manufacturers of stoneware steins in West Germany. Pictured on pages c.23, c.24 and c.25 are examples of their current production. Most of their steins may be obtained from distributors such as Bavarian Ltd. and M. Cornell Importers, through retail dealers.

Above, top row, left to right:

a. Beerwagon stein, .5L, transfer, $35-50.

b. Bayern Crest stein, .5L, relief, hand-painted, $85-110.

c. Farm Dancers stein, 1.0L, pewter relief, $110-140.

d. Mozart stein, .5L, low relief, transfer, $60-75.

e. Kaiser Franz-Josef stein, .5L, low relief, transfer, $60-75.

Above, bottom row, left to right:

f. Seven Schwaben stein, .5L, low relief, transfer, $40-50.

g. Herzog von Berry stein, .5L, low relief, transfer, $45-55.

h. Black Forest Couple stein, .5L, relief, transfer, $50-60.

i. Altenburg stein, .5L, relief, hand-painted, limited edition of 6000, sold out, $110-140.

j. Wildflower stein, .5L, relief, hand-painted, limited edition of 4000, $90-110.

k. Tiffany type stein, .5L, transfer, limited edition of 8000, $90-120.

Gerz GmbH.

Above, top row, left to right:

a. Defregger stein, 1.0L, relief, hand-painted, six different steins, $70-85.

b. Old Gerz stein, 1.0L, relief, hand-painted, $90-110.

c. Village Blacksmith, relief, transfer, $55-70.

d. Old Gerz, 1.0L, relief, glazed, $55-70.

e. Defregger stein, 1.0L, relief, $55-70.

f. Defregger stein, 1.0L, relief, hand-painted, $70-85.

Above, bottom row, left to right:

g. Neuschwanstein stein, .5L, relief, hand-painted, $140-175.

h. Diana-Huntress stein, .5L, relief, hand-painted, $110-140.

i. Rokoko stein, .5L, relief, hand-painted, $120-145.

j. Baroque Shield stein, .5L, relief, transfer, assorted cities, $55-70.

k. Old German Folk Life, 1.0L, relief, hand-painted, $80-90.

l. Fox Handle stein, .5L, relief, $45-60.

Gerz GmbH.

Above, top row, left to right:

a. Christmas stein, .5L, relief, hand-painted, $170-200.

b. Four Seasons stein, .75L, relief, hand-painted, $130-160.

c. Bürgerstein, 1.0L, relief, transfer, comes with different scenes, $100-125.

d. Weihnachtseidel, .5L, relief, transfer, $75-95.

e. Musical stein, .5L, relief, transfer, $75-95.

Above, bottom row, left to right:

f. Old Gerz stein, .5L, relief, hand-painted, $80-100.

g. Old German stein, .5L, relief, hand-painted, $110-140.

h. Sailship stein, .5L, transfer, $55-70.

i. Alp Horn Blower stein, .5L, relief, hand-painted, $75-95.

j. München stein, .5L, relief, hand-painted, transfer, $75-95.

House of Tyrol is a mail order company selling imported items, including beer steins. Many of the steins in their catalogs and pictured above are limited editions sold only by House of Tyrol.

Above, top row, left to right:

a. Stoneware, .5L, by Beyer, 1987, limited edition, $49.

b. Stoneware, .5L, by Westerwald Team, 1988, limited edition, $129.

c. Glass, .5L, by Christallerie Bavaria, 1989, overlay, $225.

d. Glass, .5L, by Schreiner & Söhne, 1988, pewter overlay, $198.

e. Glass, .5L, by Rudolf Wutschka, 1988, engraved, $298.

Above, bottom row, left to right:

f. Stoneware, .75L, Mettlach style, incised, by A.J. Thewalt, 1987, $145.

g. Porcelain, .5L, by L. Parbus, 1987, $110.

h. Porcelain, .5L, by Elisabeth Liegl, 1987, $98.

i. Porcelain, .5L, by Elisabeth Liegl, 1986, $125.

j. Glass, .5L, by Crystal Factory of Baron von Poschinger, 1987, $325.

Opa's Haus has been an importer of German beer steins for 20 years, specializing in limited edition steins. Most of the steins pictured above are available from them, through retail dealers.

Above, top row, left to right:

a. Stoneware, .5L, Lowell Davis Christmas, Second Edition, Presents for Uncle Remus, by Beyer GmbH, 1989, limited edition of 2500, $85-110.

b. Stoneware, .5L, Festival stein, by Gerz, 1982, limited edition of 10,000, sold out, $60-80.

c. Stoneware, .5L, Boxer Rebellion stein, by Gerz, 1985, limited edition of 1950, $70-90.

d. Stoneware, .5L, Winter Snows stein, by Gerz, 1985, limited edition of 1950, $100-125.

e. Stoneware, .5L, Night Stalker stein, by Gerz, 1984, limited edition of 1950, $100-125.

Above, bottom row, left to right:

f. Porcelain, .5L, Pair of Eagles stein, by Lindner, 1989, limited edition of 500, $175-225.

g. Stoneware, .5L, Skiing stein, by A.J. Thewalt, 1986, limited edition of 2500, $150-180.

h. Stoneware, .5L, Lowell Davis Christmas, First Edition, Silent Night, by Gerz, 1988, limited edition of 500, prestige edition, $110-140.

i. Stoneware, .75L, Polar Bear stein, by A.J. Thewalt, 1986, limited edition of 2500, $150-180.

j. Stoneware, 1.0L, His Majesty stein, by Gerz, 1988, limited edition of 2500, $140-170.

k. Stoneware, 2.0L, Pintail Sunset, by Gerz, 1988, limited edition of 1950, $180-220.

M. Cornell Importers, Inc. has been a major importer and distributor of beer steins for over thirty years. Most of the steins pictured here are available exclusively from them, through retail dealers.

Above, bottom row, left to right:

f.   Stoneware, .5L, relief, Beer Wagon stein, by Westerwald Team, 1987, limited edition of 4000, $100-140.

g.   Stoneware, .5L, relief, Railroad stein, by Westerwald Team, 1989, limited edition of 2000, $110-150.

h.   Glass, .5L, engraved, Cobalt Eagle stein, 1989, $200-300.

i.   Stoneware, .5L, relief, Dragon Slayer stein, by A.J. Thewalt, 1988, limited edition of 10,000, $165-220.

j.   Stoneware, .5L, relief, The Ahrens-Fox Fire Engine Stein, by A.J. Thewalt, 1989, limited edition of 10,000, $120-180.

Opposite, top row, left to right:

a.   Stoneware, .5L, relief, The Singer, by Marzi & Remy, 1989, limited edition of 5000, $85-115.

b.   Stoneware, .5L, relief, The Firefighter, by Marzi & Remy, 1989, limited edition of 5000, $85-115.

c.   Stoneware, .75L, relief, The Bald Eagle, by A.J. Thewalt, 1989, limited edition of 10,000, $150-200.

d.   Stoneware, .75L, Mettlach style, incised, Lorelei stein, by A.J. Thewalt, 1985, with castle lid, $150-225.

e.   Stoneware, .75L, relief, Carousel stein, by Werner Corzellus, 1989, limited edition of 5000, $160-220; with music box, $190-250.

Above, left to right:

a.   Stoneware, .5L, relief, Largemouth Bass, Bass Research Foundation, by Ceramarte, 1989, $25.

b.   Porcelain, .5L, transfer, Winterfest, Coors Brewery, 1989, limited edition of 9950, $40.

c.   Stoneware, .75L, relief, Frederick Miller stein, by A.J. Thewalt, 1989, limited edition of 9850, $125-200.

d.   Stoneware, .5L, print over glaze, Winter Stein, by Alwe, 1989, $20-30.

e.   Stoneware, .5L, transfer, Harley Davidson Motorcycles, by A.J. Thewalt, 1989, $60-85.

Concepts Unlimited is an importer and distributor of beer steins from Brazil (Ceramarte) and Germany, specializing in corporate and association promotional steins. The steins pictured above as well as on page c.29, a, b & c, have been distributed by Concepts Unlimited. These steins are sold by the brewery or other company featured on the stein, and, in some cases, directly by Concepts Unlimited.

Above, top row, left to right:

a., b., c., d. Miller Brewery, .5L, by Ceramarte, First Flight, 1986, sold out, First Assembly Line Car, 1987, First Transcontinental Railroad, 1988, First River Steamer, 1989, $10-20.

e., f. Coors Brewery, .5L, by Ceramarte, Brewery, 1988, Beer Truck, 1989, $14-16.

Above, bottom row, left to right:

g. Miller Brewery, .5L, by Alwe, Plank Road, 1989, limited edition of 9950, $90.

h., i., j. Ducks Unlimited, .5L, by Ceramarte, 50th Anniversary, 1987, Mallards, 1988, Canvasbacks, 1989, $50-63.

k. Stroh Brewery, .5L, by Ceramarte, Statue of Liberty, 1986, limited edition of 25,000, sold out, $30-45.

Primex International Trading Corp. represents Ceramarte of Brazil in the United States. They have been importing beer steins for breweries such as Anheuser Busch and other companies including Avon.

Generally the production quantity of these steins exceeds that of most German produced steins. This is especially true over the last five years. In addition to a large production capacity, Ceramarte has developed a technique for applying a detailed transfer to a low relief body. This has enabled them to satisfy the demands of the large volume customers.

Above, left to right:

a. Mettlach stein, .5L, #2136, stoneware, etched & print under glaze, made in 1894, *The Anheuser Busch Stein,* inlaid lid depicts the Anheuser Busch emblem, originally about $5, currently selling for over $2000.

b., c., d. Examples of three steins made by Ceramarte for Anheuser Busch. Nearly 100 different ones have been made. Most were sold for prices from $12 to $30, while some limited edition steins were sold for about $50.

e. Stoneware, .5L, The Bud Man, by Ceramarte, originally about $12.50 retail, sold out, currently selling for over $200. A new version was introduced in 1989, $30-40.

Above, six steins made by Ceramarte for Anheuser Busch, including :

a. Limited Edition V, about $35.

b. The 1983 Olympic stein, used as gifts, no selling price.

c. The Bald Eagle, about $25.

d. The Brewhouse stein, about $23.

e. The 1987 Holiday stein, about $13.

f. The 1989 Holiday stein, about $13.

Gary Kirsner Auctions specializes in selling antique beer steins. About six auctions are conducted each year. Limited edition steins are also sold in some of these auctions. Mail bids are accepted.

Gary Kirsner Auctions
P.O. Box 8807
Coral Springs, Florida 33075
Phone (305) 344-9856.

Character steins, .5L, pottery, by M. Girmscheid, c.1980, Ram, Frog, Monkey, Fox, pottery lids, $20-40.

e.   Character stein, .5L, pottery, by Beyer, c.1988,
     Money Bag, inlaid lid, $60-90.

f.   Character stein, .5L, stoneware, by Gerz, c.1984,
     Bavarian Lion, retired, pottery lid, $70-100.

g.   Character stein, .5L, stoneware, by Gerz, c.1984,
     Bartender Pig, retired, inlaid lid, $70-100.

h.   Character stein, .5L, stoneware, by Gerz, c.1987,
     Santa Claus, stoneware lid, $50-75.

New Regimental steins, .5L and 1.0L, porcelain, made by various manufacturers, generally unmarked.
From 1960 through the 1980's, transfer decorations and pewter lids, current retail store prices, $75-125.

Identification of new Regimental steins is usually not difficult, although some new steins are very similar to the originals. Many things can indicate a Regimental stein is not an original, including:

1. Porcelain steins with manufacturer's marks on the bottom are almost always new (1 in 1000 old Regimentals are marked). A common new mark is a *crown* in blue or gold.

2. A lithophane of a semi-nude woman indicates a new stein.

3. A stamped rather than cast pewter lid would indicate a modern stein.

4. Information about the unit (Regiment) that is not correct, such as putting Munich in Prussia, would indicate a new stein.

5. A sharply tapered body is frequently an indication of a new stein.

   Note: Trying to determine age using transfer vs. hand-painting is unreliable.

Regimental steins, .5L, pottery, manufacturer unknown, c.1975, pewter lids, $30-50.

Stoneware steins, 1.0L and .5L, Schultz & Dooley, made in different versions, in Germany and Brazil, first made c.1960, $10-20.

18. Bibliography and References

Journals

Der Gemutlichkeit, Stein Collectors International, *1*, September 1965, to *16*, June 1969.

Keramos, Villeroy & Boch Keramische Werke K.G., *1*, 1952, to *6*, 1978.

Mettlacher Turm, Mettlacher Steinzeugsammler E.V., *1*, 1977, to *44*, 1989.

Prosit, Stein Collectors International, *17*, September 1969, to *98*, December 1989.

General

Bernay, J. et. al., 1983. *Das Grosse Lexikon vom Bier und seinen Brauereien*, Scripta Verlag, Stuttgart.

Chaffers, Wm., undated. *Marks & Monograms on European and Oriental Pottery and Porcelain*, Borden Publishing Company, Los Angeles.

Dexel, W., 1939. *Deutsches Handwerksgut - Eine Kultur - und Formengeschichte des Hausgerats*, Berlin.

Erling, F., et. al., 1978. *Bier-Trinkgefasse*, Limpert-Verlag, Bad Homburg.

Gruhl, J., 1982. "Queen of the Drinking Vessels," *Prosit*, *70*, Stein Collectors International, pp. 978-980, December.

Hansen, H.J., 1970. *Das pompose Zeitalter zwischen Biedermeier and Jugendstil*, Gerhard Stallung Verlag, Oldenburg.

Harrell, J.L., 1979. *Regimental Steins*, The Old Soldier Press, Frederick, MD.

Kirsner, G., and Gruhl, J., 1984. *The Stein Book*, Glentiques, Ltd., Coral Springs, FL.

Kirsner, G., 1989. *German Military Steins*, Glentiques, Ltd., Coral Springs, FL.

Kohlhausen, H., 1955. *Geschichte des deutschen Kunstwerks*, München.

Lowenstein, J.G., 1974. *A Stein Bibliography*, Princeton, NJ.

Manusov, E., 1976. *Encyclopedia of Character Steins*, Wallace Homestead Book Co., Des Moines, IA.

Manusov, E., and Wald, M., 1987. *Character Steins, A Collector's Guide*, Cornwall Books, Cranbury, NJ.

Monson-Fitzjohn, G.J., 1927. *Drinking Vessels of Bygone Days*, London.

Münchner Stadtmuseum, 1976. *125 Jahre Bayerischer Kunstgewerbeverein*, München.

Oshkosh, 1969. *Antique Steins at the Paine Art Center*.

Schiedlausky, G., 1956. *Essen und Trinken*, München.

Scholz, R., 1978. *Humpen und Krüge-Trinkgefasse 16.-20. Jahrhundert*, Keyser, München.

Uhlig, O.O., 1982. *Bierkrug-Deckel*, Rosenheimer.

Wilson, R.D., 1982. "Misconceptions About Dates Implied By *Made in Germany* on Steins," *Stein Zeitung*, S.C.I. Erste Gruppe, Summer.

Glass

Dexel, T., 1977. *Gebrauchsglas*, Braunschweig.

Frankfurt a.M. Museums fur Kunsthandwerk, 1973. *Europaisches und aussereuropaisches Glas*, Frankfurt a.M.

Fuchs, F.L., 1956. *Die Glaskunst im Wandel der Jahrtausende*, Darmstadt.

Kalnein, W.G., 1978. *Das Wein Gefass*, Ariel Verlag, Frankfurt a.M.

Kampfer, F., 1966. *Viertausend Jahre Glas*, Dresden.

Klesse, B., and Reineking-von Bock, G., 1973. *Kunstgewerbemuseum der Stadt Köln: Glas*, Köln.

Lipp, F.C., 1974. *Bemalte Glaser*, München.

Saldern, A. von, 1965. *German Enameled Glass*, New York.

Schade, G., 1968. *Deutsches Glas*, Leipzig.

Schlosser, J., 1977. *Das alte Glas*, Braunschweig.

Schmidt, R., 1922. *Das Glas*, Berlin/Leipzig.

Unusual Materials

Brunner, H., 1964. *Altes Tafelsilber*, München.

Doucet, F.W., 1973. *Silber*, München.

Fritz, J.M., 1964. "Goldschmiedearbeiten des 14.-18. Jhrs. im Rhein," in *Bonner Jahrbuch*, *164*, pg. 407.

Neuwirth, W., 1978. *Markenlexikon fur Kunstgewerbe, Edle und unedle Metalle, vol. 1, 1875-1900*, Wien.

Philippovich, E.v., 1966. *Elfenbein*, Braunschweig.

Rohde, A., 1937. *Bernstein, ein deutscher Werkstoff*, Berlin.

Theuerkauff, C., 1967. *Elfenbeinarbeiten aus dem Barock*, Hamburg/Berlin.

Weinholz, G., undated. *Gefasse und Gerate aus Bernstein*, Staatliche Kunstsammlungen Dresden, Dresden.

Pewter

Dietz, A., 1903. *Das Frankfurter Zinngiessergewerbe und seine Blutezeit im 18. Jh.*, Historischen Museums in Frankfurt a.M., Frankfurt a.M.

Dolz, 1974. *Zinn*, München.

Drier, F.-A., 1959. "Die mittelalterlichen Balusterzinnkannen Norddeutschlands," in *Zeitschrift fur Kunstwissenschaft*, *13*, pp. 27-50.

Haedeke, H.-U., 1973. *Zinn, Zentren der Zinngiesserkunst von der Antike bis zum Jugendstil*, Leipzig.

Hintze, E., 1928. *Die deutschen Zinngiesser und Ihre Marken*, 7 vols., Karl W. Hiersemann, Leipzig.

Mory, L., 1975. *Schones Zinn*, 5. Aufl., München.

Ohm, A. and M. Bauer, 1977. *Steinzeug und Zinn*, Catalog of the Museums fur Kunsthandwerk, Frankfurt a.M.

Wagner, E., 1977. *Jugend-Zinn*, München.

Wuhr, H., 1957. *Altes Zinn*, Darmstadt.

Faience and Porcelain

Badischen Landesmuseum, 1975. *Durlacher Fayencen*, Karlsruhe.

Bauer, M., 1977. *Europaische Fayencen*, Museum fur Kunsthandwerk, Frankfurt a.M.

Behse, A., 1955. *Deutsches Fayencemarken-Brevier*, Braunschweig.

Behse, A., 1965. *Porzellanmarken-Brevier*, Braunschweig.

Bosch, H., 1983. *German Faience Jugs and Tankards of the 17th and 18th Centuries*, Verlag Philipp von Zabern, Mainz a.R.

Bosch, H., 1984. *Die Nürnberger Hausmaler*, Klinkhardt & Biermann, München.

Danckert, L., 1954. *Handbuch des Europaischen Porzellans*, München.

Dewiel, L., 1977. *Deutsche Fayencen*, München.

Ducret, S., 1962. *Deutsches Porzellan und deutsche Fayencen*, Baden-Baden.

Ducret, S., 1972. *Meissner Porzellan bemalt in Augsburg*, Brunswick.

Erdner, H. and Nagel, G.K., 1972. *Die Fayencefabrik zu Schrezheim, 1752-1865*, Schwabenverlag Ellwangen, Jagst.

Fregnac, C., 1976. *Europaische Fayencen*, Fribourg.

Fuchs, E. and P. Heiland, 1925. *Die deutsche Fayence-Kultur*, München.

Graesse, J.G. and E. Jaennicke, 1967. *Führer für Sammler von Porzellan und Fayence*, Brunswick.

Hauger, O., 1951. *Durlacher Fayencen*, Verlag G. Braun, Karlsruhe.

Hofmann, F.H., 1932. *Das Porzellan der europaischen Manufakturen im 18. Jahrhundert*, Berlin.

Huseler, K., 1956-1958. *Deutsche Fayencen, Ein Handbuch der Fabriken, ihrer Meister und Werke*, 3 vols., Stuttgart.

Jedding, H., 1971. *Europaisches Porzellan, vol. 1*, München.

Klein, A., 1975. *Deutsche Fayencen*, Braunschweig.

Langer, H., 1988. *Österreichische Fayencen*, Weltkunst Verlag, München.

Pazaurek, G.E., 1925. *Deutsche Fayence- und Porzellan-Hausmaler*, 2 vols., Leipzig.

Riesebieter, O., 1921. *Die deutsche Fayencen des 17. und 18. Jahrhunderts*, Leipzig.

Schnorr von Carolsfeld, L., 1956. *Porzellan der europaischen Fabriken*, Braunschweig.

Schwarze, W., 1980. *Alte Deutsche Fayence-Krüge*, Schwarze Verlag, Wuppertal.

Spies, G., 1971. *Braunschweiger Fayencen*, Klinkhardt & Biermann, Braunschweig.

Stohr, A., 1920. *Deutsche Fayencen und deutsches Steingut*, Berlin.

Ceramic

Albrecht, R., 1909. *Die Topferkunst in Creussen*, Rothenburg o.T.

Rijksmuseum Amsterdam, 1977. *Villeroy & Boch 1748-1930, Two Centuries of Ceramic Products*, Amsterdam.

Arens, F., 1971. "Die ursprungliche Verwendung Gotischer Stein- und Tonmodel," in *Mainzer Zeitschrift*, 66, p. 106.

Borrmann, R., undated. *Moderne Keramik*, Leipzig.

Clarke, P.J. and J. O'Connor, 1977. "The Mettlach Occupationalists," *Prosit*, 48, Stein Collectors International, p. 408, June.

Cohausen, A. von, 1879. "Einige technische Bemerkungen uber die groberen Thonwaaren auf der Pariser Austellung 1879," in *Mittheilungen des Gewerbevereins fur Nassau*.

Cox, W.E., 1959. *The Book of Pottery and Porcelain*, New York.

Dexel, W., 1958. *Keramik, Stoff und Form*, Braunschweig/Berlin.

Dexel, W., 1962. *Das Hausgerat Mitteleuropas; Wesen und Wandel der Formen in Zwei Jahrtausend*, Braunschweig/Berlin.

Dry-v.Zezschwitz, B., 1981. *R. Merkelbach: Grenzhausen und München, Spezialpreisliste, 1905*, Dr. Graham Dry, München.

Dry-v.Zezschwitz, B., 1982. Rosskopf & Gerz, Verlag Dry, München.

Eber, H., 1913. *Creussner Topferkunst*, München.

Engelmeier, P., 1969. *Westerwalder Steinzeugkruge mit dem Monogram GR*, in *Keramos*, 44, pp. 3-11.

Falke, O.v., 1908. *Das rheinische Steinzeug*, 2 vols., Berlin.

Finke, U.C., 1988. *Westerwälder Steinzeugkrüge der Spätrenaissance*, Kannenbäckerstadt, Höhr-Grenzhausen.

Fischer, W., 1927. *Die Saltglasur*, Coburg.

Funcke, W.F., 1927. *Die Entwicklung des rheinischen Topfergewerbes seit dem 15. Jahrhundert*, Universitat Köln, Gladbach.

Graesse, J.G., 1974. *Führer fur Sammler von Porzellan, Fayence, Steinzeug, Steingut, usw.*, Braunschweig.

Groschopf, G., 1937. *Die suddeutsche Hafnerkeramik*, in *Jahrbuch 1937 d. Bayerischen Landesvereins fur Heimatsschutz*.

Grundriss, 1879. *Der Keramik*, Paul Neff, Stuttgart.

Haedecke, H.-U., 1967. "Zur Soziologie der Topfer im Rheinland," in *Keramos*, 37, pp. 63-68.

Hillier, B., 1968. *Pottery and Porcelain 1700-1914, The Social History of Decorative Arts*, London.

Honey, W.B., 1949. *European Ceramic Art*, 2 vols., London.

Honey, W.B., 1952. *European Ceramic Art from the End of the Middle Ages to about 1815*, London.

Horschik, J., 1977. "Sachisches und Thuringisches Steinzeug," *9. Int. Hafnerei-Symposium*, Frechen.

Horschik, J., 1978. *Steinzeug*, Verlag der Kunst, Dresden.

Hughes, G.B., 1959. *Victorian Pottery and Porcelain*, London.

Jaennicke, F., 1978. *Deutsches Steinzeug*.

Jaennicke, F., 1900. *Geschichte der Keramik*, Leipzig.

Just, R., 1960. "Creussen un sachsische Steinzeug mit Emailfarbenbemalung," in *Keramik-Freunde der Schweiz, 52*, pp. 18-24, Zurich.

Klinge, E., 1977. *Creussner Steinzeug*, Neue Presse, Coburg.

Klinge, E., 1979. *Deutsches Steinzeug der Renaissance und Barockzeit*, Hetjens-Museum, Dusseldorf.

Kirsner, G., 1982. "Signatures on Etched Mettlach Steins: What Are They Worth?," *Stein Report*, June.

Kirsner, G., and J. Gruhl(ed.), 1987. *The Mettlach Book, Second Edition*, Glentiques, Ltd. Inc., Coral Springs, FL.

Kohnemann, M. 1982. *Auflagen auf Raerener Steinzeug*, Töpfereimuseums, Raeren.

Kroll, J., 1980. *Creussner Steinzeug*, Klinkhardt & Biermann, Braunschweig.

Liebscher-Willert, 1955. *Technologie der Keramik*, Dresden.

Lowenstein, J.G. and Clarke, P., 1974. *English Translation 1899 Mettlach Catalogue with Supplement Steins*, Princeton, NJ.

Lüthgen, G.E., 1981. *Deutsches Steinzeug*, Verlag Dr. Graham Dry, München.

Mettlach, 1937. *Dreitausend Jahre Topferkunst: Ein Rundgang durch das Keramische Museum von Villeroy & Boch.*

Moltheim, A.W. von, 1924. "Die deutsche Keramik der Renaissance in Nachbildung und Falschung," in *Belvedere Forum, 5*, pg. 37, Wien.

Ohm, A. and M. Bauer, 1977. *Steinzeug und Zinn*, Museum fur Kunsthandwerk, Frankfurt Besitz, Frankfurt a.M.

Pazaurek, 1927. *Steingut, Formgebung und Geschichte*, Stuttgart.

Pelka, O., 1924. *Keramik der Neuzeit*, Leipzig.

Post, A., 1975. Mettlacher Steinzeug 1885-1905, Hans J. Ammelounx, Wheeling, IL.

Reineking von Bock, G., 1970. "Steinzeug - Nachahmung, Nachbildung oder Falschung," in *Keramos, 49*.

Reineking von Bock, G., 1978. *Meister der deutschen Keramik 1900-1950*, Kunstgewerbemuseum Köln.

Reinheckel, G., 1978. *German and Austrian Ceramics*, Tokyo.

Rolfes, D., 1982. *Keramikmuseum Westerwald - Deutsche Sammlung fur historische und zeitgenossische Keramik*, Keramikmuseum Westerwald, Höhr-Grenzhausen.

Seng, A., 1983. *Dumler & Breiden - 100 Jahre Keramik*, Höhr-Grenzhausen.

Stieber, P., 1973. "Deutsches Hafnergeschirr," in *Keysers Kunst- und Antiquitatenbuch III*, München.

Stoehr, A., 1920. *Deutsche Fayencen und deutsches Steingut*, Berlin.

Strauss, K., 1925. "Die Topferkunst in Hessen," in *Studien zur Deutschen Kunstgeschichte, vol. 228*, Strassburg.

Thieler, E.R., 1909. *Making Steins in an Old Monastery*, Brochure by E.R. Thieler Co.

Thieler, E.R., 1909. *Mettlach Wares Catalog.*

Thomas, T., 1976. "Mettlacher Steinzeug - Spiegel des Zeitgeschmacks," in *Keramos*, research newspaper Villeroy & Boch, pp. 28-30.

Thomas, T.,(ed.), 1978. *Keramos, 6*, Augsburger Druck- und Verlagshaus, Augsburg.

Thomas, T. and A. Post, 1975. *Mettlacher Steinzeug 1885-1905*, Hans J. Ammelounx Publisher, Wheeling, IL.

Wald, M., 1980. *HR Steins*, S.C.I. Publications, Kingston, NJ.

Wilson, R.D., 1979. "Date Your Mettlach Steins," *Prosit, 57*, Stein Collectors International, pp. 597-598, September.

Wilson, R.D., 1980. "Mettlach's Phanolith Fabrication," *Stein Zeitung*, S.C.I. Erste Gruppe, Spring.

Wilson, R.D., 1980. "Mettlach Size Number Code," *Stein Talk, 39*, S.C.I. Thirsty Knights Chapter, December.

Zobeltiz, H. von, 1899. "Villeroy & Boch," in *Velhagen und Klassing's Monatsheften XIII, Bd. 1*, pp. 193-207.

Appendix

A. Price Adjustments for Condition

Many factors contribute to the value of a specific stein. But unlike some assets which have alternative productive uses, steins have value only as something beautiful to collect for enjoyment or speculative purposes. For this reason the value of any antique stein is simply what one person will pay another in order to own it. Dealers do not, nor could they, collude to set prices because no one need buy any stein if it is not priced at an acceptable level.

The *prices*, or *values*, on all the steins shown throughout this book have been set at the *average* U.S. retail prices of these steins in *good* condition. Deviations from these prices can occur for any number of reasons, reasons that are important to many collectors. An explanation of these is contained in this Appendix.

A.1 Normal Variations

The stein market is relatively stable, and the prices of certain types of steins generally move up in an orderly fashion. Of course, even for identical steins in good condition, one can expect to see fluctuations in day-to-day sales prices. What causes these fluctuations? Large variations can occur when the buyer or seller, or both, lack a good understanding, or reference, for the current price of a particular stein. Occasionally a stein will come up at a small auction where there are no competing interests.

Aside from the variations due to abnormal circumstances, what amount of variation in price should one expect? *Informed* variations exist when the buyer and the seller know the market price of a stein, but have decided on a different price due to personal preferences, time constraints, or speculation. Take, for example, the variations in prices of Mettlach steins. For steins under

$200, such variations might be as much as +/-20%. For somewhat more valuable steins the range decreases to about +/-10%. And for the Mettlach steins valued at over $500, variations might be in range of +/-5% to +/-10%.

The variations for other types of steins are similar. Pewter, occupational, faience, early stoneware, and etched ceramic steins will have variations slightly greater than Mettlach's. Relief pottery, glass, porcelain, very rare steins, or steins of unusual materials will generally have somewhat greater fluctuations. Character and Regimental steins tend to have variations of about the same magnitude as the lower to middle price range Mettlachs.

There are *real* costs and *time* costs involved in finding alternative sellers or buyers of the same stein, and in many cases these are the reasons for these price fluctuations. Stein prices in Germany may vary somewhat from those in this book, some being higher and some lower. Occasionally, the foreign price may be different enough to stimulate substantial shipments of steins in or out of the United States. For the most part, these temporary differences are caused by currency fluctuations, and not by sudden changes in tastes or supplies.

A.2 Original Quality of Body

The *color* on steins is generally produced using glazes or enamels that are quite resistant to fading. Thus, when there is a stein that has noticeably less attractive coloring, it is generally *not* due to original color variations or subsequent natural fading, but to repairs or improper cleaning, such as with abrasives or caustic cleaners (vinegar, turpentine, or ammonia). Most transfer-decorated porcelains or stonewares *will* be affected by caustic cleaners, although most other types of steins will not. In any event, if the aesthetic appeal of the stein is affected, the value will be adversely affected.

Blotching or sloppy decorations can occasionally be seen on steins. Of course, blotching near the handle, or away from the detail on the front of the stein, will affect the price less than imperfections which are immediately noticeable.

Firing lines are primarily a concern with etched Mettlach steins, and are due to slightly different shrinkages of the dyed clays and the body clays. Reductions in price rarely exceed 5% or 10%, unless there is a heavy concentration of firing lines in an important part of the decoration.

Occasionally, transfer-decorated steins will show a tear, gap, or distortion in the decoration, or hand-painted steins will show some similar flaws, and these again must be evaluated with respect to the effect on the overall appearance of the stein. Price adjustments in excess of 15% are occasionally necessary in order to make a fair valuation.

A.3 Body Damage and Repairs

There is a *tremendous* variation in the price reductions that generally compensate for damage to a stein. However, there are several generalities concerning these reductions which should be understood.

1. Damage is more tolerable, even acceptable, on very old steins. For example, cracks and chips would be the norm on c.1600 stoneware steins, but cracks and chips on a 1983 Mettlach Collector's Society stein would necessitate tremendous discounting in order to stimulate a sale.

2. The more visible the damage, the greater the effect on price. Chips or cracks on glass steins are more visible, and thus more important than those on stoneware. Damage to the front (opposite the handle) discounts the price more than damage to the back or to the inside.

3. Paradoxically, damage to more fragile steins reduces their value more than similar damage to steins made from sturdier materials. For example, chips and cracks on glass or porcelain cause greater price reductions than similar damage on ceramic or pewter steins.

4. Damage to common steins is more important than damage to rare or one-of-a-kind steins. If collectors know they can obtain a better example of a stein, they will wait to do so, unless the discounts are significant.

Damage to Mettlach steins is often important because of this last point. A study was made for *The Mettlach Book* of the price reductions for damage, and these are roughly summarized here. Repaired chips of sizes up to 1" reduce value from 15% to 35%. Repaired, larger chips and broken pieces can require reductions of 50% or more. Repaired hairline cracks reduce value 25% to 50%.

The cost of high quality repairs can sometimes be greater than what the finished product is worth, from $25 to $200 depending upon the extent of damage and the amount of detailed work involved. New handles or sections of a stein can cost $100 or more. Besides being aware that the stein may not be worth repairing, there are several other cautions to heed. On older pieces, where damage is more acceptable, repairs are less acceptable. That is to say, do not repair very old steins unless they can't be displayed with their damage unrepaired. It is also a fact that some parts, such as handles or inlays, are easier to make than to repair. Thus, you must insist that the original part be used in repairs unless it is missing or beyond all usefulness. Also, be aware that very few people are capable of making high quality repairs or replacement parts.

A.4 Original Mountings

The quality or type of the original lid can be an important factor in the price of a stein. The prices for steins shown in this book are based upon the stein having the specific type of lid that is shown.

Mettlach steins could almost always have been ordered originally with a choice of plain or fancy pewter lids, ceramic insert lids, or no lids. When they were ordered without lids, they were undoubtedly sent to special pewterers (often in Munich) at additional expense, to get spectacular pewter lids. The fancy pewter lids that Mettlach provided (possibly contracted locally rather than actually attached by Villeroy and Boch) were usually more expensive than the ceramic inlaid lids. The original cost of lids, however, does not relate directly to current desirability. In fact, especially on the smaller-sized etched Mettlach steins, the inlaid lids are almost always the most desirable type for today's collectors. Steins that have less desirable pewter lids will be worth about 10% to 35% less.

Other ceramic stein manufacturers either concentrated on using heavy pewter lids (such as H.R.) or generally used ceramic inlaid lids (J.W.Remy, Gerz, Marzi & Remy, and most others). There is usually little or no discount for such steins when they are found with a different type of high-quality lid.

There is, however, a *low-quality* pewter lid that will always be measurably less desirable. That lid has been made, since the early 1900's, out of a lighter weight pewter alloy, generally containing lead, that has been *stamped* into a low steepled lid. Its design is often not sharp, and the shape is more conical to accommodate the stamping process. Older steins are occasionally found with *out of period* lids which, after examination of the strapping around the middle (as described in Section 2), seem to be original. Examples include steins from the 1600's with lids typical of the 1700's, or more commonly, steins from the 1700's with 1800's lids. It should be noted that these may be old replacements. In almost all European wars people were asked to turn in any metal that could be obtained. If the lid were replaced later, of course, it would be of a more modern type. It also seems likely that some lids were intentionally changed to become more stylish. Although such steins might have more mystery or romance, collectors and museums are generally looking for archetypical steins without confusing appearances. Therefore, these steins often must be discounted somewhat in order to pass through the market.

The same is usually true of steins which have lids of materials that are not typical. For example, Mettlach steins with silver-plated, copper, or brass lids will generally be worth somewhere around 30% to 50% less than those with typical lids. Upgraded materials, such as sterling for the usual pewter, will usually increase the value except if the lids seem suspicious or incongruous (such as silver on pewter or faceted glass on pottery).

A.5 Damaged, Replaced, or Missing Mountings

Section 2 contains some important information about the mountings on steins, and about how to detect when a lid has been replaced. There is some additional information about the mountings, from the point of view of pricing, that is worth noting here.

A most common occurrence is to find a very nice stein which is, unfortunately, without a lid. Also unfortunate, lids for steins were not made in a set of standard sizes. Surprisingly, plus or minus an eighth of an inch is often not good enough to insure the proper fitting of a replacement lid. Also, the tang and the shaft must be the appropriate length, or a difficult splicing is required. Thus, particularly for older steins, a missing lid will make for a substantial price reduction. Badly damaged old steins, or unattractive c.1900 steins with nice lids, are often purchased and made into *mugs* because the lid is perfect for some other special piece for which a collector needs a lid. Intentionally seeking such matches has some of the pleasures, as well as the displeasures, of gambling.

The picture sections of this book clearly show which types of steins generally have footrings, such as faience and some glass steins. When these are missing, of course, they have much less visual impact than do missing lids, so the price reduction is much less. Yet, while it would seem to be easier to find replacements because only the diameter must match, there are precious few good footrings available, even from repairmen who are constantly trying to stock up on parts. Therefore, *do not* count on being able to find a footring for a stein you may be considering for purchase.

Although pewter is easily damaged, with dings and tears, it is also relatively easily repaired. The following are some of the more common types of damage.

Hinges occasionally bind up. Often they can be cleaned with water (do not use oil). If that doesn't work, rather than forcing the hinge, have a repairman deal with it.

A tooth or ring missing from the hinge will have only a nominal influence on value, usually less than 10%.

Tears, dents, and missing thumblifts can be fixed for about $30 to $60, and once fixed, should not reduce the value of the stein by more than about 10% to 15%. The cost of repairing the *strap* is also in this range. Recall that repairs to the strap often signify that the lid has been replaced, which can mean a price reduction in the range from 10% to as much as 25% or 35%. If the lid is not appropriate to the stein, the reduction can be 50% or more.

Some collectors and museums feel it is essential to the proper care and display of pewter and silver to have them polished. Other collectors would rather see the dark patina, especially on pewter. *Unabrasive* polishing *should* have no affect on price, but be forewarned that a few collectors will shy away from polished pewter steins. On the other hand, diseased pewter, such as pewter that is pitted, powdered, or scaled, can reduce the value of a stein by 10%, or more if the pewter is heavily damaged.

Lad carrying a hexagram, the early symbol of the brewer, from an early 1800's drawing by Ludwig Richter.

B. Important Information for Collectors

The Appendixes of *The Mettlach Book* and *The Stein Book* contain miscellaneous information that many collectors have found very helpful. Thus some of that information is again discussed here.

B.1 Sources of Steins

The first important collections of steins seem to have been started in the middle 1800's by museums vying for examples of fine Renaissance art. Private collectors became an important force in stein collecting in the late 1800's, and some astonishingly high prices were paid in those days for the best examples of Renaissance steins.

Of course, stein collections of a sort existed long before steins were being collected as antiques. In kitchens and in taverns and inns, narrow shelves along the upper parts of the walls, so-called *plate rails*, held collections of steins. In homes, the *number* of steins was a measure of hospitality; in taverns it was a measure of prosperity, signifying the number of regular customers. To increase this measure, and probably for aesthetic reasons as well, there were often more steins displayed than were really necessary.

Such stein displays have continued as important decorations in both rustic and refined tavern, inn and home settings. Such decorative tastes were brought to the United States by the early English settlers, the Pennsylvania Dutch, and the many waves of European immigrants.

Great numbers of German stoneware steins were brought to Canada and the Northeastern United States in the 1700's. Important stoneware shipments were also made in the late 1800's, and led some U.S. manufacturers at that time to begin their own production of stoneware and porcelain steins. Mettlach and other German factories actively advertised their steins in the U.S. beginning in the late 1800's. Significant quantities of steins also began flowing into the United States beginning in the 1940's. These came back with soldiers, tourists, and beginning in the late 1950's, with antique importers. With all of the political and economic turmoil in Europe, the quantity of steins which have made their way to the U.S. have become an important fraction of the world supply.

In both Europe and the U.S., the more desirable steins, once scattered throughout the countryside, have continued to become more concentrated in collections. Increasingly, the places to find good steins have become a small number of U.S. and German dealers, auctions, and fellow collectors upgrading or disposing of their collections.

If the intent of a collector is to buy a stein only occasionally and with little consideration for the type or characteristics of the stein, then shopping at antique shops and antiques shows could yield the desired results. However, if a specific objective is important, such as acquiring a nicely planned collection, it would be advantageous to develop contacts with knowledgeable and trustworthy dealers and collectors.

B.2 Collection Strategies

In varying degrees, most collectors combine the enjoyment and the investment aspects of stein collecting. First, consider the investment angle.

During the 1960's and early 1970's steins proved to be a very good investment, both in comparison to other antiques and to other investment alternatives. Their performance in the middle and late 1970's and in the 1980's, was not as strong, with some other antiques increasing in value more rapidly. Recently, most steins' prices have remained steady or increased moderately, thus having proved to be relatively strong, if unspectacular, performers.

It is difficult to predict a future price trend with precision, but based upon past performance, it is likely that steins will be a fairly good investment on a long-term basis. A general and rapid appreciation in prices over any short period of time is unlikely, but there will always be a few spectacular performers. Those steins that were relatively expensive when issued often combine beauty and rarity, and thus may offer potential for those also interested in the investment angle. Those steins that seem to a collector (after looking over all the steins in this book) to be priced disproportionately low, are likely to be good investments.

Also with respect to the future, the steady performance of most steins over recent years seems to indicate a very solid price base. It is the *collectors* who have created the demand for and prices of steins, not the *investors*. The absence of investment capital artificially forcing up the price of steins beyond the price collectors would be willing to pay, has kept stein prices firm even as other investment opportunities changed drastically. It is always possible, though not very likely, that old and new collectors could plunge into a bidding war with museums, and the resultant prices would continue upward.

As for the enjoyment of collecting steins, consider the possibilities. Since steins come in many sizes and types, and cover a wide range of prices, different approaches to collecting are possible. Collections always contain certain elements of similarity and certain elements of diversity. Most frequently, the materials are similar and the decorations vary.

Most collectors enjoy putting together sets or pairs, particularly of the scarcer or more aesthetically pleasing items. The artistic arrangement of a collection can also greatly enhance its appeal to the collector, and the use of plaques, bowls, and other items together with steins provides an additional dimension that ought to be considered.

A collection should contain what the individual collector likes, and not what seems to be rare, in vogue, or expensive. If you like a stein, there will always be a proper place for it to be displayed in your collection.

B.3 Buying Steins

If you purchase steins at prices near those in this book, you will be receiving a fair value for your money. These are prices that other collectors are willing to pay for the same pieces. Of course, this assumes that any defects that might exist have been detected and the price properly discounted.

Recognizing repaired defects has gotten to be increasingly difficult. In the last few years the techniques, materials, and experience developed by a few repairmen have resulted in some excellent repairs being performed on some steins. Many steins have been sold by dealers, and by collectors, with repairs or damages that were not indicated to the buyer. Some sellers do not know of the repairs, or do not feel obligated to point out repairs or damages to prospective buyers.

Learning to detect repairs and damage, and to distinguish them from factory flaws, takes time and requires the advice and coaching of experienced collectors or dealers. In the meantime, you will have to rely on the reputation of the individual dealer or collector from whom you make your purchase.

Do not assume that an advertisement of steins for sale, even one carried in a respectable publication such as an antiques periodical, can be relied upon for accuracy. While many dealers and collectors are honest, a lack of knowledge by some, and a tendency for the dishonest dealers to gravitate toward advertising, has left knowledgeable buyers with a cautious suspicion toward advertisements. Many advertisers do deliver what is promised, but be certain you can return the stein if you are not satisfied, and do not expect the publication to be of any help should a problem arise.

Auctions are a uniquely different way to buy. If you have a very good idea what you are doing, and you have time and patience, you might do very well. If you are not well informed or are not patient, beware! Simple rules to remember for auction buyers are:

1) some auctioneers know very little or nothing about steins and even less about repairs;

2) auctions that sell *as is* (no description or condition), naturally tend to attract merchandise with defects that sellers would rather not describe;

3) at many auctions, some items will not be sold until their prices reach a level above the price that the consignor (owner) is willing to accept, and this *reserve* price may be more than the stein is worth; not all items at auction are *protected* this way but many are; and

4) if a buyer's premium exists, usually 10%, remember to add that to your total cost before you make your bids. Should you decide to buy steins at an auction, try to arrive in plenty of time to thoroughly examine the steins at the preview. Take copious notes on conditions, qualities, and maximum bids you will make, even for items only remotely of interest to you. If possible try to frequent only those auctioneers who knowledgeably indicate damage.

5) Stein specialty auctions have come into existence since 1982, having been pioneered by Gary Kirsner Auctions. These auctions offer collectors an opportunity to see and bid on hundreds of different steins. The best of these auctions offer accurate descriptions, in catalogs, with photos and estimates. Guarantees and return privileges are usually superior to those offered at most general line auctions. Bargains are possible, but not common on better quality steins. The selection is usually much better than can be found hunting in stores, shows and general line auctions.

B.4 Protecting Your Collection

First, there are some common-sense procedures to follow so as to keep from damaging your own steins. Hot beverages should be kept out of steins, and no hot water or dishwashers should be used to clean steins. Just use lukewarm water, mild soap, and a soft brush. Displaying steins in sunlit windows, or storing them in extremely hot or cold locations, can cause stress lines to develop in the bodies of the steins. Wrapping steins in newspaper and storing them in damp basements can discolor the pewter. When choosing a place to display steins, try to find an area free from flying objects, swinging brooms, or vacuum cleaner handles. Instruct curious friends in the proper way to hold or examine steins; warn them especially not to flop closed the inlaid or heavy pewter lids.

Steins often break when transported. Wrap and box them carefully, then wrap and re-box the first box, and insure all packages that are being shipped.

Finally, valuable collections in homes should be fully covered by insurance policies; to protect larger collections, security systems should be also be considered. Stein dealers can provide you with accurate insurance appraisals of your pieces for nominal fees. Do not advertise your home address; use a post office box or work through a dealer.

B.5 Selling

Steins have always had a fairly high degree of liquidity relative to other antiques. Collectors throughout the country are always looking for desirable items to add to their collections. Many antique dealers around the country are also quite anxious to purchase a nice stein or two, in order to dress up their inventory.

Still, it is important to select the proper method, among the many available, for selling your stein or your collection. There are several avenues open for selling a *small* number of steins with a fairly low total dollar value:

1) *Direct to a collector*: This is an excellent idea, if you know a collector who wants the stein(s) that you want to sell.

2) *To a local antique dealer*: This is a fairly easy and appropriate method if a local dealer is willing to pay a fair price for your steins. Keep in mind that he has to resell them at a profit. Depending on his location, he may be able to sell them quickly, or he may have to wait a long time before buyers come along. These factors will contribute to the price he can afford to pay. Many dealers would rather take expensive steins on consignment; if they sell, then you will get a percentage of the sale price.

3) *Through a general auction*: Many auctioneers are anxious to have high quality steins to sell. Expect to pay about a 25% commission, perhaps higher. If a buyer's premium is charged, consider this part of the commission, because the buyer will keep this in mind and bid lower. Rarely do steins sell at retail prices in general auctions; generally, they will bring less than the retail price.

4) *Through a stein auction*: stein specialty auctions will reach the desired buyers. Retail prices will be obtained on most steins, depending on the abilities of the particular auction company chosen. Commissions are generally about 20% to 25%, including the buyers' premium.

5) *Advertise in an antiques publication*: Fairly good results can be achieved sometimes, but there is no guarantee that the right person will see your advertisement, and most steins are difficult to describe accurately.

6) *Respond to an advertisement from a collector or a dealer in an antiques publication*: Responding to a *want* advertisement from a collector may result in a sale, but he will have to want the stein(s) you are selling in order to pay a fair price. A dealer who specializes in steins will generally pay fair *wholesale* price. He will usually buy for resale at a fairly small margin because his turnover is probably more rapid than the average dealer, and he will know steins very well, and therefore will not have to make allowances to cover risks due to ignorance.

Should you have a large collection to sell, realizing a high percentage of the retail price could be of significant importance. A ten percent difference in the total price could amount to a large sum of money. Therefore, a number of things must be considered. Do you want to sell everything in one group, to one buyer? Do you want to sell immediately, or over a short or perhaps long period of time? Are you willing to work hard at selling your collection: communicating widely, wrapping packages, mailing the steins, and so on? To sell a large collection at *retail* prices, you would have to be prepared to undertake the expenses and do the work of being the dealer, advertiser, traveler, wrapper, and shipper. While this is possible, it is not practical for everyone. Some collectors have done so successfully, but most that have tried eventually became frustrated and impatient, and ultimately would have fared better with another approach.

A dealer specializing in steins, who is thus familiar with the market, can generally realize a retail price on a greater number of steins from a large collection, and with greater ease, than can a collector selling for the first time. Depending upon the *quality* of the collection, that is to say its desirability, diversification, and condition, a collector can expect to sell a collection to a stein dealer at a discount in the vicinity of 30% from the retail prices. This can, of course, vary greatly depending upon the collection and general business factors.

Just as for the small collection, auctions offer a convenient method for disposing of a large collection. Auctions vary in a number of ways, but certain factors do not vary substantially. It will cost about 20% to 25% to sell a collection at auction. This commission is a percentage of the *selling* price, not the retail price. Some steins may sell at auction above a fair retail price, but on average, a *large* collection will not sell at auction above a fair retail price.

This section should provide the seller with the means to calculate the range of prices that are likely to be realized in the sale of steins. Selling steins can require a substantial investment of time and resources, and it will be worthwhile for a seller to take the time to work through the mathematics of each alternative to allow for a good bottom line comparison among the alternative methods of selling the steins.

Glossary

Allegory, the representation of incidents, scenes, or characters in a way that evokes a dual interest, providing both aesthetic enjoyment and a deeper intellectual interpretation.

Apostlekrug, a stout-shaped stein with the Apostles in relief around its body.

Art Nouveau, literally *modern style*, the bold and flat sinuous motifs abstractly based upon seaweed and other plant forms; this style was popular from 1895 to 1915 and was a rebellion against the derivative style of *Historicism*; see *periods*.

Baluster shape, bulbous in the middle with a thinned neck and pedestal base; a popular shape of early earthenware vessels.

Baroque, an ornate, florid, flamboyant style popular from 1600-1770; see *periods*.

Beaker, a cup-like drinking vessel, sometimes with a handle but never with a lid; contrast with *pokal*.

Biedermeier, a *peasant style* of folk art that was important from 1810-1850; a provincial, rustic, sturdy functionalism favored by the new middle class; see *periods*.

Blockzinn, see *pewter purities*.

Britannia metal, alloy of tin and antimony.

Cameo, a type of stein design with low relief made from a translucent, porcelain-like material that allows for contrasting background colors to show through the thinnest areas; compare with *relief*.

Character stein, or *figural stein*, a stein with a shape designed to represent a person, animal, or object, often a personified object.

Chinoiseries, style of design popular in the 1700's depicting Chinese genre scenes and Chinese landscapes; see *periods*.

Chip-carving, or *Kerbschnitt*, a pattern of vertical creases, sometimes hand-cut, sometimes simulated with a mold.

Clay glaze, see *glaze*.

Clay slip, or *colored slip*, see *slip*.

Cold painting, a non-durable method of stein decoration that does not require firing; uses varnishes or gold leaf.

Crack, an open break; contrast with *hairline*.

Double firing, the process of firing biscuit (unglazed) pottery, then glazing and decorating and refiring.

Earthenware, porous ceramic material, fired to only about 800°C (1500°F); sometimes made impervious to liquids with the addition of a lead glaze, as in hafnerware and folk pottery; see *stoneware*.

Edelzinn, *Engelmarke*, and *Englischzinn*, see *pewter purities*.

Enamel, painted decoration, usually on glass.

Engobe, see *slip, colored*.

Engraved, use of abrasive material to cut lines, ornaments, or script into a hard surface.

Etched, a type of stein decoration with distinctive incised black outlining of uniformly colored design areas.

Faience, a porous earthenware, glazed with a white tin oxide (stanniferous) glaze; originally a porcelain substitute first made in Faenza, Italy.

Feinzinn, see *pewter purities*.

Footring, a pewter collar around the base of some steins to protect them against chipping and wear; see *pewter mountings*.

Four F, or *4F*, a symbol of the German gymnastic or athletic society; the F's are flipped in a pattern that puts all their corners together making a cross shape; 4F stands for *Frisch, Fromm, Froh, Frei*, meaning alert, devout, joyful, free.

Form number, or *mold number*, usually an incised number in the base of a stein used to identify the mold from which it was made, providing a catalog number.

Gambrinus, legendary king of Flanders who supposedly discovered beer; the subject of many stein decorations.

Glaze, a hard, impervious coating fired onto ceramic materials, it can be clear or colored, transparent or opaque, matte or glossy; *clay glazes* are like *slips* and were used on very early ceramics, other glazes are all forms of glass made from powdered glass, geldspar, borax, salts, or metal oxides; *lead glaze* is found on hafnerware and folk pottery; *leopard glaze* is a strong brown speckled salt glaze found especially on Frechen wares; *salt glazes* are produced by pouring large quantities of salt into the furnace at its peak firing temperature; the sodium chloride reacts with water (hydrogen oxide) to produce a glassy coating (sodium oxide) and hydrochloric acid vapors; *tin glaze*, as commonly used on faience, is made from tin oxide.

Greenware, formed pottery that is air dried but unfired and thus still raw clay.

Hafnerware, lead glazed earthenwares, including steins, made by potters best known for their oven tiles.

Hairline, a closed break that sometimes shows as a thin black line in ceramic materials; contrast with *crack*.

Hand-painted, a type of ware that is either glazed and fired, or just cold painted, with some design.

Hausmalers, or *studio painters*, often resulted from houses being rebuilt after the Thirty Years War (in the middle 1600's) with artists' studios included; these artists decorated wares, mostly porcelain or faience, as independent craftsmen in their own home studios.

Hinge, a device, usually pewter, that enables the lid to swivel open on a stein.

Historicism, the style of art that dominated the Continent from about 1840 to 1910; it sought a return to the Renaissance with powerful sculptural forms, complicated outlines and friezes, and deep reliefs or contrasting shadows; it originated with archeological findings of numerous awe-inspinring Renaissance artifacts, and in response, art schools began instructing pupils by having them copy the forms and ornaments of these artifacts; see *periods*.

Incised, refers to lines impressed into the unfired ceramic material by means of a stamp, press, or mold; sometimes used synonymously with *etched*.

Inlay, the name of a type of lid for steins that have an insert, usually ceramic, porcelain, or glass, set into the pewter or silver flange of the lid; or *inlay* can be a decorative technique where one material has been inlaid into another so as to help form the design, such as pewter inlaid wood; contrast with *overlay*.

Ivory stoneware, or *yellow stoneware*, a fine, light-colored clay fired as stoneware and used to make many steins from about 1850 to the present; frequently refered to as *pottery*.

Kayser-Zinn, not a measure of the quality of the pewter, instead indicating manufacture by the J.P. Kayser Company in Krefeld-Bockum between the end of the 1800's and the beginning of the 1900's, many pieces being of the Art Nouveau style.

Krug, literally a jug, but often used to indicate a large, or master, stein.

Liter, or *L*, the metric measure of capacity, slightly more than a quart (1.057 quarts = 1 liter).

Lithophane, a porcelain panel found in the bottom of many porcelain steins, with a relief decoration that is visible when light passes though it; lithophane molds were taken from beeswax carvings made over lighted panels.

Luster, a metal oxide decoration fired onto a stein; including occasional platinum accents on early Mettlach steins, metal alkali sheens all over some glass steins, and many other types.

Mettlach, village next to the Saar River in West Germany where Villeroy & Boch has one of their ceramics factories; commonly used as the name of the steins from that factory.

Mosaic, a type of stein on which colored glazes are painted into protruding ridged sections of the stoneware or pottery.

Muffle-fired, a lower temperature third firing achieved by protecting the ceramic materials from the main heat of the kiln by placing them behind muffling fire bricks, or chamotte capsules; this made available an almost unlimited range of glaze colors.

Mug, a cup, usually cylindrical, with a handle; a *lidded mug* is a mug with a set-on lid (not hinged), often used in spas for mineral water; contrast with *beaker* and *stein*.

Munich Child, Munich Maid, or *Munich Monk*, a common theme on steins, the symbol of the the city of Munich, supposedly showing a monk's robe on the first child born in Munich after the 10th Century massacre.

Musterschutz, literally meaning *copyright protection*, but occasionally used almost as if it were a factory name; most frequently found on porcelain character steins made by Schierholz.

Occupational stein, a stein with a decoration or shape that depicts or symbolizes an occupation, probably the occupation of the original owner of the stein.

Orivit, a pewter and silver alloy mostly used around 1900.

Overglaze, a special glass and flux mixture that provides a clear glossy coating for extra sheen and vividness on ceramic materials.

Overlay, filigree, or *latticework*, an ornamental openwork of intricate design, usually of pewter, applied to the outside of a stein.

Pate-sur-pate, marbleized porcelain, usually green and white.

Patina, an oxidation layer on metals; often indicates evidence of age.

Periods, or *styles*, the names of different types of fashionable art, see *Renaissance, Baroque, Rococo, Chinoiseries, Biedermeier, Historicism*, and *Art Nouveau*, as the most important styles for steins.

Pewter, a very workable metalic alloy containing as much as 90% tin, with the remainder made up of lead, copper, zinc, nickel, bismuth, or antimony; see the following two entries.

Pewter mountings, includes the *footring* and all the pewterwork that is used to attach the lid to the handle of a stein; the attaching pewterwork has a whole set of terminology that is important in describing damage and repairs; the *strap* encircles the handle and a usually triangular *strap support* runs somewhat down the outside of the handle; the *shank* goes from the strap to the *hinge*; a *hinge pin* will show on most steins made after about 1860; it will not show on earlier steins; an odd number of *rings* or *teeth* make up the hinge; the *tang* proceeds from the hinge to the *lid rim*; the *thumblift* can be over the hinge or fastened to the rim; if there is an *inlay*, a pewter *flange* will hold it in place; the top of some all-pewter lids may contain an ornate pewter *finial*.

Pewter purities, have been carefully marked since the Middle Ages when lead and other impurities were suspected of being health threats; *Bergzinn, Blockzinn, Feinzinn*, and *Klar und Lauter Zinn* are pewters that are quite pure and known to contain very small quantities of copper or brass (copper and tin alloy); often they had to have no recycled pewter; *Engelmarke* or *Angel-marked* is Feinzinn from the 1700's or 1800's marked with an angel and sword and scales (or trumpet and palm frond); *Englisch Zinn* or *English Pewter* is Feinzinn certified to also be lead-free; *Rosenmarke* or *Rose-marked* is a touchmark for Englisch Zinn; *Probezinn* contains lead but no more than 1/5 or a 4 tin to 1 lead ratio, *Nürnberger Probe* is 10 to 1, *Kolnische Probe* is 6 to 1, *Frankfurter Probe* is 4 to 1; *Edelzinn* is from the 1800's and contains too much lead to allow use as a utensil; *Geringes Zinn, Mankgut*, or *Low Pewter* may contain as much as 50% lead and is occasionally found in thumblifts or applied relief on steins; see also *Britannia metal* and *Orivit*.

Pokal, or *brimmer*, a large ceremonial handleless beaker with a seperate set-on lid and usually having a pedestal base.

Porcelain, a vitrified, fine white clay, quartz, and feldspar mixture that has a hard surface; hard porcelain is fired to about 1450°C (2650°F) while soft porcelain is fired to about 1200°C (2200°F); compare with *stoneware* and *pottery*.

Porcellaine, another name for faience, which was originally intended as a porcelain substitute.

Pottery, or *Steingut*, a rather imprecise term for a usually light-colored porous ceramic with a hardness dependent upon the temperature of the firing, from 960°C (1800°F) to 1300°C (2350°F); generally used to include all tan colored ceramic materials.

Print over glaze, a transfer decoration fired over the glaze.

Print under glaze, *PUG*, *transfer-printed*, or *transfer-decorated*, the name for a process of decoration that takes hand-painted, silk-screened, or printed decals, transfers those decals to a smooth surface, then fires them in place.

Probe, a mark occasionally found on trial or test pieces; *Probe* can also refer to the lead content of pewter; see *pewter purities*.

Prunts, *bosses*, or *Nuppen*, glass drops, sometimes with an impressed design, found attached to the sides of glass vessels as decoration.

Pug mill, a device somewhat like a blender, but very large, previously horse driven, used for refining and mixing clay recipes.

Regimental stein, *reservist's stein*, or *military stein*, a stein that was purchased as a souvenir of service in the military; most often refers to those purchased by reservists upon discharge from the Imperial German Armies in the years 1890 to 1914.

Relief, the name of a type of ware that has figures or designs of opaque material, usually tan or white, that stand out substantially from the smooth or textured background; compare with *cameo*.

Renaissance, the style of art, and the name of the time period from about 1300 to 1600 that was characterized by a revival of the Classical influence, and vigorous aesthetic and intellectual activities; see *periods*.

Reservist's stein, see *regimental stein*.

Rib, a wooden scraper or forming die, used for smoothing sides and forming the bands and moldings of steins on a potter's wheel.

Rococo, the last, less colorful but more figurative, phase of the Baroque period, from about 1735-1770; see *periods*.

Rorken, or *sampler*, a shape of stein that has a pedestal base then becomes slightly wider with height.

Salt glaze, formed when salt is added to the kiln to form a glassy mist that coats all the wares; should not be confused with painted metal oxide glazes such as cobalt oxide blues and manganese oxide violets that are merely glazes that can withstand the intense stoneware firing temperatures; see *glazes*.

Slip, a watered down clay or porcelain recipe that is sufficiently liquid for use in coating, gluing, or casting pieces of ceramic material; *clay slip*, *colored slip*, or *engobe* are terms used to describe slips that have been combined with coloring agents and used primarily as decorative coatings or paints, such as clay glazes; see *glazes, clay*.

Slurry, a recipe of clays, water, and other additives which have been filtered, mixed, and poured into backs, or settling tanks.

Smoother, either a wooden paddle for smoothing the sides of wet, freshly turned pottery, or the person who smooths out turning marks with a wet cloth.

Stack marks, firing variations on the bottom of stoneware or pottery steins that show how they were stacked in the kiln, occasionally circles or parts of two or three circles are seen on some very old steins.

Stein, literally meaning *stone*, is a shortened form of *Steinzeugkrug* or *stoneware tankard*; generally expanded to mean any drinking vessel with a handle and an attached lid; a *lidless stein* did have, or was intended to have, a lid that is now missing; contrast with *mug*, *beaker* and *pokal*.

Stoneware, a vitrified ceramic material, usually a silicate clay, that is very hard, rather heavy, and impervious to liquids and most stains; achieved at temperatures between 1200°C (2200°F) and 1300°C (2350°F); *early stoneware*, or *Fruhsteinzeug*, does not quite reach those temperatures or was made from clays needing higher temperatures to vitrify, and was common from the 1300's to the early 1500's; color is usually gray or tan, but can be found in terra cotta and other colors; see *earthenware*, *pottery*, and *porcelain*.

Tankard, technically synonymous with *stein*, but since this was the British term, some reserve its use for the typically British silver or pewter steins.

Threading, a low, fine, wire-like relief decoration, with colors usually painted between the raised lines; the reverse of etching.

Touchmark, a small stamp, usually found on pewter, that may indicate the name or symbol of the master pewterer, his city, or the pewter's purity.

Transfer-decorated or *transfer-printed*, see *print under glaze*.

Waldglas, or *forest glass*, made from sand and wood ashes and generally having a grayish green color with small impurities and air bubbles.

Walzenkrug, cylindrical tankard, or *straight-up tankard*, a cylindrically shaped stein about twice as high as it is wide; the most common shape in the 1700's.

White gold, a name that was used for porcelain, porcelain clays, or for the valuable stoneware clays with low vitrification temperatures and minimal warping and cracking potential.

Wiremark, concentric whorls on the base of some older stoneware or faience steins that indicates the 'hump' was cut off the potter's wheel by pulling a wire across the base of the turning piece, as opposed to being cut off with smooth knives.

Zig-zag decor, or *Knibistechnik*, decorative ribbons of tight, wide, incised zig-zags made by wadding a wooden chisel across the surface of unfired clay.

Price Changes

The following chart illustrates the change in price for steins appearing in both this book and *The Stein Book* (1985). The average of the low and high price comprising the price range in this book has been used for comparison to the single price listed in *The Stein Book*, to arrive at the percentage change versus the 1985 price.

Page		1985 Price	Range Low	Range High	Percent Change	Page		1985 Price	Range Low	Range High	Percent Change
Section 3 Early Stoneware						52	d	2000	2200	2800	25%
28	a	2000	3000	3600	65%	52	e	1300	1400	1800	23%
28	f	3000	2600	3200	-3%	52	f	1300	1400	1800	23%
29	e	2500	2500	3000	10%	52	g	1600	1800	2400	31%
31	d	2500	2700	3200	18%	52	h	1500	1400	1800	7%
31	e	3000	3000	3600	10%	53	a	1500	1400	1800	7%
31	f	5000	7000	10000	70%	53	b	1700	1800	2200	18%
32	e	2000	1200	1600	-30%	53	c	2500	2600	3200	16%
32	f	2000	1700	2200	-3%	53	d	2500	2600	3200	16%
32	g	3500	4000	5000	29%	53	e	1200	1200	1600	17%
35	a	800	400	700	-31%	53	f	2000	2000	2600	15%
35	b	1200	1000	1300	-4%	53	g	1000	1000	1400	20%
35	c	600	500	700	0%	53	h	1200	1100	1500	8%
35	d	300	300	400	17%	54	c	2000	1800	2400	5%
35	f	800	800	1100	19%	54	e	2000	1800	2400	5%
35	g	2000	1700	2200	-3%	54	h	1500	1600	2200	27%
36	a	1500	900	1300	-27%	55	f	2500	2600	3400	20%
36	b	1500	900	1300	-27%	55	g	3000	2600	3400	0%
36	c	1000	700	1000	-15%	56	b	1800	1500	1900	-6%
36	d	600	400	600	-17%	56	c	1500	1400	1800	7%
36	e	1500	1000	1400	-20%	56	d	1200	1100	1500	8%
37	d	2000	1200	1600	-30%	57	a	800	700	1000	6%
38	d	1500	1200	1600	-7%	57	b	950	1200	1600	47%
38	e	2500	2000	2500	-10%	57	c	950	1000	1400	26%
38	f	2000	1400	1800	-20%	57	d	2000	2200	2700	23%
38	g	1800	1200	1600	-22%	57	g	1600	1500	1900	6%
40	a	3000	3000	3600	10%	58	a	3000	2600	3400	0%
40	d	700	400	600	-29%	58	b	2000	2000	2600	15%
40	e	1300	700	900	-38%	58	c	800	900	1300	38%
40	f	1000	600	800	-30%	58	d	1200	1000	1400	0%
40	g	1200	700	900	-33%	58	e	800	700	1000	6%
41	a	1300	800	1000	-31%	58	f	2000	2000	2500	13%
41	b	750	500	750	-17%	58	g	1500	1200	1600	-7%
41	c	850	600	800	-18%	58	h	2500	2200	2700	-2%
41	d	550	350	500	-23%	59	e	2000	2800	3400	55%
41	e	1000	500	700	-40%	59	f	2500	2400	3000	8%
41	f	3000	2200	2700	-18%	59	g	1200	1200	1600	17%
41	g	1100	600	800	-36%	59	h	1200	1200	1600	17%
41	h	800	500	700	-25%	60	a	1800	1400	1800	-11%
						60	b	1200	900	1300	-8%
Section 4 Faience						60	c	600	500	700	0%
48	b	600	600	800	17%	60	d	1200	1000	1400	0%
48	c	800	700	1000	6%	60	e	1000	900	1300	10%
48	d	800	700	1000	6%	60	f	1000	1000	1400	20%
48	e	600	600	800	17%	60	g	2000	2400	3000	35%
49	c	4000	4000	5000	13%	61	a	1200	1100	1500	8%
49	d	2000	3500	4500	100%	61	b	1200	1100	1500	8%
49	e	2000	3000	4000	75%	61	c	900	1000	1400	33%
49	f	4000	4000	5000	13%	61	d	1500	1400	1800	7%
49	g	1500	1800	2400	40%	61	e	1300	800	1100	-27%
49	h	4000	3500	4500	0%	61	f	1000	900	1200	5%
50	a	5000	5000	6000	10%	61	g	1000	900	1200	5%
50	b	1200	1200	1600	17%	61	h	1000	1000	1400	20%
50	c	1000	1100	1500	30%	62	a	1100	1000	1400	9%
50	d	3000	2400	3000	-10%	62	b	950	800	1100	0%
51	c	4000	3400	4200	-5%	62	c	850	700	1000	0%
51	d	800	600	900	-6%	62	e	1000	700	1000	-15%
51	e	1000	700	1100	-10%	62	f	1000	900	1200	5%
51	f	800	600	900	-6%	62	g	700	500	700	-14%
51	g	900	700	1100	0%	62	h	1300	1000	1400	-8%
52	a	3000	3000	3600	10%	64	d	800	600	900	-6%
52	b	2000	2000	2600	15%	64	e	600	500	700	0%
52	c	2000	2000	2600	15%	64	f	600	500	700	0%

Page		1985 Price	Range Low	Range High	Percent Change	Page		1985 Price	Range Low	Range High	Percent Change
Section 5 Pewter						87	d	275	225	325	0%
67	e	750	600	800	-7%	87	e	400	400	600	25%
67	f	500	300	500	-20%	88	a	400	350	450	0%
67	g	225	150	250	-11%	88	b	375	300	400	-7%
68	a	475	300	450	-21%	88	e	400	350	450	0%
68	b	475	400	550	0%	89	a	250	200	300	0%
68	c	550	450	600	-5%	89	b	300	275	375	8%
68	d	550	450	600	-5%	89	c	250	225	325	10%
68	e	450	400	550	6%	89	f	225	200	300	11%
68	f	450	400	550	6%	90	a	450	475	550	14%
69	a	500	450	600	5%	90	b	475	400	550	0%
69	b	500	450	600	5%	90	c	600	600	800	17%
69	c	500	450	600	5%	90	d	475	400	550	0%
69	d	1000	700	900	-20%	90	e	400	350	450	0%
70	a	200	100	175	-31%	90	f	550	500	700	9%
70	b	250	100	175	-45%	90	g	400	325	425	-6%
70	c	275	150	250	-27%	91	b	350	250	350	-14%
70	d	275	150	250	-27%	91	c	325	275	375	0%
70	e	450	250	350	-33%	91	d	400	350	450	0%
70	f	225	100	200	-33%	91	e	450	400	550	6%
70	g	350	150	250	-43%	91	f	450	450	550	11%
70	h	275	150	250	-27%	91	g	400	350	450	0%
71	a	150	50	100	-50%	91	h	325	300	400	8%
71	b	125	50	100	-40%	93	b	200	150	250	0%
71	c	125	50	100	-40%	94	f	400	350	450	0%
71	d	100	40	70	-45%	95	b	350	350	450	14%
71	e	75	40	70	-27%	95	c	275	300	400	27%
71	f	100	50	100	-25%	96	a	325	250	350	-8%
71	g	375	200	300	-33%	96	b	350	300	400	0%
71	h	425	200	300	-41%	96	c	350	300	400	0%
71	i	300	150	250	-33%	96	d	375	300	400	-7%
72	d	550	300	400	-36%	96	e	300	275	375	8%
						98	b	350	300	400	0%
Section 6 Glass						99	a	350	200	300	-29%
75	a	1800	3000	4000	94%	99	b	150	100	160	-13%
76	a	1000	1000	1400	20%	99	c	150	100	160	-13%
76	b	800	700	1000	6%	99	d	375	225	325	-27%
76	c	900	900	1200	17%	99	e	375	300	400	-7%
77	a	1200	2000	2600	92%	99	f	425	350	450	-6%
77	b	1000	1700	2200	95%	99	g	325	250	350	-8%
77	d	700	600	800	0%	100	e	150	175	250	42%
77	e	500	500	650	15%	100	f	75	60	100	7%
77	f	550	500	650	5%	100	g	75	60	100	7%
77	g	350	300	500	14%	100	h	125	100	160	4%
78	a	1200	1500	2000	46%	102	a	700	600	800	0%
78	b	1400	2000	2600	64%	102	b	500	500	700	20%
78	c	800	700	1000	6%	102	c	1000	800	1200	0%
78	d	900	800	1100	6%	102	d	650	600	800	8%
79	e	600	700	1000	42%						
81	g	900	2200	2800	178%	**Section 7 Unusual Materials**					
82	c	800	600	800	-13%						
82	d	700	600	800	0%	105	b	3500	7000	9000	129%
82	e	1300	1800	2300	58%	105	c	700	1100	1300	71%
83	b	500	450	600	5%	105	e	4000	3000	5000	0%
83	c	550	500	700	9%	106	a	1300	8000	12000	669%
84	b	900	1400	1800	78%	106	b	1600	14000	18000	900%
84	c	900	1000	1400	33%	106	d	4500	15000	20000	289%
84	d	650	500	700	-8%	107	a	500	600	800	40%
84	e	650	550	750	0%	107	b	600	600	900	25%
85	a	750	700	900	7%	107	c	650	700	1000	31%
85	b	750	700	900	7%	107	d	750	700	1000	13%
85	c	1100	1400	1800	45%	107	e	600	600	800	17%
85	d	1300	2000	2600	77%	108	a	2500	2000	2800	-4%
85	e	800	600	800	-13%	108	b	700	1200	1600	100%
85	f	700	600	800	0%	108	c	600	600	800	17%
85	g	700	600	800	0%	108	d	1200	2000	3000	108%
85	h	650	500	700	-8%	109	a	750	1800	2300	173%
86	b	750	800	1100	27%	109	b	450	500	700	33%
86	c	900	2000	2500	150%	109	c	650	600	900	15%
86	d	350	300	450	7%	109	d	400	400	600	25%
86	e	700	650	850	7%	110	a	950	1000	1400	26%
86	f	750	800	1100	27%	110	b	400	400	600	25%
86	g	900	2000	2500	150%	110	c	275	250	350	9%
87	a	175	175	250	21%	110	d	225	200	300	11%
87	b	900	900	1200	17%	110	e	175	150	250	14%
87	c	275	225	325	0%	110	f	300	250	350	0%

Page		1985 Price	Range Low	Range High	Percent Change	Page		1985 Price	Range Low	Range High	Percent Change
111	e	3000	2000	3000	-17%	140	g	290	225	300	-9%
111	f	6000	5000	7000	0%	140	h	320	250	350	-6%
112	a	4000	3000	4000	-13%	141	a	290	225	300	-9%
112	b	3200	1800	2600	-31%	141	b	300	250	350	0%
112	c	2400	1000	1800	-42%	141	c	300	250	350	0%
112	d	5500	3000	4000	-36%	141	d	300	250	350	0%
112	e	6500	4000	5000	-31%	141	e	200	200	250	13%
113	a	2500	1400	2000	-32%	141	f	170	150	200	3%
113	b	2800	1500	2200	-34%	141	g	250	200	275	-5%
114	e	2500	4000	6000	100%	141	h	170	150	200	3%
115	e	2500	2000	3000	0%	142	a	225	250	350	33%
116	a	700	600	800	0%	142	b	375	300	400	-7%
116	b	1400	1300	1700	7%	142	c	375	350	450	7%
116	c	900	800	1100	6%	142	d	375	375	475	13%
116	d	1800	2000	2800	33%	142	e	300	225	275	-17%
116	g	4000	3000	4000	-13%	142	f	300	225	275	-17%
117	b	2500	2800	3800	32%	142	g	300	225	275	-17%
119	b	3500	3000	4500	7%	142	h	325	250	300	-15%
120	b	1200	1000	1500	4%	143	a	975	900	1100	3%
						143	b	950	850	1050	0%
Section 8 Porcelain						143	c	1600	2000	2400	38%
						143	d	1600	2000	2500	41%
123	a	6000	10000	13000	92%	143	e	700	550	750	-7%
123	b	8000	12000	15000	69%	143	f	900	550	750	-28%
123	c	2000	1800	2300	3%	143	g	550	350	450	-27%
123	d	2300	2000	2500	-2%	143	h	900	700	900	-11%
123	e	1700	1500	2000	3%	144	a	550	450	550	-9%
123	f	2400	2000	2500	-6%	144	b	550	500	600	0%
123	g	2000	1700	2200	-3%	144	c	575	500	600	-4%
124	a	2000	1700	2200	-3%	144	d	650	575	675	-4%
124	b	1700	1300	1700	-12%	144	e	550	500	600	0%
124	c	2200	1800	2300	-7%	144	f	2400	2300	2900	8%
126	a	1300	1600	2000	38%	144	g	1850	1800	2200	8%
126	b	1300	1600	2000	38%	144	h	700	550	700	-11%
126	c	1200	1600	2000	50%	145	a	450	375	450	-8%
126	d	1300	1600	2000	38%	145	b	2300	2400	3000	17%
126	e	1500	1700	2100	27%	145	c	700	550	675	-13%
126	f	1500	1700	2100	27%	145	d	1600	1400	1800	0%
126	g	800	1000	1300	44%	145	e	2100	1500	1800	-21%
126	h	800	1000	1300	44%	145	f	900	700	850	-14%
127	a	1300	1200	1600	8%	145	g	900	700	850	-14%
127	b	1500	1600	2000	20%	145	h	900	700	850	-14%
127	c	850	900	1200	24%	146	a	775	600	700	-16%
128	a	2500	2600	3200	16%	146	b	900	650	775	-21%
128	b	500	600	800	40%	146	c	2600	2200	2600	-8%
128	c	500	600	800	40%	146	d	800	650	800	-9%
131	f	500	400	600	0%	146	e	300	250	325	-4%
131	g	500	400	600	0%	146	f	400	350	450	0%
132	a	150	150	250	33%	146	g	500	375	475	-15%
132	d	150	250	350	100%	146	h	450	375	475	-6%
132	e	100	75	125	0%	147	a	1200	900	1200	-13%
132	f	100	75	125	0%	147	b	700	500	600	-21%
132	h	175	150	250	14%	147	c	1100	750	950	-23%
133	b	100	75	125	0%	147	d	1250	950	1200	-14%
133	d	200	125	200	-19%	148	e	550	450	550	-9%
133	e	200	150	250	0%	148	f	550	450	550	-9%
133	f	200	150	250	0%	148	g	675	575	675	-7%
133	g	225	200	300	11%	148	h	675	450	550	-26%
133	h	200	200	300	25%	149	a	950	900	1100	5%
134	e	125	75	125	-20%	149	b	800	650	750	-13%
134	f	100	100	175	38%	149	c	650	500	600	-15%
134	g	125	75	125	-20%	149	d	600	500	600	-8%
134	h	200	200	300	25%	149	e	650	550	650	-8%
						149	f	625	500	600	-12%
Section 9 Mettlach						149	g	550	450	550	-9%
						149	h	675	575	675	-7%
138	c	165	130	170	-9%	150	a	700	550	650	-14%
138	e	175	130	170	-14%	150	b	1650	1500	1800	0%
138	g	275	200	300	-9%	150	c	700	500	600	-21%
139	a	325	325	425	15%	150	d	2000	2200	2600	20%
140	a	225	150	225	-17%	150	e	1650	1500	1900	3%
140	b	290	225	300	-9%	150	f	1650	1500	1900	3%
140	c	285	225	300	-8%	150	g	1400	1000	1200	-21%
140	d	340	275	375	-4%	150	h	1400	1000	1200	-21%
140	e	300	250	325	-4%	151	a	925	700	850	-16%
140	f	290	225	300	-9%	151	b	900	750	850	-11%

Page		1985 Price	Range		Percent	Page		1985 Price	Range		Percent
			Low	High	Change				Low	High	Change
151	c	950	850	1000	-3%	167	h	150	100	175	-8%
151	d	950	850	1000	-3%	168	c	225	200	300	11%
151	e	550	425	525	-14%	168	d	225	250	350	33%
151	f	600	550	650	0%	168	f	125	100	175	10%
151	g	1100	900	1100	-9%	169	a	400	400	550	19%
151	h	700	550	650	-14%	169	b	175	125	200	-7%
152	e	450	400	500	0%	169	c	275	200	300	-9%
152	f	300	300	400	17%	169	e	250	300	400	40%
152	g	300	300	400	17%	169	f	250	300	400	40%
152	h	450	400	500	0%	169	g	200	150	250	0%
153	b	950	700	900	-16%	169	h	150	125	200	8%
153	c	1500	1500	1900	13%	170	a	175	100	175	-21%
153	f	375	350	450	7%	170	f	200	150	250	0%
155	f	600	475	575	-13%	171	b	225	150	250	-11%
156	f	700	600	750	-4%	171	c	150	100	175	-8%
157	a	2000	1300	1700	-25%	171	d	150	100	175	-8%
157	e	1175	900	1100	-15%	171	e	250	300	400	40%
158	a	1800	2200	2600	33%	171	f	250	300	400	40%
158	c	2500	2100	2500	-8%	172	c	175	100	175	-21%
						172	e	150	100	175	-8%
						172	f	150	100	175	-8%

Section 10 Other Etched Ceramics

Page		1985 Price	Range		Percent	Page		1985 Price	Range		Percent
			Low	High	Change				Low	High	Change
						172	g	150	100	175	-8%
160	a	300	300	400	17%	173	b	225	200	300	11%
160	b	250	300	400	40%	173	c	175	150	250	14%
160	c	250	250	350	20%	173	d	175	150	250	14%
160	d	275	300	400	27%	174	a	475	250	350	-37%
160	e	300	350	450	33%	174	b	175	100	175	-21%
160	f	325	350	450	23%	174	c	225	150	250	-11%
160	g	300	300	400	17%	175	a	400	225	325	-31%
160	h	300	300	400	17%	175	b	400	225	325	-31%
161	a	300	300	400	17%	175	c	400	250	350	-25%
161	b	275	300	400	27%	175	d	425	250	350	-29%
161	c	300	350	450	33%	175	e	425	300	400	-18%
161	d	300	300	400	17%	175	f	375	275	375	-13%
161	f	275	300	400	27%	175	g	225	150	250	-11%
162	a	300	350	450	33%	175	h	225	125	200	-28%
162	b	300	350	450	33%	176	a	375	250	350	-20%
162	c	225	200	300	11%	176	b	400	300	400	-13%
162	d	250	300	400	40%	176	c	375	250	350	-20%
162	e	175	250	350	71%	176	d	375	250	350	-20%
162	g	250	200	300	0%	176	e	400	250	350	-25%
162	h	225	200	300	11%	176	f	425	275	375	-24%
163	a	225	150	225	-17%	176	g	425	250	350	-29%
163	b	175	125	200	-7%	176	h	425	250	350	-29%
163	c	200	125	200	-19%	177	a	375	225	300	-30%
163	d	175	125	200	-7%	177	b	325	200	300	-23%
163	e	200	175	275	13%	177	c	350	200	300	-29%
163	g	150	125	200	8%	177	d	375	250	350	-20%
163	h	200	150	250	0%	177	e	350	200	300	-29%
164	a	275	250	350	9%	177	f	375	225	325	-27%
164	b	275	250	350	9%	177	g	350	225	325	-21%
164	c	275	250	350	9%	177	h	375	225	325	-27%
164	d	275	250	350	9%	178	e	350	200	300	-29%
164	e	175	150	225	7%	178	f	350	200	300	-29%
164	f	175	150	225	7%	178	g	375	225	325	-27%
164	g	200	200	300	25%	178	h	325	200	300	-23%
164	h	200	200	300	25%	179	a	475	1000	1400	153%
165	a	225	150	250	-11%	179	b	475	350	450	-16%
165	b	150	100	175	-8%	179	c	425	350	450	-6%
165	c	150	100	175	-8%	179	d	325	200	300	-23%
165	d	150	100	175	-8%	179	e	375	250	350	-20%
165	f	225	250	350	33%	179	f	400	300	400	-13%
165	g	225	250	350	33%	179	g	500	500	700	20%
165	h	225	250	350	33%	179	h	500	500	700	20%
166	a	175	125	200	-7%	180	a	400	250	350	-25%
166	c	150	100	175	-8%	180	b	425	250	350	-29%
166	d	150	100	175	-8%	180	c	500	400	500	-10%
166	f	200	150	250	0%	180	d	550	450	550	-9%
166	g	175	125	200	-7%	180	e	550	450	550	-9%
167	a	175	125	200	-7%	181	a	325	300	400	8%
167	b	175	125	200	-7%	181	b	300	300	400	17%
167	c	250	250	350	20%	181	c	200	150	250	0%
167	d	225	150	250	-11%	181	e	250	200	300	0%
167	e	150	100	175	-8%	182	a	450	450	600	17%
167	f	150	100	175	-8%	182	b	375	400	500	20%
167	g	150	100	175	-8%	182	d	175	200	300	43%

Page		1985 Price	Range Low	High	Percent Change
183	a	325	300	400	8%
183	b	275	250	350	9%
183	c	425	450	600	24%
184	a	400	350	450	0%
184	b	375	350	450	7%

Section 11 Pottery and Stoneware

Page		1985 Price	Range Low	High	Percent Change
187	e	125	150	225	50%
187	f	60	50	80	8%
187	g	70	80	120	43%
187	h	60	50	80	8%
189	e	150	150	250	33%
189	f	100	100	175	38%
189	g	150	150	225	25%
189	h	150	150	225	25%
190	a	175	150	225	7%
190	b	100	75	125	0%
190	c	150	150	225	25%
190	d	125	125	200	30%
190	e	125	120	180	20%
190	f	100	120	180	50%
190	g	125	140	200	36%
190	h	90	120	180	67%
193	a	200	150	250	0%
193	b	200	200	300	25%
193	c	175	200	300	43%
193	d	175	200	300	43%
195	e	200	350	500	113%
195	f	100	80	120	0%
196	a	90	80	120	11%
196	b	80	60	100	0%
196	c	80	60	100	0%
197	d	250	500	700	140%
197	e	90	100	160	44%
197	f	100	120	180	50%
197	g	100	140	200	70%
198	e	125	120	180	20%
198	f	125	120	180	20%
198	g	125	120	180	20%
198	h	110	120	180	36%
199	d	150	140	200	13%
199	e	125	175	250	70%
200	d	350	400	500	29%
201	a	250	250	350	20%
201	b	125	80	120	-20%
201	c	175	120	180	-14%
201	d	175	90	140	-34%
201	e	150	80	120	-33%
201	f	150	80	120	-33%
201	g	175	120	180	-14%
201	h	175	120	180	-14%
203	a	60	50	80	8%
203	b	70	60	90	7%
203	c	80	60	90	-6%
203	e	100	120	180	50%
203	g	90	75	125	11%
203	h	90	75	125	11%
206	d	120	120	180	25%
207	b	100	300	400	250%
207	e	90	80	120	11%
207	f	80	80	120	25%
207	h	100	70	100	-15%
208	e	70	60	90	7%
209	f	60	50	80	8%
210	a	80	250	350	275%
211	h	90	300	400	289%

Section 12 Occupational

Page		1985 Price	Range Low	High	Percent Change
217	a	275	300	400	27%
217	b	250	250	350	20%
217	c	225	250	350	33%
217	d	250	250	350	20%
217	e	325	400	500	38%
217	f	275	300	400	27%
217	g	250	250	350	20%
217	h	225	200	300	11%
218	a	400	500	700	50%
218	b	250	250	350	20%
218	c	250	250	350	20%
218	d	275	250	350	9%
218	e	275	250	350	9%
218	f	250	225	325	10%
218	g	375	350	450	7%
218	h	250	225	325	10%
219	a	250	225	325	10%
219	b	325	350	450	23%
219	c	250	300	400	40%
219	d	300	350	450	33%
219	e	375	400	500	20%
219	f	350	400	500	29%
219	g	300	275	375	8%
219	h	225	250	350	33%

Section 13 Regimental

Page		1985 Price	Range Low	High	Percent Change
224	e	600	550	700	4%
224	f	400	350	450	0%
224	g	400	350	450	0%
224	h	575	550	700	9%
226	a	475	450	550	5%
226	b	500	475	600	8%
226	c	575	550	700	9%
226	d	675	650	800	7%
226	e	475	425	525	0%
226	f	650	650	800	12%
226	g	650	600	800	8%
226	h	550	500	700	9%
227	a	325	350	450	23%
227	b	350	375	475	21%
227	d	350	325	425	7%
229	b	350	300	400	0%
229	c	525	600	750	29%
229	d	325	300	400	8%
230	a	475	450	600	11%
230	b	500	500	650	15%
230	c	475	550	750	37%
230	e	350	325	425	7%
230	f	325	300	400	8%
230	g	350	400	550	36%
230	h	325	325	425	15%
231	b	375	400	500	20%
231	c	475	450	600	11%
231	d	375	350	450	7%
232	a	425	400	500	6%
232	b	375	375	475	13%
232	c	350	325	425	7%
232	d	800	700	900	0%
232	e	950	1100	1500	37%
232	f	1400	2000	2500	61%
233	a	800	700	900	0%
233	b	1300	1400	1700	19%
233	c	1500	1600	2000	20%
233	d	600	500	700	0%
233	e	1200	1100	1400	4%
233	f	1600	2000	2400	38%
234	a	950	800	1000	-5%
234	b	800	700	900	0%
234	c	1050	1100	1300	14%
234	d	1100	1200	1400	18%
234	e	1500	1500	1800	10%
234	f	1100	1400	1700	41%
234	g	1300	1400	1700	19%
234	h	1000	1100	1400	25%
235	a	1100	1100	1400	14%
235	b	1050	1100	1400	19%
235	c	1050	1100	1400	19%
235	d	1050	1100	1400	19%
236	a	900	1000	1200	22%
236	b	850	1000	1200	29%
236	c	850	1000	1200	29%

Page		1985 Price	Range Low	Range High	Percent Change	Page		1985 Price	Range Low	Range High	Percent Change
236	d	850	800	1000	6%	250	f	1200	1300	1600	21%
236	e	900	1000	1200	22%	251	a	1150	1200	1400	13%
236	f	900	1000	1200	22%	251	b	1250	1300	1600	16%
236	g	900	1100	1300	33%	251	c	1100	1400	1700	41%
236	h	875	700	900	-9%	251	d	1450	1500	1900	17%
237	a	650	500	700	-8%	252	a	1100	900	1100	-9%
237	b	750	600	800	-7%	252	b	1200	1100	1400	4%
237	c	800	700	900	0%	252	c	900	700	900	-11%
237	d	850	800	1000	6%	252	d	1000	900	1100	0%
238	a	1000	1100	1300	20%	252	e	900	700	900	-11%
238	b	900	1000	1200	22%	252	f	950	750	1000	-8%
238	c	850	1000	1200	29%	252	g	1000	800	1100	-5%
238	d	850	900	1100	18%	252	h	900	700	900	-11%
238	e	900	1100	1400	39%	253	a	850	600	800	-18%
238	f	1200	1500	2000	46%	253	b	750	550	700	-17%
239	a	575	450	575	-11%	253	c	750	550	700	-17%
239	b	600	450	575	-15%	253	d	900	600	800	-22%
239	c	600	500	650	-4%	254	a	850	700	950	-3%
239	d	650	550	700	-4%	254	d	850	650	850	-12%
239	e	1800	1800	2200	11%	254	e	1800	1600	1900	-3%
239	f	1200	1400	1800	33%	255	a	700	550	750	-7%
240	a	750	650	800	-3%	255	b	700	550	750	-7%
240	b	800	650	800	-9%	255	c	700	550	750	-7%
240	c	700	550	700	-11%	255	d	750	550	750	-13%
240	d	800	600	750	-16%	255	e	1300	1000	1300	-12%
240	e	1100	1200	1500	23%	255	f	1400	1100	1400	-11%
240	f	750	575	725	-13%	256	a	800	600	800	-13%
240	g	700	475	625	-21%	256	b	725	600	750	-7%
240	h	700	475	625	-21%	256	c	750	600	750	-10%
241	a	700	500	650	-18%	256	d	775	600	800	-10%
241	b	750	500	650	-23%	256	e	800	600	800	-13%
241	c	750	550	700	-17%	257	a	700	600	750	-4%
241	d	700	500	650	-18%	257	b	700	650	850	7%
242	a	600	450	600	-13%	257	c	650	475	625	-15%
242	b	575	450	600	-9%	257	d	800	750	1000	9%
242	c	600	450	600	-13%	257	e	700	500	700	-14%
242	d	1400	1300	1700	7%	257	f	750	550	750	-13%
242	e	1000	1000	1300	15%	258	a	775	600	750	-13%
242	f	800	600	750	-16%	258	b	900	700	900	-11%
242	g	1200	1100	1400	4%	258	c	650	500	700	-8%
242	h	775	600	800	-10%	258	d	750	600	800	-7%
243	a	750	600	800	-7%	258	e	1200	1100	1400	4%
243	b	1000	900	1100	0%	258	f	1000	800	1000	-10%
243	c	700	600	750	-4%	258	g	900	800	1000	0%
243	d	800	700	900	0%	258	h	1000	900	1100	0%
244	a	900	800	1000	0%	259	a	750	600	750	-10%
244	b	775	600	800	-10%	259	b	750	600	800	-7%
244	c	750	600	800	-7%	259	c	775	600	750	-13%
244	d	1000	1000	1200	10%	259	d	775	600	750	-13%
244	e	1150	1100	1400	9%	260	e	1000	900	1100	0%
244	f	1300	1200	1500	4%	260	f	1400	1400	1700	11%
244	g	1200	1100	1400	4%	260	g	1100	1000	1200	0%
246	a	500	450	550	0%	260	h	1300	1300	1600	12%
246	b	450	400	500	0%	261	a	1250	1200	1500	8%
246	c	550	550	700	14%	261	b	1350	1200	1500	0%
246	d	550	550	700	14%	261	c	1350	1200	1500	0%
246	e	475	425	525	0%	261	d	1200	1100	1400	4%
246	f	500	450	550	0%	262	a	1400	1300	1700	7%
246	g	500	450	550	0%	262	b	1100	1000	1200	0%
246	h	700	600	800	0%	262	c	1100	900	1100	-9%
247	a	700	550	750	-7%	262	d	1250	1200	1500	8%
247	b	550	500	650	5%	262	e	1350	1200	1500	0%
247	c	475	450	575	8%	262	f	1050	900	1200	0%
247	d	850	700	1000	0%	262	g	1200	1100	1400	4%
248	e	650	550	750	0%	262	h	1250	1200	1500	8%
248	f	500	450	550	0%	263	a	1100	1000	1300	5%
248	g	550	450	600	-5%	263	b	1000	800	1000	-10%
248	h	400	350	450	0%	263	c	800	700	900	0%
249	a	625	500	650	-8%	264	a	2200	2500	3000	25%
249	b	675	500	650	-15%	264	b	2200	2500	3000	25%
249	c	700	500	700	-14%	264	c	2300	2800	3400	35%
249	d	1200	1200	1500	13%	264	d	1800	1600	2000	0%
250	a	650	400	600	-23%	264	e	2200	2600	3200	32%
250	b	700	600	800	0%	265	a	2200	3500	4500	82%
250	c	1600	1800	2200	25%	265	b	2400	3500	4500	67%
250	d	1000	1100	1300	20%	265	c	1200	1100	1400	4%
250	e	1250	1400	1700	24%	265	d	1000	800	1100	-5%

Page		1985 Price	Range		Percent Change	Page		1985 Price	Range		Percent Change
			Low	High					Low	High	
265	e	1500	1400	1800	7%	285	a	900	800	1100	6%
266	a	1100	1500	2000	59%	285	b	1100	900	1200	-5%
266	b	1000	1100	1400	25%	285	c	1500	1200	1600	-7%
266	d	1150	1600	2200	65%	285	d	900	800	1100	6%
267	a	800	700	900	0%	285	e	1100	1000	1400	9%
267	b	700	700	1000	21%	285	g	800	700	900	0%
267	c	1250	1400	1700	24%	285	h	800	700	1000	6%
267	d	2300	3500	4500	74%	286	b	1000	1100	1400	25%
267	e	1700	1600	2000	6%	286	c	800	700	900	0%
267	f	1600	1800	2200	25%	286	g	450	400	550	6%
268	a	900	900	1100	11%	287	a	800	800	1100	19%
268	b	875	900	1100	14%	287	b	500	450	600	5%
268	c	975	800	1000	-8%	287	c	1300	1200	1600	8%
268	d	975	850	1100	0%	287	d	850	700	900	-6%
268	e	1250	1100	1400	0%	287	e	400	350	500	6%
268	f	1150	1000	1300	0%	287	f	350	250	350	-14%
268	g	1100	900	1200	-5%	288	a	850	700	900	-6%
268	h	1600	1800	2300	28%	288	e	450	450	550	11%
269	a	1800	2400	3000	50%	289	g	375	350	450	7%
269	b	750	650	850	0%	290	a	400	400	500	13%
269	c	1700	2000	2500	32%	290	e	350	300	400	0%
269	d	1500	1800	2200	33%	291	b	400	350	500	6%
270	a	1300	1200	1500	4%	291	d	300	250	350	0%
270	b	1350	1300	1600	7%	291	e	475	500	650	21%
270	c	1400	1300	1600	4%	292	b	250	250	350	20%
270	d	1300	1100	1400	-4%	293	b	275	225	325	0%
270	e	1200	1000	1300	-4%	293	c	225	250	350	33%
270	f	1200	1000	1300	-4%	293	d	275	250	350	9%
270	g	1150	1000	1300	0%	293	e	300	350	450	33%
270	h	1100	950	1250	0%	293	h	225	200	300	11%
271	a	1200	1000	1300	-4%	294	c	300	200	300	-17%
271	b	875	800	1000	3%	294	e	300	225	325	-8%
271	c	875	800	1000	3%	294	f	275	225	325	0%
271	d	1100	1100	1400	14%	294	g	250	225	325	10%
272	a	1600	1800	2200	25%	294	h	275	225	325	0%
272	b	1600	2000	2400	38%	294	j	350	350	450	14%
272	c	1600	1400	1800	0%	295	a	400	350	450	0%
						295	d	250	200	300	0%
Section 15 Character						295	g	300	275	375	8%
						296	b	375	350	450	7%
278	a	950	900	1300	16%	296	c	350	400	500	29%
278	b	1000	900	1300	10%	296	f	300	250	350	0%
278	c	1200	1000	1400	0%	296	g	250	200	300	0%
278	d	1600	1800	2300	28%	297	a	350	350	450	14%
279	a	1000	900	1300	10%	297	d	350	350	450	14%
279	b	1600	1500	2000	9%	297	e	350	350	450	14%
279	c	1000	900	1300	10%	298	i	250	300	400	40%
279	d	2000	2000	2500	13%	298	j	350	350	450	14%
279	e	375	350	450	7%	298	k	350	350	450	14%
279	g	550	500	650	5%	298	l	350	400	500	29%
279	h	950	900	1300	16%	299	a	300	275	375	8%
280	b	1100	1000	1400	9%	299	b	300	275	375	8%
280	d	700	700	1000	21%	299	c	300	300	400	17%
280	e	950	700	1000	-11%	299	e	375	300	400	-7%
280	g	1200	1500	2000	46%	300	a	325	300	400	8%
280	i	500	700	1000	70%	300	d	2000	1800	2200	0%
281	b	1100	1000	1400	9%	300	f	1400	1300	1700	7%
281	c	1600	2600	3400	88%	301	h	275	200	300	-9%
281	d	1700	1400	1800	-6%	302	d	750	600	800	-7%
281	f	1200	1100	1500	8%	302	e	750	600	800	-7%
281	g	850	700	900	-6%	303	a	375	325	425	0%
281	h	700	600	800	0%	303	b	950	800	1100	0%
282	a	700	600	750	-4%	303	c	375	325	425	0%
282	b	650	600	750	4%	303	d	475	450	550	5%
282	c	750	600	800	-7%	304	a	225	200	300	11%
282	d	550	500	650	5%	304	c	250	225	325	10%
282	i	750	600	750	-10%	304	d	475	425	550	3%
282	k	700	600	750	-4%	304	e	400	400	500	13%
282	l	850	700	900	-6%	304	g	325	300	400	8%
283	a	475	600	800	47%	305	b	625	500	700	-4%
283	b	475	600	800	47%	305	d	550	550	750	18%
284	a	150	120	180	0%	306	b	2800	3600	4200	39%
284	c	225	250	350	33%	306	d	2000	2600	3200	45%
284	f	175	150	225	7%	306	e	2000	2400	3000	35%
284	g	150	140	200	13%	306	f	2000	2400	3000	35%
284	h	175	150	250	14%	307	b	1000	1000	1300	15%
284	j	325	300	400	8%	307	e	1000	900	1200	5%

Page		1985 Price	Range Low	High	Percent Change
307	g	1700	1400	1800	-6%
308	a	850	800	1000	6%
308	b	1000	900	1200	5%
308	c	900	800	1100	6%
308	d	850	700	900	-6%
308	e	350	300	400	0%
309	c	700	600	750	-4%
309	f	900	800	1100	6%
309	g	325	275	375	0%
309	h	500	400	600	0%
310	c	300	300	400	17%
310	d	300	400	550	58%
310	e	300	400	550	58%
310	f	300	250	350	0%
310	g	300	225	325	-8%
310	h	300	350	450	33%
311	e	350	350	500	21%
312	a	800	700	1000	6%
312	b	600	500	650	-4%
312	c	550	575	625	9%
312	d	500	450	600	5%
312	e	375	300	400	-7%
312	f	325	300	400	8%
312	h	250	225	325	10%
313	a	300	275	375	8%
313	c	325	300	400	8%
313	e	850	900	1200	24%
313	g	275	275	375	18%
313	i	250	275	375	30%
314	a	375	350	450	7%
314	e	275	250	350	9%
314	g	275	250	350	9%
315	e	250	250	350	20%
316	a	250	350	450	60%
316	c	250	300	400	40%
316	d	350	300	400	0%
316	e	275	250	350	9%
317	c	225	250	350	33%
317	d	275	250	350	9%
317	e	325	300	400	8%
317	g	250	250	350	20%
318	a	275	300	400	27%
318	b	225	200	300	11%
318	c	225	225	325	22%
318	d	350	400	500	29%
318	e	300	300	400	17%
318	f	300	300	400	17%
318	g	300	300	400	17%
319	a	400	350	450	0%
319	c	400	350	450	0%
319	e	275	225	325	0%
319	f	450	400	550	6%
320	a	250	175	250	-15%
320	d	150	120	180	0%
320	e	300	275	375	8%
320	f	375	300	400	-7%
320	g	450	400	500	0%
321	c	350	300	400	0%
321	f	275	200	300	-9%
322	b	350	350	450	14%
322	c	350	350	450	14%
323	b	250	200	300	0%
323	c	375	300	400	-7%
323	d	550	500	600	0%
323	e	350	300	400	0%
323	f	350	350	450	14%
323	h	300	250	350	0%
323	j	1700	1500	2000	3%
324	a	225	200	300	11%
324	b	600	500	700	0%
324	e	1500	1700	2100	27%
324	g	800	700	900	0%
325	e	850	700	900	-6%
325	f	850	700	900	-6%
325	g	750	700	900	7%

Page		1985 Price	Range Low	High	Percent Change
325	h	650	500	700	-8%
326	b	225	200	300	11%
326	f	225	350	450	78%
326	g	225	300	400	56%
327	a	1000	1000	1300	15%
327	b	375	375	500	17%
327	c	850	800	1100	12%
327	d	450	400	500	0%
328	a	180	140	200	-6%
328	b	200	150	225	-6%
328	c	150	150	225	25%
328	d	175	140	200	-3%
328	f	250	300	400	40%
328	g	225	175	250	-6%
328	h	300	250	350	0%
328	i	200	150	250	0%
328	m	225	175	250	-6%
329	a	900	700	1000	-6%
329	b	1000	1000	1400	20%
330	d	650	500	700	-8%
330	g	850	800	1100	12%
331	a	325	400	550	46%
331	c	350	500	700	71%
331	f	300	250	350	0%
332	d	475	400	500	-5%
332	e	425	400	500	6%
332	h	250	175	250	-15%
332	j	250	200	300	0%
333	a	300	250	350	0%
333	e	400	300	450	-6%
334	a	200	150	220	-8%
334	b	300	250	350	0%
334	d	325	300	400	8%
334	f	375	300	400	-7%
334	h	300	275	375	8%
335	c	250	200	275	-5%
335	d	250	200	275	-5%
336	d	450	400	500	0%

Color Sections

Page		1985 Price	Range Low	High	Percent Change
c5	f	4400	3000	4000	-20%
c7	g	450	500	700	33%
c8	b	3000	4000	5000	50%
c8	d	2000	2000	2600	15%
c8	e	3000	3000	4000	17%
c8	f	3500	4000	5000	29%
c9	a	1000	900	1300	10%
c9	b	900	800	1100	6%
c9	c	2000	3000	4000	75%
c9	d	1100	1100	1400	14%
c9	e	700	600	750	-4%
c9	g	2000	2600	3200	45%
c9	h	900	800	1000	0%
c9	i	1500	1200	1600	-7%
c10	a	1800	1600	2200	6%
c10	b	1800	1600	2200	6%
c10	d	1500	1600	2200	27%
c10	f	1000	1200	1600	40%
c10	g	1200	1300	1700	25%
c10	h	1300	1200	1600	8%
c11	b	1000	2000	2500	125%
c11	c	2600	3400	4000	42%
c11	e	1800	1800	2400	17%
c11	h	2000	2200	2800	25%
c11	k	950	1500	2000	84%
c11	l	800	1100	1500	63%
c13	g	1300	1200	1600	8%
c14	c	375	550	700	67%
c14	d	275	200	300	-9%
c14	f	900	550	750	-28%
c14	g	550	450	550	-9%
c16	a	475	450	550	5%
c16	e	1300	1500	2000	35%

INDEX

Advertisements
    buying from, 365
    selling by, 366
Allegory, see *Motifs, allegorical*
Alloys, 15, see also *Pewter, Brittania metal*
Altenburg, 26
Amber, 104
Anheuser Busch, 337
Annaberg, 26
Ansbach, 45
Antimony, see *Recipe, Brittania metal*
Antwerp World's Fair (1885), 135
Appraisal, 365
Apprentice, see *Labor, apprentice*
Art Nouveau, 5, 12, 65, 136
Auctions,
    buying from, 365
    selling in, 366
Austria, 9, 25, 65

Baluster, 25, see also *Steins, shapes illustrated*
Baroque, 9, 12, 73
Bas-relief, see *Relief*
Bavaria, 8, 9
BAVARIA, 136
Beakers, 9, 103
Beer, 8, 9, 12, 103, 104
Beyer GmbH, 347
Biedermeier, 9, 12, 44, 73, 135, see also *Steins, shapes illustrated*
Birnkrug, 43
Bisque, see *Glaze, bisque*
Black Death, 7, 8
Black salt, 26
Blotching, see *Factory flaws*
Boch-Buschmann, 135
Bohemia, 9, 65
E. Bohne Söhne, 277
Johann Böttger, 43, 121

Brass, 104
Brazil, see *Ceramarte*
Bremen, 8
Brewery steins, 5, 337
    quantities produced, 337
Brittania metal, 66
Bubonic plague, see *Black Death*
Bunzlau, 26
Buyers' premium, see *Auctions, buying from*
Buying, see *Collecting, strategies*

Cameo, 135
    difference from relief, 136
Casting, 15, 66, 103
    mountings, see *Mountings, cast*
Castle trademark, 135
Catalogs, 19, 159, 185, see also *Auctions, buying from*
Ceramarte, 14, 347
Ceramics, see also, *Earthenware, Hafnerware, Porcelain, Pottery, Stoneware*
    hand-thrown, 18
    production of, 18
    slip-molded, 18
Character steins, 14, 18, 221, 277-278
    color variations, 278
    quantities produced, 278
Chicago, 337
Chinoiseries, see *Motifs, Oriental*
Chip-carving, 26
Chromolith, see also *Mettlach, etched*
    theories, 136
Clay, 12, 18
    faience, 45
    mining, 25
    porcelain, 121
    pottery, 186
    Rhenish, 185
    stoneware, 25, 26

Cleaning, 17, 365, see also *Patina*
    damage caused by, 361
Cloisters, 8
Coal, 74, 135
Coconuts, 104
Cold-painting, see *Painting, cold-*
Collecting,
    as an investment, 361, 364
    strategies, 27, 45, 75, 186, 215, 222, 278, 337,
        364-365
Cologne, see *Köln*
Copyright, see *MUSTERSCHUTZT*
W. Corzellus, 347
Covered container law, 8, 9, 15
    origin of, 7
Creussen, 26, 27
Cross hatch mark, 277
Crystal, see *Recipe, crystal*
Cylindrical, see *Walzenkrug*

Damage, 361-363, see also *Faience, damage*
    caused by cleaning, 361
    diseased pewter, 66
    due to war, 137, 159, 273
    impact on price, 27, 362-363
    prevention, 365
Dates, see *Marks, dates*
Dealers, 5, 365, 366
DEC, 137
Decals, 186, 221
    silk-screened, 74, 221
Decolorizers, see *Metal oxides, as decolorizers*
Decoration number, 137
Defregger, 186
Delft, 8, see also *Mettlach, Delft*
Deutsche Wehrmacht, see *Nazi Army*
Diamond-cut, 73
Displaying steins, see *Damage, prevention*
Duingen, 26
Peter Dümler, 12, 185, 186
Dümler & Breiden, 185, 277, 347
Dutch trade, 43
Dutch East Indies Trade Co., 104

Earthenware, 8, 18, 25, 277
Eckhardt & Engler, 185, 347
Empire, 135
Enameled, 65, 73, 74
Enghalskrug, 43
England, 9, 121
Englishzinn, see *Pewter, purity*
Engraved, 9, 65, 73, 74, 103, see also *Diamond-cut,*
    Wrigglework, Zig-zag
Etched, 12, 74, 159, 337, 348
    techniques, 159
Exports, 347

Factory flaws, 362
Faenza, Italy, 43

Faience, 9, 12, 14, 43-47, 65, 121, 348
    damage, 45
    factories, 44
    identifying reproductions, 45
Feinzinn, see *Pewter, purity*
File marks, see *Replacement parts, identifying*
Finials, 73
Firing,
    duration, 8
    temperature, 8, 18, 25, 45, 122, 186
Firing lines, see *Factory flaws*
Folk art, 12, see also *Biedermeier, Motifs, folk art*
Footrings, 15, 45, 363, see also *Mountings*
Form number, 137
Franco-Prussian War, 221, 223
Frankfurt, 43
Frechen, 26, 27
Freiberg, 26
Frieze bands, 136
Furnace, 8, 25, 74

Genuine, see *Pewter, purity*
Geringen, see *Pewter, purity*
German flowers, 73, 121
German Imperial Armies, 221
Germany,
    map of, 13
GERMANY, see Marks
Simon Peter Gerz, 159, 185, 277, 362
Gerz GmbH, 347, 348
Geschützt, 137
GESCHÜTZT, 19
Gilded, see *Gold*
Matthias Girmscheid, 159, 347
Glass, 8, 9, 12, 14, 65, 73-75, 221, 337, 348
    acid etched, 12
    coloring agents, 73
    colors, 9, 73, 74, 75, see also *Waldglas*
    flashed, 75
    jewels, 74
    molded, 12, 74
    overlaid, 12, 74, 75
    pewter overlaid, 12
    stained, 74
Glasshouse, 74
Glaze, 8, 12, 45, 137, 221, 348
    bisque, 26, 277
    cobalt, see *Stoneware, cobalt-glazed*
    colors, 26
    glass-based, 186
    lead-based, 25, 186
    on lithophanes, 277
    porcelain, 122
    salt, see *Saltglaze*
W. Goebel, 347
Gold, 65, 73, 103, see also *Glass, coloring agents*
    decoration, 121, 122
GR (Georgius Rex), 27

Grain surplus, 8, see also *Beer*
Greek art, 12
Guilds, 8, 9, 44, 45
Johann Gutenberg, 215

Hafnerware, 18, 25
Hamburg, 8
Kurt Hammer, 347
Hanau, 43
Handles, 66
    attachment, 18, 45, 136
    illustrated, 26
    pewter, 65, 74
Hand-painted, 185, 186, 221, 348
    identifying, 186
Reinhold Hanke, 12, 185, 347
Hash mark, 277
Hauber & Reuther (HR), 159, 185, 362
Hausmaler, 43, 44, 45, 121
Hesse, 27
Hinges, 9, 15, 103, 277, 363, see also *Wood, hinge*
    origin of, 7
    pin, 15
Historicism, 12, 14, 65, 66, 73, 75, 103, 135, 185
Höhr-Grenzhausen, 27, 159, 185, 273
Horn, 9, 104
HR, see *Hauber & Reuther*
Hump, see *Ceramics, hand-thrown*
Hungary, 65

Incising, see *Engraved*
Inlaid clays, see *Etched, techniques*
Inlays,
    porcelain, see *Lids, porcelain inlaid*
    repairs to, 362
Iron Cross, 273
Ivory, 9, 103, 104
    workmanship, 104

Japan, 347

Kaiser Wilhelm II, 221
Kaolin, 121, 122, 186, see also, *Clay, porcelain* and *pottery*
KAYSERZINN (KZ), 66
Kiln, see *Furnace*
KL (klar und lauter), see *Pewter, purity*
Koblenz, 9
Köln, 8, 9, 12, 26, 185, 186, also called Cologne
Kulmbach, 65, 104

Labels, paper, 19
Labor,
    apprentice, 44
    -intensive processes, 9, 12, 15, 18, 135
Lathework, 15, 104
Lautere, see *Pewter, purity*
Lead, 15, see also *Recipe, pewter*
Lichtenhainer, 65, 103

Lids, 9, 15, 25, 45, 66, 74, 222, see also *Mountings*
    atypical, 363
    ceramic inlaid, 362
    cut glass inlaid, 74
    impact on price, 337, 362
    origin of, 7
    out of period, 362
    porcelain, 121
    porcelain inlaid, 12, 74, 121, 185, 337
    silver, 43
    steepled pewter, 74, 121, 337, 362
Elisabeth Liegl, 347
Limited edition, 14, 348
Lindner Porzellan, 347
Lithophane, 12, 222, 277
Lost-wax process, 15
Low, see *Pewter, purity*

Made in Germany, 19
Map, see *Germany, map of*
Marking Law (1891), 19
Marking rule (1884), see *Silver, marking rule*
Marks, 17, 19, 27, 136, 137, 348
    dates, 17, 137
    faience, 46-47
    illustrated, 20-24
    pewter, 66
    porcelain, see *Cross hatch mark, Hash mark, Marks, illustrated*
Marzi & Remy, 159, 185, 273, 277, 347, 362
Mass-production, 12, see also *Molds*
Master stein, 9, see also *Steins, shapes illustrated*
Meissen, 43, 121
Melon, 26, see also *Stein, shapes illustrated*
Merchants, influence on marks, 19, 27, 45
Reinhold Merkelbach, 159, 185, 273
Merkelbach & Wick, 159, 185, 273, 277
Metal oxides, 9
    as coloring agents, 73, 74
    as decolorizers, 75
Mettlach, 12, 135-137, 222, 277, 364, see also *Villeroy & Boch*
    brewery steins, 337
    Delft, 136
    etched, 136
    faience, 136
    marks, illustrated, 137, see also *Marks, illustrated*
    Rookwood, 136
    secret formulas & techniques, 136, 159, 348
Mettlach Book, 5, 19, 135, 137, 362, 364
Middle Ages, 103
Middle class,
    emergence as a market, 9, 43
    tastes, 44
Military,
    steins, 273
    glossary, see *Regimental, terminology*
Milk glass, 73
Mining, see *Clay, mining*

Molds, 12, 66, 136, 185, 348
    clay, 66
    iron, 66
    metal, 66
    number, 19
    plaster, 12, 18, 66, 277
    stoneware, 66
Monasteries, as breweries, 12
Mosaic, 136
Motifs, 9, 104, see also *German flowers*
    allegorical, 12, 26, 65
    folk art, 26, 65, see also *Biedermeier*
    genre, 185
    influences on, 12, see also *Greek art, Roman art,*
        Renaissance art
    Oriental, 43, 73, 121
Mountings, 362
    attachment, 15
    cast, 45
    illustrated, 17
    pewter, 15, 17, 73
    replacing, 363
    silver, 73, 121
    silver gilt, 121, see also *Gold*
Muffle painting, Muffle bricks, Muffle firing, 45, 122
Mugs, 221, 363
    defined, 7
Munich, 337, 362
Museums, 5, 14, 27, 44, 65, 122, 363, 364
Muskau, 26
MUSTERSCHUTZ, 19, 277

Names, on steins, 19, 27, 44, 66, 122
Napoleon, 222
Nazi Army, 273
Neo-Classical, see *Historicism*
Neo-Renaissance, see *Historicism*
Numbers,
    incised, see *Marks*
    painted, see *Marks*
Nürnberg, 65, 104

Occuptional steins, 215
Overlaid,
    glass, see *Glass, overlaid*
    pewter, see *Glass, pewter overlaid*

Painting,
    cold-, 45, 73
    durability of, 12
Patina, 17, 45, 348, 363, see also *Replacements parts,*
    identifying
Pewter, 8, 9, 12, 17, 65-66, 221, 277, 348, see also
    Patina
    contents of, 15
    diseased, 363
    expense of, 15
    genuine, 66
    low, 66, 362
    purity, 66
    repairs, 363

Pewter Guild, see *Guilds*
    records, 17
Piercework, 74, see also *Glass, pewter overlaid*
Plaster, see *Molds, plaster*
Plate rails, 364
Plaue, 277
Pokal, 9, see also *Stein, shapes, illustrated*
Polishing, 66, 363,
    gilding to avoid, 103
Pontil, 74
Porcelain, 12, 14, 18, 121-122, 221, 277, 278, 348, 364
    Chinese, 9, 43
    substitutes, see Faience, Milk glass
Porcellaine, see *Faience*
Porzellanmanufaktur Plaue, 277
Post-World War II, 14, 347-348, see also *Limited*
    editions, Ceramarte
Potters' Guild, see *Guilds*
Potter's wheel, illustrated, 18
Pottery, 12, 14, 18, 185, 186, 221, 277, 337
Price, 5, 27, 75, 222, 277, 361-363
    original cost, 12, 221
    reduction for damage, 362-363
    retail, 361, 366
    trends, 364
    variations, 361
    wholesale, 365
Print over glaze, 337
Print under glaze (PUG), 121, 136, 222, 273, 337,
    see also *Transfer-decorated*
Probe, Probezinn, Proved, see *Pewter, purity*
Prunts, 73, 74
Public health laws, see *Covered container law*
Punty, see *Pontil*

Raeren, 26, 27
Rastal, 347
Recipe, 18
    Brittania metal, 66
    crystal, 75
    faience, 45
    glass, 74
    pewter, 66
    porcelain, 122
    pottery, 186
Regimental steins, 221-223, 347
    terminology (glossary), 223
Reichsprobe, see *Pewter, purity*
Reichswehr Army, 273
Relief, 12, 65, 103, 104, 121, 136, 185, 186, 337
J.W. Remy, 159, 185, 347, 362
Renaissance, 8, 9,
    art, 12, 73
Repairs, 362
    identifying, 17, 365
Replacement parts, 363
    identifying, 45
Reproductions, 14, 27, 44, 45, 66, 75, 347
    identifying, 45, 75, 103, 122, 222
Reserves, see *Auctions, buying from*

Reservist, see *Regimental*
Reverse painting, see *Chromolith, theories*
Rhineland, 25
Ribs, see *Ceramics, hand-thrown*
Rigaree, 74
Franz Ringer, 186
Roman art, 12
Roman Catholic Church, 8, 9
Rorken, 65, see also *Stein, shapes illustrated*
Rosters, 221

Hans Sachs, 215
Salt, 19
Saltglaze, 8, 12, 26, 277
Saxony, 65
Scandinavia, 9, 65, 104
Schierholz & Söhn, 277, 347
Schlesien, 65
Schrezheim, 45
Scraper, see *Ceramics, hand-thrown*
Seams, see *Molds*
Selling steins, 366
Siegburg, 26, 27, 185
Silicic acid, see *Recipe, glass*
Silk-screened, see *Decals, silk-screened*
Silver, 8, 9, 12, 65, 103, 121
    and copper alloys, 103
    lids, see Lids, silver
    marking rule, 103
    purity, 103
Slip molding, 18, 277
Slurry, see *Ceramics, hand-thrown*
Spinmarks, see *Lathework*
Stained glass, 74
Stein Book, 5, 6, 364
Steinau, 27
Steingut, 18, 186, see also *Pottery*
Steins,
    brewery, see *Brewery steins*
    buying, see *Collecting, strategies*
    caring for, 66, 75, 365
    decorations, 9, 12, 26, 27, 43, 65, 73, 74, 75, 104,
        121, 136, 185, 215, 221, 222, see also *Chip-
        carving, Motifs, Prunts, Rigaree, Zig-Zag*
    defined, 7
    factories, 44, 277, 347
    materials, 9, 12, 15, 73, see also *Earthenware,
        Faience, Glass, Gold, Hafnerware, Horn,
        Ivory, Pewter, Porcelain, Pottery, Silver,
        Stoneware, Wood*
    military, see *Military steins*
    occupational, see *Occupational steins*
    post-World War II, see *Post-World War II steins*
    regional characteristics, 9
    Renaissance, 364
    selling, see *Selling steins*
    shapes, 9, 12, 25, 26, 44, 45, 65, 73, 74, 103, 121,
        185, see also *Baluster, Birnkrug, Character
        steins, Enghalskrug, Melon, Walzenkrug*
    shapes, illustrated, 10-11

Steinzeug, see *Stoneware*
Steinzeugkrug, see *Steins, defined*
Steinzeugwerke, 159, see also *Reinhold Merkelbach,
        Simon Peter Gerz, Marzi & Remy*
Stone, 104
Stoneware, 8, 9, 12, 14, 18, 25-27, 65, 121, 185, 186,
        221, 273, 277, 337, 364
    cobalt-glazed, 185
    identifying reproductions, 27
Storage, see *Damage, preventing*
Strap, 363, see also *Mountings*
St. Louis, 337
St. Louis Silver Co., 104
Switzerland, 65
Symbols, see *Marks*

Tankard, see *Steins, defined*
Taverns, 8, 185, 364
Temperature,
    firing, see *Firing, temperature*
    melting metals, 15
A.J. Thewalt, 159, 185, 347, 348
Thumblifts, 66, 73, 103, 222, 363, see also *Mountings*
    shapes, 15, 104
    shapes illustrated, 16
Thumbpieces, see *Thumblifts*
Thüringen, 277
Tin, 15, see also *Recipe, pewter*
Touchmarks, see *Marks, pewter*
Transfer-decorated, 121, 185, 186, 221, 337, 348, 362
Transporting, see *Damage, preventing*
Ehrenfried (Walter) von Tschirnhaus, 43, 121

Veterans' organization, 273
Villeroy and Boch (V&B), 12, 135, 136, 277, 347, 348,
    see also *Mettlach*
    marks, see *Marks, illustrated*
Vitrification, 8, see also *Clay*

Waldenburg, 26
Waldglas, 9
Walzenkrug, 12, 43, 65, 73, 103, 121
WEST GERMANY, see *Marks*
Westerwald, 12, 25, 26, 27, 273
Westerwald Team, 347
White gold, 25, 43, see also *Clay, stoneware*
Wick-Werke, 273, 347
Wood, 8, 9, 65, 103, see also *Lichtenhainer*
    hinge, 9, 103
    pewter inlaid, see *Lichtenhainer*
    pewter overlaid, 9
World War I, 273, 337
    impact on stein production, 12
Wrigglework, 65
Würfel & Müller (King), 347

X, see *Pewter, purity*

Zig-zag, 26, 27, 65
Zoeller & Born, 347